D1520319

Ranking Business Schools

Ranking Business Schools

Forming Fields, Identities and Boundaries in International Management Education

Linda Wedlin

Assistant Professor and Lecturer, Uppsala University, Sweden

Edward Elgar

Cheltenham, UK • Northampton, MA, USA

Published by
Edward Elgar Publishing Limited
Glensanda House
Montpellier Parade
Cheltenham
Glos GL50 1UA
UK

Edward Elgar Publishing, Inc.
136 West Street
Suite 202
Northampton
Massachusetts 01060
USA

A catalogue record for this book
is available from the British Library

Library of Congress Cataloging in Publication Data

Wedlin, Linda.
    Ranking business schools : forming fields, identities, and boundaries in
international management education / Linda Wedlin.
        p. cm.
    Includes bibliographical references and index.
    1. Business schools—Europe—Evaluation. 2. Master of business administration
degree—Europe—Evaluation. I. Title.

    HF1140.W43 2006
    650.071′14—dc22   2005052810

ISBN–13: 978 1 84542 515 9
ISBN–10: 1 84542 515 4

Typeset by Cambrian Typesetters, Camberley, Surrey
Printed and bound in Great Britain by MPG Books Ltd, Bodmin, Cornwall

Contents

Figures

Tables

Abbreviations

AACSB	Association to Advance Collegiate Schools of Business, Tampa, FL, USA
AMBA	Association of MBAs, London, UK
Efmd	European Foundation for Management Development, Brussels, Belgium
EIU	Economist Intelligence Unit, London, New York, Hong Kong and Vienna
EMBA	Executive MBA
EQUIS	European Quality Improvement System
ESADE	Escuela Superior de Administración y Dirección de Empresas, Barcelona and Madrid, Spain
ESCP-EAP	Ecole Supérieure de Commerce de Paris – Ecole Européenne des Affaires, Paris, London, Berlin, Madrid and Torino
FT	*Financial Times*, London, UK
GMAC	Graduate Management Admissions Council, McLean, VA, USA
HEC	Ecole des Hautes Etudes Commerciales, Paris, France
IE	Instituto de Empresa, Madrid, Spain
IESE	Instituto de Estudios Superiores de la Empresa, Barcelona and Madrid, Spain
IMD	International Institute for Management Development, Lausanne, Switzerland
INSEAD	Institut Européen d'Administration des Affaires, Fontainebleau and Singapore
LBS	London Business School, London, UK
MBA	Master of Business Administration
MBS	Manchester Business School, Manchester, UK
MIT	Massachusetts Institute of Technology, Cambridge, MA, USA
UCLA	University of California, Los Angeles, Los Angeles, CA, USA

Preface

At a time when systems of higher education and research are under reform, there seems to be an increasing desire to regulate, to monitor and to control the production of knowledge and learning in universities and higher education organizations. Increasing political efforts to create international markets for education and research are noticed. In recent years we have also seen an increase in other efforts to compare, assess and monitor education; among them an increasing production of ranking lists and league tables. Despite strong interest and intense debates, there is little research trying to entangle what rankings really are, why they have become influential and widely diffused, and what it means for higher education that such efforts are proliferating.

Taking seriously the idea that rankings are influential and important, this book is an attempt to provide a critical analysis of the proliferation of rankings in management education. I do not attempt to determine whether rankings are good or bad, but rather to thoroughly analyse, empirically and theoretically, the development of rankings and its implications for the field of management education. In doing so, the book will focus on questions of how and why the rankings have developed, how business schools have responded to the changes, and what the implications are for the field of management education. By integrating different theoretical approaches and traditions, including organization theory, sociology of knowledge and education, the book is also an attempt to explain the role of classifications and other monitoring activities in forming social order and fields of practice. This is important for understanding the development of transnational monitoring systems and new modes of governance in many areas of society.

Acknowledgements

I have enjoyed the help and support of many people and institutions in putting this book together. I am grateful to all the people in business schools around Europe who have generously shared their experiences, thoughts and opinions about the rankings and about their business schools with me. I am also grateful to the journalists who have taken time to explain their rankings and to tell their side of the story to me.

I have benefited greatly from the thoughtful advice and intellectual support of Lars Engwall and Kerstin Sahlin-Andersson. As my dissertation advisors, they have carefully guided this work through the various stages, and have provided both criticisms and endless support and encouragement. Kerstin has provided invaluable inputs in the final stages of revising this work into a book. I am greatly indebted to Walter Powell for putting forward intriguing questions and wise comments at my dissertation seminar, and for his encouragement to publish this book. I also want to express my thanks to colleagues and friends at the Department of Business Studies at Uppsala University for constructive criticisms and inspiration, particularly Stefan Jonsson for his insightful comments on various drafts of this manuscript and to Tina Hedmo for inspiring collaboration. Special thanks also to my partner, Lars, for his patience and his support.

I have had the opportunity to present this study and drafts of the manuscript at seminars and workshops around the world, which have given me valuable insights for this book. I particularly thank Royston Greenwood, Marc Ventresca, and Kerstin Sahlin-Andersson for these opportunities.

Financial support for this research is gratefully acknowledged from several sources. Uppsala University and the Department of Business Studies, and the 'Jan Wallander and Tom Hedelius Foundation' have provided financial support for my doctoral and post-doctoral work. This study has also been part of the research projects 'Creation of European Management Practice', financed by the European Commission, and 'Transnational Regulation and the Transformation of States', financed by the Swedish Research Council.

Linda Wedlin
Uppsala, July 2005

1. European management education and the proliferation of business school rankings

INTRODUCTION

Ranking lists of business schools and management education programmes are flourishing in newspapers and magazines around the world. National and international media, specialized business magazines, and general news media companies are all involved in producing and publishing rankings and league tables of business schools and of MBA and other management education programmes. The London-based *Financial Times* published a ranking list of European business schools and MBA programmes in 1998, which was followed by an international list the following year. This ranking was one of the first attempts to produce an international comparison of schools from the United States and Europe, primarily, in a single ranking list. Other rankers have since picked up this international profile and produce ranking lists of business schools and management education programmes from around the world, for instance *Business Week*, the *Wall Street Journal*, *The Economist* and *Forbes*. Although business school rankings are prominent in business media, these rankings follow a number of national or regional efforts to rank universities and higher education organizations in different countries, for instance Canada, Germany and the UK. International comparisons and rankings of universities in general are also increasing, noting for instance the ranking from Shanghai Jiao Tong University, and the *Times Higher Education Supplement* 'World University Rankings'.

Ranking lists have taken a significant step into academic life and have become a fact of life for members of business schools and universities. However, the proliferation of rankings has put business school and university administrators, leaders and academic members in a dilemma: Should we love them or should we hate them? Rankings are believed to be beneficial for schools that score well, but detrimental to schools that score badly or get a poorer rank than expected. For the larger number of European management education organizations, the proliferation of international league tables and comparisons has meant an opportunity to be included in business school rankings for the first time. This development has resulted in a lot of discussion where the existence as well as the methodology of rankings has been debated and, in some instances, also heavily criticized. The issue was, for instance, debated at an MBA directors meeting in the fall of 2001, and the grapevine has it that debate was intense and that the criticism of the *Financial Times* ranking from some European business schools was heavy:

> When the group turned its attention to rankings, it became clear that we were waving a red flag at a bull! The journalists who joined us . . . knew in advance that they were venturing into the lion's den, but bravely sallied forth to defend their point of view both eloquently and vigorously. . . . If we had chosen to allow it, this thorny topic could have taken over the whole meeting. (*efmd Bulletin*, February 2002, p. 2)

Faced with such ranking lists and league tables, business schools feel the need to participate and, in their own words, 'play the rankings' game'. It is not always clear what it means to play this game, however, and the business education community is battling to understand what ranking lists are, what they represent, and what the game of being ranked in these lists entails for participants. Rankers and the media, faculty and deans at universities and business schools, politicians, students and others all take part in discussions of these issues, debating the criteria, the methodology, and the very existence of rankings – in order to make sense of what is happening.

Explaining some of the intense reactions and anxiety in response to rankings, Elsbach and Kramer (1996) propose that rankings are potential identity threats to business schools and universities. They show how rankings can create 'identity-crises' in business schools, threatening the perceived core identity of the school as well as the perceived position of the school relative to other schools, which causes distress and identity dissonance inside the business schools (Elsbach and Kramer, 1996, p. 464).

The anxiety of business schools when faced with rankings is furthermore enhanced by the fact that there is no clear understanding of what the rankings are and what the ranking number represents. Dichev (1999, p. 209) concludes that rankings should not be viewed as comprehensive and efficient measures of 'school quality', largely because they incorporate 'noisy information' that makes business schools move up and down in the rankings without any substantial changes in performance. The results of his study show that changes in rankings have strong tendencies to revert, meaning that a school that has moved up in the list one year is most likely to move down in the next ranking issue, and the reverse. There is also a noted lack of co-movement between the two main American ranking lists, suggesting that rankings only partly reflect changes in performance of schools. Similarly, Segev et al. (1999) show that there is no relation between a certain structure of the MBA programme and the ranking of the school. They conclude that there is no one 'best' structure of programmes that yields a high rank in the lists (Segev et al., 1999, p. 562). The fact that rankings are no clear measures of quality, and that there are no clear linkages between a good rank and a specific model or approach to management education, may thus enhance uncertainty for business schools and increase their identity anxieties.

We can thus argue that the volatility of the rankings and the problems of measurement are causing insecurity and uncertainty among business schools about how they should relate and respond to the rankings, increasing the identity dissonance and anxiety in response to the rankings. However, even with insights about identity threats and uncertainty in relation to rankings, it is difficult to understand exactly why rankings are so powerful and what kind of influence they have on the business schools and their work. Why are rankings so important that they threaten the identities of business schools? If they are not exact measures of quality or performance then what are they, and what do they mean?

The questions raised above suggest that there is another side to the story of rankings. To frame them as influencing and being part of the identity formation of business schools is not enough; we also need to understand why and how they have become so powerful that they influence the identities of schools. To understand this we need (a) to investigate how and why they have developed, and (b) to consider the fact that they may have implications beyond threatening individual organizations' identities. This book thus attempts to make a contribution to the ongoing debate in business schools and universities by answering two main research questions: What are rankings and why are they here? What impact does the introduction of rankings have on business schools and on the field of management education?

Answering these questions can also help us to understand better the role of ranking lists and other monitoring and scrutinizing activities in a society that is increasingly interested in 'knowledge', often expressed as information, and in making social practices and performance of various kinds transparent and visible to audiences (Power, 1997; Strathern, 2000b; Tsoukas, 1997). The questions about rankings can be formulated in more theoretical terms, focusing on the function of classifications mechanisms in forming social order in different areas of society. What is the role of classification mechanisms in forming and organizing the field of management education? In this book I thus argue for a field perspective on the development of rankings as classifications, focusing on issues of how organizational and cultural fields are formed and shaped. The book thus attempts to make a theoretical contribution to our understanding of the role of classification mechanisms in forming social order and organizational fields. Beginning to craft out the answers to these questions, the following section will provide a theoretical as well as an empirical background, and present some further arguments to why current understandings of rankings are insufficient.

EXPLAINING RANKINGS – A FIELD PERSPECTIVE

To be able to answer the questions of how and why rankings have developed and what they mean, I will conceptualize rankings as part of a developing field of international management education. The concept of organizational fields is used in institutional theory to depict an area of social life or a group of organizations that compete for the same resources and legitimacy, as well as live by the same institutional frameworks in terms of laws, regulations, normative rules, and cognitive belief systems (cf. Powell and DiMaggio, 1991; Meyer and Rowan, 1977; Scott, [1981] 1998). Organizational fields influence how organizations within them are structured and carry out work, and what are considered legitimate activities. This definition of field is inspired by Bourdieu, who claims that fields are made up of organizations struggling for something that they have in common, as for instance, the definition of good art in the field of arts (Bourdieu, 1993). A common belief in and adherence to a definition of what constitutes the field holds the field together (cf. Sahlin-Andersson, 1996).

Providing an analytical frame situated between the level of organization and society, a field perspective has been particularly useful in the social sciences to explain regularities in actions across a community or group of actors that is not caused by explicit rules or in any way formally organized or dictated (DiMaggio and Powell, 1983; Martin, 2003, Scott and Meyer, 1983). It directs attention to processes formed between and among organizations and individuals rather than on separate actors, and it provides opportunities for explanations that reach beyond a simple rule-like causality (Martin, 2003). Understanding rankings as part of an organizational field thus provides a different perspective from that of earlier studies on what rankings mean and on what they are. First, a field approach demands a contextual understanding and a concrete analysis (Martin, 2003) of the process whereby the rankings have developed, taking account of the institutional conditions and specific characteristics of the management education field. Second, it proposes a relational approach that accounts for the relations and interactions between organizations in a particular field, the struggles to determine the characteristics and stakes of that field, and the reactions to the changes introduced in a specific area of society. This allows for an understanding and conceptualization of not just the reactions and responses of individual organizations to changes in the environment, but also the interrelated efforts of organizations to respond and contribute to developments such as rankings. This way it is possible to reach beyond simple explanations of rankings as quality measures and 'identity-threats'.

In order to do so, we need a framework for understanding the role of rankings in field formation processes. I claim that the rankings are important classification mechanisms that contribute to constructing perceptions of who is part of the international management education field, and are an arena where management education organizations participate in debates and struggles about what constitutes the field. To set the stage for such a framework, however, it is necessary to take a brief look at some developments that have paved the way for the expansion and proliferation of international rankings. Focusing on the European experience with rankings, this study will depart mainly from the developments in the European management education field. The following sections describe first the development of rankings in relation to an expansion of media interest, and second, show that the development of rankings is closely tied to, and part of, field-specific developments such as the expansion of the MBA label in Europe, increasing competition in and internationalization of, the field of management education, and the development of different forms of regulations and standards within the field. This overview will show that while such developments have provided important conditions for rankings to develop, they are not sufficient to explain the current surge in them.

International Business School Rankings in the Media

It is important first to note that despite intuitive perceptions that the ranking phenomenon is new and different, at least from a European perspective, MBA and business school rankings are far from a new invention. Business school rankings appeared as early as in the 1970s in the United States, and grew steadily throughout that decade. Daniel (1998) reports several attempts by university researchers, professors and students to compile rankings that were intended to assess the relative standings of business schools in the United States. In 1973, a group of researchers at Columbia University undertook a survey about the reputation of schools, asking business school deans to list other professional schools in their fields. At about the same time, two professors at Georgia State University came up with a rating system that was based on the number of articles published in major journals by the faculty members of each school (Daniel, 1998, p. 215). Students at Columbia University compiled a ranking based on assessments of the employment value of graduates; they simply asked recruiters to name the business schools they considered best. In 1974 a ranking was performed by *MBA* magazine, which combined criteria for academic quality with that of employment value in surveys of both deans and students/graduates (Daniel, 1998, p. 215).

Efforts to rank business schools and other educational establishments continued in the United States in the 1980s, although the introduction of new business school rankings introduced a significant change in the rankings trend. Business school and MBA rankings now began to spread outside a strict academic setting and move into general newspapers and business magazines. The *US News & World Report* started producing rankings of business education organizations in 1987, and since 1990, has ranked not only business schools but a wide set of college and university disciplines; and *Business Week* started their biennial ranking of MBA programmes in 1988. Both these rankings have gained attention outside strict academic settings, and have spread to a wide audience of prospective students, parents, employers, and so forth (Elsbach and Kramer, 1996).

The development of rankings is thus related to an increasing interest in management education issues generally, inside and outside strictly academic settings. But not until the early 1990s, however, did management education make a significant breakthrough in popular as well as academic discourse. Moon (2002) notes a very dramatic increase in both the number of management periodicals and the number of articles featuring management education topics in both academic and popular publications in the early 1990s, particularly in 1991 (Moon, 2002, p. 66–7). The number of management periodicals covering management education topics, specifically represented by the MBA, increased from around five each year in the 1980s to approximately 15 each year in the 1990s (Moon, 2002, p. 67). Thus, the discourse on management education became prominent publicly in the early 1990s.

Several newspapers and magazines, for instance the *Financial Times* (*FT*), thus increased their coverage of management education issues during the 1990s. The *Financial Times* started a standing section on business education on 2 October 1995. The aim was to create a consumer guide to the many options of management education programmes and organizations. From writing about management education issues generally under the management page of the paper, from this year, business education got not only a standing section under the heading 'Inside track' in the Monday paper, but also an appointed editor (business education correspondent). The section contains a column, 'News from campus', featuring brief notices about business schools and programmes, as well as one or more feature articles every week. The section is also accompanied by advertisements for MBA programmes and schools. The coverage of business education in the *Financial Times* has, since the dedicated section was first started, increased more than fourfold: from producing 800 words a week it now produces about 3000 to 4000 words a week and the number of dedicated surveys, or special issues, has increased from two to six per year (Business education correspondent *FT*, 2001).

It is in this context that we should understand the introduction of rankings in the late 1990s. They became part of an effort to launch a credible business education section for the *Financial Times*, and to compete with other newspapers and magazines: 'Because we are the *FT* we have to produce something that is hard, and that is factual, and something that is going to have an authority. And I felt very strongly that we could only do that if we had rankings.' (Business education correspondent, *FT*, 2001). The wording in this quote, interestingly, stresses that the ranking and the business education section need to have 'authority' in the management education field, and that this is largely what the newspapers and the different rankers compete for. A newspaper with authority sells not only newsstand copies of the ranking edition of the paper, but attracts interest, resources, and influence beyond the individual rankings.

The competition between newspapers was clearly an argument for the increase in and expansion of rankings in the late 1990s. As a reaction to the American rankings, which featured only schools in the United States, the 1999 *Financial Times* ranking list featured business schools from both the United States and Europe in a ranking of 50 full-time MBA programmes. The expressed intent of the *Financial Times* first international ranking list was to make explicit the differences between the two continents, or the 'Atlantic divide' (*Financial Times*, 25 January 1999). Other newspapers picked up this international profile of rankings at this time. In 2000, *Business Week* published a separate list of seven non-US schools together with their biennial ranking of US schools (*Business Week*, 2 October 2000) and in April 2001, the *Wall Street Journal* followed suit and published their first ranking of business schools, which also included both North American and European schools (*Wall Street Journal*, 30 April 2001). During 2002, *The Economist* presented their first international ranking list comparing schools on a single ranking scale.

The rapid expansion of international rankings in the late 1990s and the early 2000s thus introduced yet another change in the attention of the business school rankings game. Business school and MBA rankings, which have moved even farther from specialized magazines and the academic corridors, have also left a strictly American setting. Competition between the rankers has also driven an increase in the number of lists, and there are currently ranking lists of executive MBA programmes and executive education courses alongside the full-time MBA rankings. Rankings have become the business of the large media companies, which continue to spread management education topics to an even wider general public.

Diffusion of the MBA and Expansion of Management Education in Europe

One of the important drivers for this increasing media interest in management education and the competition between newspapers is the growing market for higher education in business and management in Europe, and internationally. The field of management education, which is diverse and competitive, has expanded dramatically after the Second World War (cf. Locke, 1989). There are many types of programmes for graduate management training, geared to students with or without work experience as practicing managers. With more than 1600 institutions around the world offering an MBA programme in 1999 (Moon, 2002), this has become one of the most visible business education programmes in many parts of the world. The MBA is originally an American graduate degree in business, which has spread to Europe and other parts of the world after the war. The first MBA programme in Europe was set up in the late 1950s, and several new programmes were started during the following decades. The expansion of the MBA increased dramatically in Europe during the 1980s and 1990s (Mazza et al., 2005). With 400 new business schools established in Europe during the late 1980s, together with many of the traditional universities starting MBA programmes, the competition in the MBA market today has become fierce (Daniel, 1998, p. 266). An estimate is that over 700 MBA programmes are offered in Europe in 2003 (MBA Info, 13 October 2003).

Together with the expansion of the MBA, internationalization of business schools and their programmes has also notably occurred. An increasingly global market for education seems to have arisen, within which schools are starting campuses in other countries and offer 'global' educational programmes, as for example, INSEAD's Asian campus in Singapore, the Chicago GSB campuses in Europe and Asia, and the Duke 'Cross Continent' MBA programme. This internationalization, together with the establishment of new schools locally, has radically increased the competition among business schools and universities. Management education programmes thus compete for financial resources and for students, faculty, and support from businesses.

The developments within the field are not restricted, however, to business schools and universities. Increased competition since the 1980s is partly due to several attempts by the corporate world to develop their own learning programmes for their executives and trainees, challenging traditional universities and business schools. Companies with specialized management education/training divisions, often called corporate universities, increased from 400 to more than 1600 in the United States between 1990 and 1999 (*Academy of Management News*, October 2000). This development is also likely to be under way in Europe. In addition, professional business advisory firms have been tending to move into education, with a subsequent 'colonization' of knowledge that changes the relationship between the business community and academia (Suddaby and Greenwood, 2001).

This expanded market for MBA programmes and for management education generally in Europe and elsewhere is an important element in the development of the field. With an increasing number of corporate universities and attempts to colonize knowledge production processes, the need and desire to create systems that evaluate, assess, and define good and proper management education has been accentuated. The expansion of business education as well as an increasing globalization has not just increased competition, but has also enhanced the need and desire to regulate and set standards for business education institutions that provide guidance as to which schools and types of organizations are considered part of the field. Together with a deregulation of national educational systems and the increased globalization of higher education, the role of the nation state in higher education thus seems to have diminished, and demands for new forms of regulations and standards have been evoked (Hedmo et al., forthcoming). This development has increased the attention given to various forms for control and regulation of educational programmes in Europe (Durand and McGuire, 2005) and an expressed tendency for the production of more external quality assessments and evaluations (Trow, 1998), such as accreditation and rankings.

With a large and seemingly quite diverse market for MBA and other business education programmes, the need for transparency, comparability, and also standardization has thus been evoked. The diffusion of the MBA label has also created possibilities for comparing programmes from different countries and regions, or for comparing different organizations, largely by creating expectations of similarity. Moon (2002) notes the perceived necessity of a transferable degree, such as the MBA, when management education institutions want to be part of globalization and of 'the global society'. The diffusion of the MBA title has thus provided conditions as well as incentives for international comparisons and new forms of regulations. This has caused a number of organizations, such as accreditation organizations and the media, to engage in standardizing and regulatory activities (Hedmo et al., forthcoming). Assessments such as accreditation and rankings have thus arisen partly from a quest for universities and business schools to be accountable to their external supporters and to society at large, for pursuing their missions faithfully and for meeting legitimate expectations (Trow, 1998, p. 20).

In this sense, the development of rankings is part of a demand for increased scrutiny, control and regulation. Efforts to assess, evaluate, and scrutinize performances of all kinds are increasingly popular in many areas of social and cultural life (Miller, 1996; Power, 1997), not just in management education. The trend to evaluate and audit is particularly emphasized by Power (1997), who claims that we have entered an 'audit society' where performances of all kinds are, by external pressures, subject to being audited, and claims that activities to an increasing extent are organized in order to be auditable (Power, 1997, p. 87). While tracing this explosion of audit activity to the history of financial audits, Power (1997) uses a very broad definition of audit activity that includes various forms of auditing but also monitoring and scrutinizing activities in general. In some instances, audits can be seen as 'rationalized rituals of inspection' (Power, 1997, p. 96). In this sense, this idea of an audit society is consistent with the arguments of a rationalizing movement in society through which a rationalized world order is being formed (e.g. Meyer, 1994; Meyer et al., 1997).

Explaining the proliferation of various forms of audit activity, Power (1997) argues that audit activity carries a technological element, which includes the particular tasks and routines performed by practitioners, as well as a programmatic content, referring to the norms, ideas, and concepts that follow the pragmatics and that attach the practice to broader policy objectives. It is thus the programmatic content of audits and accounting that has been transferred and embodied in other forms of assessments and evaluations expressed, for example, as demands for accountability to external constituents, transparency, quality and quality control, and efficiency and control (cf. Miller, 1994; Power, 1997; Strathern, 2000b; Tsoukas, 1997). Shore and Wright (2000) show that as the concept of audit entered British higher education in the 1980s, the term was separated from its largely financial meaning and became associated with a cohort of other terms, such as performance, accreditation, accountability, value for money, efficiency, benchmarking, and stakeholders (Shore and Wright, 2000, p. 60).

Regulatory Pressures and Market Demand

The above accounts show that rankings follow from specific developments in the field of management education; a diffusion of the MBA label and expansion of management education generally, and an increasing media coverage of management education issues in the popular business press, partly as a result of competition between newspapers. Picking up on demands for order and transparency as well as comparability and market information, the media seem to have developed rankings as a response to market pressures: pressures from consumer groups as well as from competitive forces in the media market. Indeed, these are the most common explanations to rankings. It is also clear, however, that mechanisms such as rankings develop as part of consumer movements (cf. Rao, 1998), with the expressed need for market mechanisms that ensure accountability and help students make informed choices about where to study, and an increasing use of and demand for various forms of audit activity. Although these two pressures may seem slightly contradictory, with one being a demand from the bottom-up (consumers) and the other being a pressure for control (audit), in the case of rankings the two trends seem to merge. Being a consumer-oriented mechanism, claiming to provide students with market information, the rankings have followed closely on, and become associated with, other control mechanisms and have incorporated the programmatic content of other audit activities, mainly accreditation, and an increasing demand for accountability, transparency and comparability.

However, while market explanations are important to understand the development of rankings they are in themselves insufficient, for two main reasons; there is no easy way to understand and conceptualize markets and market demand, and such explanations tend to ignore the specific mechanisms that trigger changes in practices and understandings among actors in the field. Let's investigate these suggestions further.

First, the concept of markets and the understanding of market demand are problematic. Miller (1996) calls attention to a number of dilemmas of accountability, one being that it is not always clear who the customers are, and what the market is. Who are the customers in education? What is the market? Rather than taking markets as given, theories of fields and institutions suggest that markets are logics, or social constructions that are the result of institutionalization processes (cf. Fligstein, 1996; cf. Thornton and Ocasio, 1999). Institutional logics change over time and undergo field-specific developments, and cannot therefore be uniformly taken for granted (Friedland and Alford, 1991). Thornton and Ocasio (1999), for instance, show how the higher education publishing industry changed from an 'editorial' logic to a 'market' logic, as conceptualizations of publishing changed from that of a profession to that of a business. Understood this way, conceptions of customers and markets are shaped in the field, and in processes of institutionalization of fields.

Conceptualizing markets as logics and constructions leads us to question the assumption that rankings have been driven solely by market demand. With this view, markets and perceptions of a market may well be a result (intended or unintended) of rankings rather than a precondition. Not denying the importance of students, companies and other interest groups and stakeholders in and around business schools, placing demands and putting pressure on organizations in different ways, it is difficult to define or get a clear perception of one market and specific market pressures. This was also one of the arguments used by the founder of the *Business Week* ranking:

> The schools didn't seem to care very much about the attitudes or the perceptions of their customers: the people who actually buy their product. . . . I felt there was no marketplace, really, to make the schools even pay attention to demand. . . . So what I thought was this, one thing that a ranking would actually do is to create a market where none had existed. Create a market where schools could be rewarded and punished for failing to be responsive to their two prime constituents: the students and the corporations. (Selections Interview 3, *Business Week*, pp. 1–2)

Along these lines, I argue in this book that the proliferation of international ranking lists in the business press has helped to create a notion of an international market for business schools and for MBA programmes, rather than being solely a result of market forces. By incorporating the demands and opinions of students and companies into the rankings, they help form, shape and direct this demand towards the business schools.

A related argument to the market explanation is that this is following from wider developments in the field of education. Looking beyond the specific context of management education, it is reasonable to consider the wider educational field in which business schools and universities are a part. Although failing to provide clear explanations to how rankings have developed, this helps us with a few answers, particularly to the question: Why now? Rankings coincide in time with discussions and efforts within Europe to create a uniform internal market for education, and to standardize and make comparable educational systems and educational programmes across the EU. This process was formalized in 1999, when the Bologna declaration was signed. This could be described as a process of deinstitutionalization (Greenwood et al., 2002), whereby an existing social order – of regulations, norms and taken-for-granted assumptions – are weakened or disappear. Through this process, national educational systems are being questioned and challenged, and discussions about new forms of regulations and standardized and comparable practices are taking shape.

The development of rankings and accreditation procedures in management education is thus closely related to political efforts in Europe to open national educational markets and standardize practices and regulations within the EU (Hedmo, 2004). However, as these developments coincide in time, with 1998–99 as the peak of events, it is difficult to view the introduction of rankings as a simple result of the restructuring and opening of European educational markets. Rather, the proliferation of rankings, and other developments in management education, is one element of the deinstitutionalization processes taking place in European higher education at this time. It gives an understanding for the conditions under which changes were introduced, but it does not provide clear answers to what triggered the proliferation of international rankings and what has made them so popular, not only in Europe but also in other areas of the world. Those explanations, I argue, need to be sought within the management education field.

Thus, the second reason the market explanations are insufficient to explain the current ranking proliferation is that they localize the impetus for change only in the external environment of management education organizations; in the media and in the market. No consideration is taken of those being subject to the rankings, the business schools, who are the ones responding to, reacting to and handling this development. While the media is an important actor in developing, producing and promoting the rankings, it has not done it alone. I will argue that business schools and members of the business school community have also been important in driving the development of rankings. This forces us, however, to seek additional answers to the question of how rankings have developed and what they mean.

Arena for Boundary-work of Fields

The arguments above lead us to challenge two main assumptions about the development of rankings: that rankings are externally imposed on the field management education, and that they are reflections of developments and of status and reputation rather than having any substantial influence on the field or on management education organizations. This book thus proposes a more complex answer to the questions of why rankings have developed and what they mean. Returning to the starting point for this section, I argue that this requires a field perspective on the developments and a framework that takes account both of larger field processes and individual responses to field developments.

Putting a slightly different interpretation on the developments described above – the expansion of management education, increasing international competition, and demands for new forms of regulation – it is possible to argue that there is a blurring of the boundaries of business education, such that a clear distinction between 'traditional' business education and other forms of management training is increasingly difficult to make. A multitude of actors, such as universities, business schools, and corporate universities, each claiming to produce knowledge and to educate and train managers and students of business, makes it unclear as to who is inside and who is outside the field of management education. It was also argued that the expansion of the MBA and the blurring of boundaries have created a desire among business schools and regulators to bring order and discipline to the market. This uncertainty and the desire for order have led to subsequent development of new regulations and rankings that aim to distinguish the serious from the less serious management education providers, and the rankings provide a mechanism to separate the 'good' schools from the 'bad' ones. In this view, rankings have developed partly as a response to unclear boundaries of the field.

Research on the development of management education as an academic discipline and a distinct intellectual field show that insecurity about work procedures and tasks is high in management studies compared to other university disciplines (Engwall, 1992, 1995; Whitley, 1984). External validations and evaluations are therefore assumed to be particularly important and powerful within management education. Characterizing management education as a fragmented adhocracy, Whitley (1984) claims that it is, and has always been, open to many audiences for legitimacy and reputation, and to standards set by non-intellectuals and a 'management elite', as for instance, a commitment to vocational training of managers (Whitley, 1984, pp. 338–40). This leads to a discipline where 'knowledge production and validation ... is rather frag- mented and disjointed' (Whitley, 1984, p. 341), implying that insecurity about the performance standards and evaluative procedures is high, and that intel- lectual standards and procedures for gaining legitimacy are divergent. This implication means, in turn, that there is high insecurity about who are consid- ered good and bad in management education, and about which standards should be allowed to judge the performance of individuals as well as organ- izations within the field. The boundaries and the definition of the field are hence unclear.

With this interpretation, the questions raised can be formulated in more theoretical terms, addressing questions about how fields are formed and deter- mined. Although perhaps particularly salient in contemporary management education, the questions and concerns raised here have broader theoretical implications that involve the ongoing construction of organizational fields and field boundaries. Who, or what, counts within the field, and who are consid- ered as legitimate players and part of the field? On the other hand, consider- ing the many actors and principles to judge and evaluate management education that have developed in recent years, the question arises as to who, or what procedures, have the legitimacy to determine who counts and who does not count? In broader terms, this is about the construction of an organ- izational field, and about the mechanisms that determine field structures and set boundaries of a field.

The struggle to construct and constitute an organizational field, such as the field of business and management education, is an ongoing process involving many diverse actors. Fields can be described as places of struggle over symbolic capital, where each field has its own specific logic that determines which characteristics can be used as capital, and which types of capital are required for participation (Bourdieu, 1984, p. 112). Because of this struggle, the boundaries of the field are flexible and constantly changing, requiring actors to engage in activities and efforts to construct and determine the bound- aries of a field or a community (Gieryn, 1999). Gieryn (1999) has labelled this 'boundary-work'. This boundary-work can be expressed as a struggle to deter- mine insiders and outsiders, to determine the criteria that define actors in the field, and to determine who has the authority to judge and set field boundaries.

Using the concept of boundary-work it is possible to conceptualize the ongoing struggle to determine the field. The concept also implies, however, that somebody is doing the work, i.e. performing activities that help construct boundaries for the field. Our framework thus needs a concept to understand the role of actors and field members in forming fields and field boundaries. Understanding and conceptualizing the actions and reactions of business schools to the development of rankings, the concept of identity and identity-formation of actors can help us to do this. To link the two concepts of identities and fields is not new, however. In the Scandinavian research tradition in neo-institutional theory, the concept of identity and identity-formation has been perhaps particularly elaborated (Czarniawska, 1997; Czarniawska and Sevón, 1996; Sahlin-Andersson, 1996; Sahlin-Andersson and Sevón, 2003; Sevón, 1996). Here, identity has been treated as an important part of field processes: for instance, as grounds for imitation processes and isomorphic pressures (Sahlin-Andersson, 1996). Other researchers have also made the connection between institutions and identities, regarding identity processes as an important component in field formation and institutional change (Oakes et al., 1998).

I will build on these studies to further develop the connection between identities and fields, and to more explicitly take the view that the forming of individual organization identities is a vital part of the forming and reforming of organizational fields. The process of identity formation is seen as part of the creation and recreation of fields and of boundaries of fields. This will help me to describe and understand field construction in more detail, as well as to see wider consequences and effects of individual identity processes. Hence, regarding both field formation and identity formation as interrelated two-way processes becomes necessary: identities are influenced by, and contribute to, the forming and reforming of fields and the structuring of fields.

Empirically, this means treating rankings as classification mechanisms. The role of classification mechanisms such as rankings provides an important link between identity processes and fields. Classifications and categorizations are used in processes of identity-formation and identification (for instance Bowker and Star, 1999; Sahlin-Andersson and Sevón, 2003; Sevón, 1996), and are central aspects of the forming and reforming of organizational and cultural fields (for instance Bourdieu, 1988; DiMaggio, 1987; Oakes et al., 1998). In order to understand the functioning of fields, the principles of classification that exist in fields, which help to construct and diffuse norms and practices, must be understood. Business school rankings are here understood as one such principle of classification, among many others. The rankings, in being such measuring or classification mechanisms, are thus perceived to contribute to field processes by setting and diffusing norms and standards for what business schools should do and how they should do it, and by playing a role in the identity formation of business schools. This way, rankings and other classification mechanisms are perceived as constitutive systems, which construct knowledge and perceptions of the objects being classified (Bowker and Star, 1999; Townley, 1993).

Having determined the continuous work that go on to structure fields and field boundaries, and the procedures and actors involved in this boundary-work, it is possible to go one step further and also conceptualize rankings and

classification mechanisms as arenas where identity formation and field struggles are being played out. Classification mechanisms are not only diffusing
norms and standards, they are also hosting debates and discussions about
values and interests, and could be used in struggles for capital of fields. This
way, we can conceptualize classifications as the place where struggles to set
boundaries of fields are being carried out. Thus, I will conceptualize the rankings as an arena where boundary-work is being performed, that is an arena for
boundary-work of fields.

The main theoretical question for this work can thus be formulated as
follows: What is the role of classifications in forming fields and field boundaries? Providing an important framework for understanding changes in fields
and in field boundaries, the theoretical argument and frame is developed
farther in Chapter 2 of this book. In this chapter, the forming of fields and
identities is elaborated and the role of rankings and other forms of classifications in such processes are elaborated. This theoretical excursion will lead to
the formulation of three specific analytical themes to be used for understanding the role of rankings in forming fields and the boundaries of fields. These
themes will then guide the structure of the rest of the book.

STUDYING RANKINGS – METHODS AND OUTLINE

The main effort in this book is to analyse the proliferation of international
ranking lists of business schools in the popular business press. The study
reported on was conducted during a five-year period between 1999 and 2004,
and is based on empirical studies of the development of rankings and the
responses and reactions to this development among European business schools
and universities. While the proliferation of rankings is prominent in many
areas of education, management education provides a good example of a
recent and rather fast development of new and extended ranking lists with an
international or global coverage.

Although the study covers international developments, I will analyse the
development of rankings mainly from a European perspective. I will investigate reactions and responses to the developments among European business
schools and universities, and I will use the development of the *Financial Times*
rankings of international business schools, which began in 1999, as particular
examples of new, international ranking lists. This European approach is important for many reasons. First, it is a significant supplement to previous work on
rankings, which has had a strictly American focus (see for instance Dichev,
1999; Elsbach and Kramer, 1996; Gioia and Corley, 2002; Segev et al., 1999;
Trieschmann et al., 2000) with the *Business Week* and *US News & World
Report* rankings as particular examples. Because of the wide proliferation of

rankings outside the United States since the late 1990s, inspired by but not led by the American rankings and magazines, it is reasonable to attempt to understand this development from a European perspective. Second, the European context is a particularly good place to study the introduction and impact of rankings because the rankings are reasonably new to this area, and the reactions to the development have been extensive among European business schools and universities. Europe around the turn of the century (1999 and onwards) provides an opportunity to study the introduction and proliferation of international rankings in a field from the early beginnings and to follow reactions to and discussions about rankings in real time. Third, although presented here as a 'European' ranking, the *Financial Times* is a newspaper with wide international coverage, and its rankings cover programmes and schools on all continents. The launch of the *Financial Times* international business school ranking in 1999 led the way for many other international ranking lists, and it is today one of the most cited and influential international MBA rankings. This ranking is thus important beyond the European context. Taken together, the results of this study are important to understand rankings and the development of rankings for an international management education field, and the general implications are applicable to many educational settings and geographical areas.

The study builds on three sets of empirical data: published material on the rankings and the media coverage of business education since the mid-1990s; interviews with media representatives as well as business school representatives; and a survey of European business school deans. The first data set includes an investigation of the most prominent business school rankings in the international business school field, as well as analyses of how the ranking lists are constructed and what they measure. Information about the rankings and the media coverage of management education has been gathered through the published newspapers and the information provided on the web pages of the respective organizations. Interviews have also been conducted with representatives of the *Financial Times* in order to find out how and why the rankings were introduced, how they were constructed, and how the media representatives perceive the development of rankings and the reactions from the business school community.

Interviews have also been conducted with various representatives and members of European business schools and universities in order to understand the development of rankings in relation to those that receive and react to them, and in relation to the understandings of rankings that these business schools create. More than 30 interviews were conducted with representatives of six European business schools. The aim was to find out how business schools handle and perceive business school rankings, and how they have responded to them, but also to get an understanding of how business school representatives perceive the field and the role and function of their school in this field. Interviews were conducted with the dean or the director at each school, and additional interviews were conducted with various other representatives such as MBA directors, executive education directors, senior faculty members, admissions directors, alumni coordinators, and members of PR/media and career services departments.[1]

The third and last set of data is a quantitative study of the responses and reactions to the rankings, conducted as a mail survey using a standardized questionnaire. The survey was addressed to deans/directors of European business schools and management education organizations. The aim of the survey was to map the views of each of these deans on the issue of rankings and on the current position/standing of their school and its current activities, as well as to map the reactions and actions taken by deans in relation to the introduction of rankings. The questions were aimed at capturing the main themes from the interview study regarding reactions and responses to the rankings.[2]

The remainder of this book is used to analyse the ranking phenomenon and to explore the role of rankings in forming the field of international management education. Chapters 3 through 6 discuss the rankings in relation to the identity-formation of schools as well as the forming of a European field of management education, and investigate different aspects of the rankings as part of the everyday lives of European business schools. Chapter 3 provides an empirical context, describing briefly the field of European business schools and management education and describing in detail two business school narratives. These narratives are constructed as ideal-type business schools representing the ends of a perceived business school continuum: one representing an academic business school inside a university and one representing a business-oriented school developed independently of the university system. The two narratives provide the basis for an analysis of the way business schools in the field are forming identities and positions within that field. Doing so, this chapter also gives a background for understanding the development of an international field for business schools, and how the rankings and perceptions of an international market are making its way into business schools' everyday activities.

Moving to the analysis of rankings and the introduction of rankings in the European field of management education, Chapter 4 investigates the rankings as a measuring mechanism. What do rankings measure, and why does it matter what they measure? In this chapter, the idea of the ongoing formation of a business school field is developed, arguing that the field is increasingly forming around a template for what a good business school should be. Furthermore, this chapter illustrates how the rankings are part of forming, reforming and diffusing this template and its contents. Chapter 5 continues with an investigation of the outcomes of rankings, i.e. the ranking lists. How do rankings construct and present the order of schools, and what does this order mean? In this chapter, the importance of positions in fields is discussed, and the procedures whereby rankings construct and reconstruct status orders and positions among members of the business school field are analysed. The relative importance of high versus low ranking, is discussed. Chapter 6 takes the investigation of rankings beyond its initial focus on the measures and its results, and moves to discuss the rankings as an arena for authority and influence and the relative influence of rankings on management education organizations. In this chapter, a discussion of the implications and importance of rankings is provided. Chapters 7 and 8 conclude the book, elaborating on the main empirical and theoretical findings and contributions of this study, respectively. Chapter 7 develops the idea of an emerging international field of management education, discussing how boundaries are shaped in response to rankings and how perceptions of a market have been formed in this field. Chapter 8 develops the idea of rankings as arenas for boundary-work, elaborating on the role of classification mechanisms in constructing fields, boundaries and identities.

NOTES

1. The interviews have been referenced with the title of the person and the year the interview took place.
2. For a more elaborate discussion on the survey and the methodology, see Appendix A.

2. The role of classifications in organizational fields

Arguing for a field perspective, the previous chapter introduced the idea of rankings as arenas for bounday-work of organizational fields, where the boundaries of such fields are being shaped. The aim of this chapter is to develop this idea further, and clarify the theoretical standpoints from which this study builds. What is the role of classifications in forming fields and field boundaries? Thus, I will develop a theoretical framework for studying business-school rankings as part of a continuous process to shape and form an international field of management education.

To articulate the role of classifications in organizational fields, I will integrate several theoretical concepts and ideas, and draw on various research traditions. First, it is important to establish the concept of 'organizational field', as this forms the basis for this study. Thus, in the first section I will examine the work of Bourdieu (1984, 1988, 1993) and his conceptualization of the construction of fields and field dynamics, particularly his analysis of the French academic field. Bourdieu's theory of field formation is in many ways the basis for the neo-institutional approach to fields, used for instance by DiMaggio (1987, 1997) and others (Oakes et al., 1998; Powell and DiMaggio, 1991) and I will also relate the analysis to these more recent theoretical approaches. Integrating different theoretical traditions will provide the basis for a dynamic and processual view of fields and the forming of field boundaries. In conceptualizing boundaries and the process to construct and define boundaries, I also review and draw on literature on boundaries in sociology and cultural studies (Gieryn, 1999; Lamont, 1992).

In order to understand how processes of field creation are enacted, supported, and driven by organizational actors within the field, the identity concept in the second section of this chapter provides a bottom-up perspective on field formation by focusing on the processes whereby actors participate in defining, constructing and understanding field boundaries (cf. Scott, 2001, p. 138). Recognizing that boundaries of fields are partly shaped by 'cultural-cognitive conceptions of identity and a sense of "being in the same boat" ' (Dacin et al., 2002, p. 51), this section will link the development of social structures and processes to cognitive constructions and understandings of field members. This helps amend a lack of agency often noted in studies of field formation processes (Borum and Westenholz, 1995; Davis and Powell, 1992; Galaskiewicz, 1991; Hoffman, 1999; Oliver, 1991; Perrow, 1986; Powell, 1991; Scott, 2001).

Drawing on the insights from the first two sections, the third section of this chapter focuses on the role of classification mechanisms and systems of measurement in forming social order. Drawing on Foucault-inspired research traditions, this section will specify the function of classifications (Bowker and Star, 1999; Strathern, 2000a; Townley, 1993), and show how they contribute to forming fields and field boundaries. This way, we can shift the focus from the constitutive functions of classifications, to their role as arenas for field struggles and identity formation processes, where debates and discussions about the field and its boundaries are being played out. This discussion will end with a specification of the analytical themes to be used for the analysis of rankings in this book.

FIELD STRUGGLES AND THE CONSTRUCTION OF FIELD BOUNDARIES

The concept of fields and the definition of fields is a critical issue for the present study. In line with the definition of organizational fields as a recognized institutional area (DiMaggio and Powell, 1983), the concept of fields has been used to depict shared meaning systems among organizations, or to define a set of organizations that are formed by the same regulatory processes (Scott, 1994, p. 71; 1995). Bourdieu's (1988) concept of cultural and social fields is more inclusive than that, and can be loosely defined as a restricted group of individuals or organizations struggling over something that they have in common. Using examples from the fields of art, literature and education, he shows that what is at stake within fields is the authority to judge what is right, proper, and suitable practice (Bourdieu, 1984; 1988). An essential conception in this field definition is the struggle for capital: the characteristics and qualities recognized as relevant, effective, and suitable for participation in the field. Capital is a relational concept and depicts a social state of order produced and reproduced within a certain field, where it is ascribed value by the participants in the field. Something is only capital if it is recognized by the players of the field to be an asset in field struggles (Bourdieu, 1988).

A field can contain several forms of capital. One of the main forms is symbolic capital, which is the capacity to define and create cultural and symbolic value (Oakes et al., 1998). For instance, symbolic value in art (as a field) is created by, among other things, critics and gallery owners who contribute to defining good art (Bourdieu, 1993). A specific kind of symbolic capital is cultural capital, which is abstract and includes for instance academic capital in the university field (Bourdieu, 1988). Other forms of capital are social and economic capital, which depicts not only material assets but also the knowledge associated with such capital forms, as for instance, the ability to act in socially accepted ways in various social settings. A given form of capital can at any time be transformed to a different form, changing the relative positions of power as well as the mechanisms and strategies governing the distribution of capital within the field. Capital is field-specific; the field determines which characteristics can be used as capital, and which types of capital are required for participation (Bourdieu, 1984, p. 112).

Capital is in this sense a specification of institutional logics (Friedland and Alford, 1991), or field frames (Lounsbury et al., 2003), in that the struggle for capital creates unique logics for fields (Bourdieu, 1984, p. 112; cf. also Oakes et al., 1998, p. 261). Logics thus refer to larger systems of meaning, identified over time, in which the struggle for capital is a part. Studies have shown how logics of fields, as shared norms and rule systems, change over time, and how they have implications for the organizational arrangements and practices within a defined area or field (Haveman and Rao, 1997; Lounsbury, 2002; Thornton and Ocasio, 1999). For instance, Lounsbury (2002, pp. 255–6) described the transformation of the field of finance and identified a shift from a 'regulatory' logic to a 'market' logic, which, in turn, shaped the professionalization of finance occupations.

One of the problems with conceptualizing field logics this way is that it assumes that we know a priori the boundaries of the field and which organizations are included in it. The studies of shifting institutional logics thus started with predefined fields, industries, or markets, and identified the changes in norms, rules, and practices that form the basis for the shifting logics. As Lounsbury et al. (2003) notes, this makes logics exogenous to actors of the field, and implies that logics are 'analytically removed from the more active struggles over meaning and resources' (Lounsbury et al., 2003, p. 72). Suggesting instead that struggles over meanings and frames are part of what constitutes fields, it is necessary to focus on what makes up large-scale changes in institutional logics. Focusing on the struggle for capital, which is at the micro level of fields, thus incorporates ongoing struggles and debates in the field.

When defining the concept of field as involving struggle for capital, which results in defining good and legitimate practices, it is similar to the concept of 'issue-based field', used for instance by Hoffman (1999) in a study of corporate environmentalism and the forming of a field around environmental protection issues. Issue-based fields are formed around specific issues and current debates in society, and do not necessarily restrict inclusion to organizations within a particular industry or geographic area. Rather, this delineation of issue-based fields includes organizations that take part in defining an issue and establishing good and proper practice around it. While Hoffman (1999) separates the forming and definition of an organizational field from the construction of specific institutions, defined as norms and ideas about environmental issues, he concludes at the same time that fields and institutions co-evolve (Hoffman, 1999, p. 352).

Focusing on the struggle for capital as a process in the forming of fields is thus mostly important because it incorporates the construction of fields with the development of logics and meanings. Thus, it makes the norms and values of institutional fields both a process and a property measure. Norms and values become part of the struggle that determines fields and field participation, and the outcome of these struggles. This allows a more processual view of field formation and institutionalization, a view in which the continuous struggles for capital and legitimacy and the creation of norms and values among organizations are in focus. This conceptualization also allows for conflict within fields, and recognizes that norms and value frames can be contested (DiMaggio, 1991; Hoffman, 1999; Oakes et al., 1998). A prerequisite for struggle and conflict over capital is that fields contain many forms of it that are valued differently by members of the field. The struggle for capital can thus lead to shifting logics, but can also be ongoing and can draw on one or several existing logics. In this sense, the concept of capital allows for competing logics of fields that can create competing, and sometimes inconsistent, demands on organizations (Friedland and Alford, 1991).

The Linking of Structure and Agency

The view of fields, field struggles, and capital presented thus far are those structural aspects of Bourdieu's theory that are most often referenced and described. But this focus on capital, positions, and structures is supplemented in his work with a discussion of actors, power, and interests of members of cultural and social fields, which requires renewed attention. Taking the notion of competing capital of fields seriously, and integrating the forming of fields with the active struggles of actors, we thus need a conception of agency. Agency has been lacking in many studies of institutional structures and processes, although, as Friedland and Alford (1991, p. 254) note, 'Without actors, without subjectivity, there is no way to account for change'. I therefore need to make a brief detour that presents Bourdieu's conceptualization of agency and the habitus, which represents the 'subjective' side – emphasizing cognitive understandings and the liberty of actors to transcend structural limits.

Agency is defined as something in between objects submissive to structure and rational actors, labelled 'socialized agents'. These agents, which have characteristics and motives transcending individual dispositions (Bourdieu, 1988, p. 150), pursue goals and practices according to interests and demands created in relations with others in the field. Forming the basis of this agency is the habitus, defined as a system of acquired, enduring, and generative dispositions, which means a system of faculties that are acquired through past practices and at the same time guiding future practices. These systems of faculties are collectively orchestrated without being formally organized or dictated. Habitus generates practices and products but functions at the same time as a system that classifies those same practices. This system of classifications is the work of taste, that is, the ability to distinguish and evaluate the practices produced (Bourdieu, 1984, p. 170). The concept of habitus thus tells us that the interpretations and meanings created by agents are both historically and institutionally dependent.

Agency is here thus conceptualized as actors' abilities to act and reflect on their actions, positions, and the situations that they face, building on the acquired experiences and past practices and dependent on past actions and socially internalized, or institutionalized, values of other agents. This conception of agency, and the reproduction of social structure, is similar to that of Giddens (1984), who points out that being reflexive, as agents, does not mean that actions are dependent on intentions or that they imply rationality, but only that actors have the capacity to reflect upon their actions and monitor the actions of others (Giddens, 1984, p. 9). Giddens (1984) also gives priority to the 'routinized' practices of agents and their constitutive influence on structuration processes, much like the focus on the habitus and on habitual actions. This gives the field stability and points to the continuity of dispositions and positions (cf. Prichard and Willmott, 1997), because the actions tend to reproduce the structures of social relationships already in place (Emirbayer and Mische, 1998).

However, practices can also change the existing structures and positions if there is dissonance between the habitus and the social contingencies met by the agents. Habitus thus partly contains the concept of habit: we act according to what we are used to rather than in line with a predefined, conscious goal, but there is in fact room for agents to break with habits and contribute to changes in fields. Scott (1995) also points this out, defining agency as 'an actor's ability to have some effect on the social world' (Scott, 1995, p. 76). With Bourdieu's conceptualization of fields, agents are provided with a 'repertoire of possibilities' for them to pursue in accordance with their interests, given their positions in the field (Bourdieu, 1996). Even habitual action thus requires effort and reflexivity, and opens possibilities for changing existing practices. This leaves room for agency, while recognizing the constraining and constructing function of fields and field structures (cf. also DiMaggio, 1997).

Flexible Boundaries of Fields

With the conception of fields, field struggles, and agency launched here, the focus is on the ongoing construction and formation of fields through struggles and contestations between members of the field. Fields are thus continuously redefined and constructed or, as noted by Oakes et al. (1998, p. 286), 'Fields are in a constant state of flux'. This understanding of fields thus makes us focus on change and on the way fields are formed and reformed.

One of the ways in which processes of field change and of institutionalization have been theorized in institutional theory is field structuration (DiMaggio, 1991; DiMaggio and Powell, 1983; Giddens, 1984; Greenwood et al., 2002), whereby a gradual 'maturity' and specification of the roles, behaviours, and interactions within fields takes place. There are four elements in the structuration process: increase in interactions among organizations; emergence of inter-organizational structures of domination; increase in information exchange between organizations; and increase in awareness among members that they belong together (DiMaggio and Powell, 1983; Hoffman, 1999). The concept of structuration points to the formation of social structures over time and across space, in that structures are produced and reproduced through ongoing actions and interactions in society (Giddens, 1984; Scott, 2001). The main argument in DiMaggio and Powell (1983) is that an increasing structuration of fields leads to isomorphic pressures that forces organizations within the field to become more alike. Coercive, mimetic, and normative isomorphic pressures are identified, leading organizations to change and incorporate standards, norms, and practices diffused within the field.

Scott (2001, p. 200) argues that most empirical studies of structuration processes have focused on the initial forming of fields and on processes promoting increasing levels of structuration in fields (e.g. DiMaggio, 1991). Some studies have also problematized the de-structuration or de-institutionalization of fields, as for instance Røvik (1996) describing how ideas and logics lose legitimacy within fields. Greenwood et al. (2002) propose, however, that it is time for institutional theory to pay attention not only to the effects of field dynamics and structuration processes, that is isomorphism, but also on the processes through which such isomorphism is brought about.

While institutional theories thus often describe stability and isomorphism (DiMaggio and Powell, 1983), Bourdieu's concept of field allows a better understanding of continuous change in fields as well as for processes of resistance and non-conformity in fields. With a field concept inspired by Bourdieu, change becomes part of the way fields work (Oakes et al., 1998, p. 264). His conceptualization of fields focuses on the ongoing process to define the field, and on the struggle to define and distribute capital in the field. Returning for a moment to this argument, the struggle over capital that creates and makes up the field can also be described as a struggle aiming to reproduce, sustain, or undermine the existing structures and relations within fields (Bourdieu, 1988, p. 74). Thus, it is not the structures and positions per se that are important for understanding fields and field processes, but rather the relations between different positions and the procedures creating/reforming these positions and relations. Thus, the hierarchies of power and the hierarchies of criteria for 'judging' or measuring need to be determined and then described.

Understood in this way, the field defines a legitimate hierarchy of properties – a classification of agents within fields. A field thus contains several independent but competing hierarchies and principles of classification (Bourdieu, 1988, p. 113); the relations between them are continuously reworked; and their hierarchical order can vary over time. The field can also be described, therefore, as a place of struggle over classifications, and over hierarchies of different classifications. Because the principle of classification is often unclear, the boundaries of the field become flexible, versatile, and debatable (Bourdieu, 1988, p. 77); and the definition of who is inside and who is outside the field is therefore also unclear at a given point in time. This implies that not just the outcome of the decisions about criteria and membership are of concern and interest, but also the struggle over how these criteria and conditions are determined (Bourdieu, 1988, p. 11). Hence, the field is not only a fight over legitimate actions, dispositions, and characteristics of the members considered to be included in the field, but equally, a fight over the procedures for determining what is legitimate and right, and thus a fight over the authority to judge.

There is thus a duality between continuity and constant change in fields and in field boundaries. Multiple classificatory systems working simultaneously, and ongoing struggles to define and distribute symbolic capital within fields, are dynamic processes that create flexible and changing boundaries of fields. Through the work of habitus, however, there is also a certain continuity and stability in fields. Because of this duality, the procedures for deciding legitimate criteria and classificatory systems, which form the basis for the ongoing field struggles, are therefore as important as the actual structures or visible boundaries.

Such a processual conceptualization of field structuration leads us to a slightly different set of questions than posed in earlier studies of field formation and change. It poses questions, then, about how the field is defined and how its boundaries are delineated (Czarniawska and Sevón, 1996, p. 38). Greenwood et al. (2002) point out that field boundaries are not fixed, but are shaped by claims and counterclaims made to, for instance, professional authority (cf. Abbott, 1988). They do not, however, theorize further on how boundaries are shaped by these struggles and contesting claims. With an explicit focus on processes of field formation and structuration, it becomes possible to address specific issues of how field boundaries are created, recreated, and maintained in processes of field change. Suggesting that struggles for boundaries of fields are central aspects of field formation and reformation, we thus need concepts to understand the continuous negotiation of boundaries that abound in any given field, and to understand the role of actors in such processes of field creation.

Boundaries and Boundary-work in Fields

Issues of boundaries and the role of boundaries are a topic in many areas of research, as for instance, in anthropology, history, political science, social psychology, and sociology; but there is little integration between different lines of research (Lamont and Molnár, 2002). Boundary issues have dealt with class (Bourdieu, 1984; Lamont, 1992), culture (DiMaggio, 1987), professions (Abbott, 1988, 1995), and science (Gieryn, 1999; Nader, 1996), for example. A common theme in these studies is a desire to understand and explain the role of symbolic resources in societies and social systems (Lamont and Molnár, 2002, p. 168). Although such symbolic resources are central to the concept of fields, boundaries have not been explicitly addressed in relation to conceptions of field and field development (cf. Dacin et al., 2002).

Gieryn (1999) has used the concept 'boundary-work' to describe processes that determine the epistemic and cultural authority of science, which can help us to conceptualize the continuous construction of fields and field boundaries. He describes the field of science as a 'credibility contest'. Boundary-work is here aimed at defining insiders and outsiders, that is, to define science and scientists, and separate these from 'others': for example, from pseudoscience, ideology, faith, or nonsense. He claims that boundary-work takes place in arenas where scientific claims meet with different audiences, such as in courtrooms, boardrooms and in the media. It is here that science and scientific claims are interpreted, and where credibility is attached or removed when the audience decides who to believe and which claims to consider scientific. In this sense, 'boundary-work would be expected in settings where tacit assumptions about the contents of science are forced to become explicit: where credibility is contested; . . . and where allocations of epistemic authority are decided and consequentially deployed' (Gieryn, 1999, p. 24).

When considering fields such as science as a cultural space constructed in boundary-work, it becomes local and episodic, pragmatic and strategic, contingent, and constructed (Gieryn, 1999, p. 27). Through this conceptualization of ongoing boundary-work, Gieryn brings in the work of actors and specifies the role of individuals/organizations and their actions in the forming and reforming of fields and field boundaries. Actors thus engage in boundary-work by producing stories and accounts of their activities, engaging in discussions and debate over the procedures and contents of science, and defending or propagating ideas and scientific claims. From this perspective, the boundaries of science are considered variable, inconsistent, and volatile, and are constantly being drawn and redrawn depending on who does the boundary-work, against whom, and for whom (Gieryn, 1999, pp. 11, 22).

In this constructivist approach, Gieryn (1999) also raises the question of who has the authority to 'map' science – thus who has the authority to judge. This reasoning is very close to that of Bourdieu. Gieryn claims that scientists themselves would prefer to have their credibility grounded in secure knowledge-making processes controlled by insiders, but often find their credibility tried by others and in other arenas (Gieryn, 1999, p. 28). The media is one such arena that is controlled largely by outsiders (i.e., non-scientists), and one that uses other than purely scientific measures to allocate credibility and locate epistemic authority.

Gieryn (1999) furthermore identifies three genres of credibility contests, each calling for a different kind of boundary-work. The first is expulsion, where rival authorities compete to define authority within science. It is a definition of who is inside the authoritative cultural space, and which claims and claimants are to be left outside. In setting the boundaries for inclusion, boundary-work also becomes a means of social control, as the field provides a basis for legitimacy and norms of conduct for those included. This can be compared to claims of social control and pressures for isomorphism in institutional theory (cf. Meyer and Rowan, 1977). The second type of contest is one of expansion. Boundary-work takes place when authorities seek to extend their frontiers and make claims on other domains. Rival authorities thus contest the definition of science and seek to distinguish it from less reliable or less relevant sources of knowledge. This can also be compared to and described as struggles of professional authority and as the mapping of jurisdiction in the professions (cf. Abbott, 1988; Greenwood et al., 2002). The third and slightly different kind of boundary-work, protection of autonomy, results from efforts of outside powers to exploit epistemic authority 'in ways that compromise the material and symbolic resources of scientists inside' (Gieryn, 1999, p. 17). Such efforts to exploit authority can be implemented by, for instance, legislators and the mass media when making science a tool in political or market struggles.

Fields of Organizations and Ideas – the Creation of Symbolic Boundaries

In neo-institutional theory, as discussed briefly above, the definition of the field and its boundaries are often set on a geographical area, a distinct industry, or a common normative framework. With this definition the field is constituted by a group of organizations, mostly thought of as those producing largely the same things, and the field includes some organizations and not others. Incorporating the struggle over common normative frameworks and ideas about good practice in the struggle of fields as we have done here, however, the field is more clearly about a set of ideas as well as a set of organizations. The struggle to define fields and the boundaries of fields thus includes both a struggle to define a group of organizations, and a struggle to define ideas about what is good and suitable practice within the field. There is correspondence between a social field of individuals or organizations, with social structures, and a field of ideas as perceptions and principles of division between individuals (cf. Bourdieu, 1996, p. 2). Through the habitus, the social order is progressively inscribed in the minds of people, and 'Social divisions become principles of division, organizing the image of the social world' (Bourdieu, 1984, p. 471).

This view of the correspondence between social and mental structures makes it possible to conceptualize the cognitive character of boundaries. In line with Gieryn (1999), boundaries can therefore be conceptualized as being made up of the perceptions that people have of what is proper and good practice within a field, as for instance, within science. The boundaries are not in this sense 'real', because they do not describe a social structure or order, but rather a mental structure (as people's perceptions of boundaries) and a field of ideas. These boundaries, however cognitive and mental, can contain perceptions of both which organizations are included and which practices and principles are considered good and proper. Inspired by Bourdieu, Lamont (1992) labels such boundaries 'symbolic boundaries', which are conceptual distinctions that individuals make to categorize objects and practices, that are subjectively drawn by individuals between themselves and others. Although separating conceptually such cognitive boundaries from social boundaries is necessary, these two types of boundaries should be viewed as equally real (Lamont and Molnár, 2002, p. 169).

Fields and Agency

We have thus far developed concepts of fields, and seen how fields are continuously developed and defined as actors struggle to define capital and to claim authority. The field is characterized by continuous change, with fluid and flexible boundaries of who and what constitutes it. The struggles of capital within fields also define the boundaries for the field, in terms of who is included and what is considered good, proper and legitimate practice. These boundaries are symbolic in character, and are produced by cognitive conceptions that members hold of who and what are inside the field. Furthermore, the concept of boundary-work has been introduced to conceptualize what these boundaries are, and how they are created and defended in ongoing construction of the field.

The concept of boundary-work and the construction of symbolic boundaries imply, however, that someone or something does the work, that is, carries out the task of drawing symbolic boundaries and of defining the field. We are therefore back to the question, introduced in the beginning of this section, of agency. The conceptualization of agency presented here so far is, however, rather limited. By focusing on the routinized practices (Giddens, 1984), the constitutive function of the habitus (Bourdieu, 1993; 1988), and the taken-for-grantedness of institutionalized practices (Scott, 2001), all tend as theories to focus on the historical dimension of agency, the repetitive and reproducing aspect of human action. The concept of habitus has been important here to understand the link between social structures and symbolic categorizations, but we also need a framework to investigate the contemporary enactment and construction of boundaries and field change.

To capture a dynamic and temporally contingent view of agents, the following section will develop the concept of identity that draws attention to the sense-making, actions, and understandings of individual actors to current situations and problems. Drawing on the work of George Herbert Mead, Emirbayer and Mische (1998) argue for the need to study the ability of actors to actively constitute their environments and to direct attention towards their own pattern of action and response to situational factors, not just in a historically dependent fashion (habitus) but also in present time. This will be provided here through the concept of identity, investigating closer the construction and constitution of the 'self' in reaction to field changes and field formation. This study of the construction of organizational fields thus needs to be linked to issues concerning the identities of actors, identity formation, and the ability of actors to interpret, react to, and act upon social structures and the principles of classification that constitute the field.

IDENTITY, INSECURITY, AND IMPLICATIONS FOR INSTITUTIONAL CHANGE

The common use of identity in social theory gives the impression of something durable, persisting, and objective in an organization's character. Probably the most cited reference to a definition of organizational identity is the one presented by Albert and Whetten (1985): it is the features of an organization that the members perceive as the central, enduring, and distinctive in character (see Dutton and Dukerich, 1991; Elsbach and Kramer, 1996; Gioia and Thomas, 1996). This definition implies that the identity is to be found within individuals, something that Czarniawska (1997) labels an 'essential self' definition of identity. This view of organizational identity, which is rather static, does not allow conceptualizations of identity changes, and of identity formation and reformation in a more open and generative way. Other studies have offered an alternative approach to issues of identity, an approach that links identity to the concept of image (Dutton and Dukerich, 1991; Gioia et al., 2000; Gioia and Thomas, 1996), and thereby acknowledge the fact that identities are dynamic and fluid. Although recognizing the social construction of identities by linking internal identity to externally construed images, this does not allow for a conceptualization of organizational identities that links to field level and institutional change. To capture such dynamics, there is also a need to account for members' interpretation of actions and structures (Zilber, 2002, p. 236).

Identification

Introducing a connection between identity and institutional change, an identity concept is needed, one that does not just define identity as an internal property, but rather, allows it to be shaped and formed in continuous interaction with the environment, and in a social context (Czarniawska, 1997, p. 44; cf. also Sevón, 1996). Being thus contingent, identity is constructed in an ongoing process (Townley, 1993) involving interactions, by which identities are not only created and defined, but also by which society is simultaneously reproduced or changed (Czarniawska, 1997). This makes it possible to see how agency and structure interact, as expressed by Davis: 'Framing identity and difference theoretically as always constructed within webs of complex social interaction would resist reductionisms and offer enhanced possibilities for understanding both determinisms and human agency' (Davis, 2000, p. 7).

Identity is thus received from the outside environment, equally as much as it is an inherent property of individuals or organizations. Stressing that identity is received from the outside, theorists have pointed to the 'social identity' that individuals hold apart from their 'personal identity' of basic characteristics (Ashforth and Mael, 1989). The social identity is created through social classifications, which enable the individual to 'locate or define him- or herself in the social environment' (Ashforth and Mael, 1989, p. 21). Groups engage in categorization, identification, and comparison in their construction of a self-identity. This identification with a social group or category thus provides part of the answer to the question 'Who am I?' (Ashforth and Meal, 1989). Much earlier, Goffman (1963) also used the term 'social identity', to signify how people get put into categories and classifications and to discuss the norms that follow from such a classification. He claims that the categories are received from society: 'Social settings establish the categories of persons likely to be encountered there' (Goffman, 1963, p. 2).

The concept of social identity points to the importance of self-identification and the relational character of identities that neo-institutionalists have picked up. Sevón (1996, p. 57) points to the importance of self-identification in processes of organizational imitation and change, because it is the matching of identities (i.e., questions of 'What am I like' and 'Whom/what do I look like') that drives imitation, and hence contributes to mimetic isomorphism in fields. Such self-identification can only be made, however, in relation with and in reference to others (Sevón, 1996, p. 57). Identity is thus relational, as Clegg (1989, p. 159) notes, and as he states: 'one can only ever be seen to be something in relation to something else'.

In creating a sense of self and an identity, the organization compares itself with others perceived as being similar, and hence the recognition of 'being in the same boat' (Dacin et al., 2002) contributes to individual and organizational identity. Identities are thus socially produced by actors who place themselves in social categories and act and relate to others in terms of these categories. Identities are 'self-meanings' acquired in particular situations (Burke and Reitzes, 1991, p. 242), and are thus formed, maintained, and confirmed through the forming of social categories. Actors take part in such processes through engaging in self-representation and actions that negotiate and confirm the meaning of these social categories (Burke and Reitzes, 1991). The concept of identity is thus also linked to action. Such considerations of identities and self-identity (Giddens, 1984) draw attention to 'an active and reflexive self that creates, sustains, and changes social structures' (Scott, 1995, p. 24).

The formation of identity is not just dependent on the self-perception and the placing of oneself in relation to others. This self-identification is also dependent on the perception of others, and how others view and recognize the organization; thus, others' perception of the 'self' is important in the construction of identities. This argument is similar to the one made above, that of the organizational identity being linked to the image of the organization, and of others taking part in interpreting and shaping the identity. This argument has been taken farther, however, to argue that the identity also has to be understood and recognized by others. The socially constructed identity is thus dependent on 'what is possible to recognize and name, with the help of typifications and classifications that others share' (Sahlin-Andersson, 1996, p. 73). Hence, identity is also about being identified as somebody and something. Unlike self-identification, this classification and identification is not always possible to control (Bowker and Star, 1999; Goffman, 1963).

Recognizing both the importance of self-identification and the need for identities to be recognized by others, Czarniawska (1997) goes even further to suggest that identities are performed and constructed in conversations, in that 'the Self is produced, reproduced, and maintained in conversations, past and present' (Czarniawska, 1997, p. 45). Thus, she treats identities as narratives, or 'as a continuous process of narration where both the narrator and the audience are involved in formulating, editing, applauding, and refusing various elements of the ever-produced narrative' (Czarniawska, 1997, p. 49). In so doing, identities are not just reflected in, but also created through, the construction of self-narratives; and the identity is continuously constructed and reconstructed in the interaction with other organizations and the audience.

The Self and the Generalized Other

This conceptualization of identification links back to Mead (1934) and his theories about the construction and development of a self and an identity. Emirbayer and Mische (1998) argue that Mead also stresses the 'sociality' of identity, claiming the self is constructed in social interaction and in processes of dialogue and conversation. Stressing the inter-subjective character of identity-formation, the self-concept of individual is developed from their capacity to project themselves into the experiences of others (Emirbayer and Mische, 1998, p. 988). Mead (1934) uses the concept of the 'generalized other', which is an abstract other that to the individual reflects social relations and produces organized views of a social system. The generalized other is the organized community or social group that gives the individual his 'unity of self' (Mead, 1934, p. 154). The reference to a general other provides people with a self, and helps a person determine himself in his relationship with the group to which he belongs (Baldwin, 1986, p. 111). Mead (1934) claims that children do this through playing games: in order to play a game the child must know the roles of all other players in the game, and to see himself as others see him in that game, and thus see himself as a generalized other. This helps the child acquire a personality, and to determine himself in relation to the group. He points out, however, that the child must not only be able to take the other's view of himself, but also take their attitudes towards the common social activity in which they are all engaged in order to develop a full sense of self (Mead, 1934, p. 155). This way, it is also through the generalized other that things or concepts acquire the same general meanings for all members of the group (Baldwin, 1986, p 100). Thus, the conceptualization of the generalized other is important for the forming of fields and common understandings of members of fields.

We can learn two important lessons from Mead's discussion of the generalized other. First, just like children in Mead's work are 'active agents in their own socialization' (see Baldwin, 1986, p. 97), so are actors perceived here as active in their own categorization and identity formation. Through the generalized, abstract other, actors determine themselves in relation to the group to which they want to belong, and it provides them with a self, or an identity. This is, however, also dependent on the perceptions of 'other'. Hence, the conception of an abstract other contributes to the identity formation processes. Second, through organized actions in response to the generalized other, the actions of the whole group or community are created and organized. The concept of the generalized other thus creates not only the roles of the individual actors, but does also define the roles and understandings of all other members in that group, or in the game. Identity formation is thus intimately connected to the forming of general meanings and 'rules of the game' in larger social systems in which individuals or other actors are a part.

Identities and Field Formation

The approach to organizational identity presented here and Mead's (1934) concept of the generalized other links the forming of identities to broader issues of field formation and change. As has been shown above, fields contribute to organizational identity-formation by providing a common reference system, norms, and classifications that are shared among the members of the field and used in processes of identification and self-identification. With this approach, identity is both received from the institutional environment and through interactions with others, and created and recreated by the organization itself through a process of self-identification and through comparing with others.

Identity-formation processes of actors do also contribute to changes in society (Czarniawska, 1997, p. 44). Local identity formation processes contribute to the forming of fields as common meanings and classifications are created, recognized, and used by members of the field. The link between fields and identities can be further understood through the concept of capital of organizational fields (Oakes et al., 1998). Capital is essentially linked to identities because it structures relationships between organizations and between actors of organizational fields, creating 'positions of possibility', or relative positions within the field that reflect various possibilities to act. The structure and distribution of capital in the field, created in a continuous struggle over classifications and definitions of legitimate activities, thus create relations and positions through which interaction between members of the field takes place. This, in turn, contributes to organizational identity-formation. Oakes et al. (1998) show how business planning can change organizational identities by changing what is at stake, that is, the capital of the field. Implicit in their analysis is also that these changes in identity contribute to institutional and field changes (Oakes et al., 1998, p. 287). This suggests that field-level changes do not just lead to identity-formation processes, but can also be driven partly by changes in actors' identities and in identity-forming processes.

Lamont (1992) shows that boundary-work is also an intrinsic part of this process of constituting the self and creating a stable sense of identity, both as individuals and as groups, and that instances of boundary-work emerge when actors try to define who they are. 'By generating distinctions, we also signal our identity and develop a sense of security, dignity, and honor; a significant portion of our daily activities are oriented toward avoiding shame and maintaining a positive self-identity by patrolling the borders of our groups' (Lamont, 1992, p. 11). This way, boundary-work can be conceptualized as both driven by, and the result of, identity-formation processes, and as grounded in procedures to classify and categorize actors in fields.

Essential to this understanding of identity, and its relation to field change and formation, are the socially produced and shared classifications and typifications that organize actors into socially recognizable groups or categories. Such classifications include grouping mechanisms that are both used by individual organizations, and recognized and used by others to classify and categorize the organization. Putting identity formation processes of actors together with field change and boundary-setting of fields, thus requires an understanding of the place, time and situation in which classifications are enacted and used, and local identity-processes activated. One way to do this is to focus on classification mechanisms and their importance in forming recognizable categories of organizations and the processes whereby these become recognized and shared among organizations.

CLASSIFICATIONS AS ARENAS FOR BOUNDARY-WORK OF FIELDS

To be able to analyse the interrelatedness of these processes – local identity-formation and field formation – I will use the concept of arena, and classifications as arenas, to understand and capture both processes and actors that form the field and the symbolic boundaries of fields. This concept has been used in institutional theories of fields (Greenwood et al., 2002; Rao, 1998) to conceptualize and localize processes of change, and by Gieryn (1999) to locate credibility contests and instances of boundary-work. Studies have shown how organizations such as professional associations play important roles as arenas for change, by hosting debates, framing and reframing professional identities, and justifying and legitimating solutions and change (Greenwood et al., 2002, pp. 59–60). Although used, the concept of arena has not been extensively theorized.

A better conceptualization and understanding of arenas for field change can contribute to theories of fields by introducing a means for analysing not the outcome of field struggles, but the processes and actors taking part in such processes (cf. Greenwood et al., 2002). Arenas specify where field struggles take place, as well as how fields and boundaries are shaped and reformed in debates and interaction between actors. Scott has pointed out that most analysts use a top-down approach to field formation and boundaries, stressing the role of global institutions, nation states, or professional groups in shaping field definitions (Scott, 2001, p. 137). A number of studies of field formation and change focus on professional organizations and governments/states as agents (see, for example, DiMaggio and Powell, 1983; Greenwood et al., 2002; Lounsbury, 2002) and on the formulation of norms, formal rules, laws, and the like, and thus concentrate on large-scale changes in regulations, standards, and logics (Dacin et al., 2002).

However, with such top-down conceptualizations of fields and field formation, a number of mechanisms and processes that contribute to field processes are not accounted for. Focusing more directly on mechanisms and classification systems that are not traditionally understood as 'governance mechanisms' or as important constitutive systems that influence organizational and organizational fields, I wish to extend the notion of arenas and suggest that a large number of evaluation and classification systems can potentially have an influence on field development and change. Inspired by a line of research investigating audit and accounting practices, it is reasonable to assume that a wide set of measuring and evaluation systems can have governing and regulatory effects even though they are not formally constituted as laws or regulations (Miller, 1996, 2001; Shore and Wright, 2000).

Various procedures for categorizing, describing, measuring, and evaluating practices and objects have been shown to influence the behaviour and perceptions of actors. The functioning and effects of measurement techniques and evaluating procedures have been investigated in various areas and settings, as for instance, in describing business planning as a 'pedagogic practice' (Oakes et al., 1998), in audits as 'political technologies' (Shore and Wright, 2000; Strathern, 2000a), or more generally, in measuring mechanisms as 'disciplinary practices' (Townley, 1993; cf. Foucault, 1977) or as expressions of 'governmentality' (Foucault, 1991) and technologies of government (Miller, 2001; Rose and Miller, 1992). As the naming of these practices and procedures suggest, they are not just reflections and objective descriptions or assessments of activities that go on in society; they are also, to a large extent, used by agents in setting standards and contributing to defining and 'disciplining' the activities and actors within certain areas or fields. Such systems operate collectively both as an external control system, and as an internalization of new norms that make individuals freely conform to the norms set by these practices (Shore and Wright, 2000, p. 61).

Making Visible through Classifications

It is not only the constitutive and regulatory functions of classifications and measuring mechanisms that are important for influencing and shaping fields and field boundaries. To understand their role as an arena for field struggles, it is important also to understand what it is that these practices do and how they do it, i.e. how they set norms and standards and what that means. One of the main characteristics of classification systems, which is important for their role in both field processes and identity processes, is the way these systems make things and objects visible. Classifications are thus not neutral instruments for presentation, but are procedures for naming, making visible, diffusing, and constructing knowledge about the objects or individuals being classified (cf. Bowker and Star, 1999; cf. Townley, 1993). They make comparisons, group individuals and organizations, and create distinction as well as sameness and belonging. By making things visible, these systems also create and diffuse norms, standards, and role models, and contribute to determining the capital of fields.

Bowker and Star (1999) separates two types of classifications that have different ways of defining categories and assigning places within categories and classes, and thus make different things visible. The first type is labelled an Aristotelian classification, which works according to a set of (binary) features or characteristics that the object being classified either has or does not have (Bowker and Star, 1999, p. 62). An Aristotelian classification thus sets up a series of criteria that puts objects into one, and only one, class or group. The authors also show, however, that the practical act of classifying is often much fuzzier and more complex than this, and that we often resort to prototypical classification. This type of classifications is based on an assessment of the appearance of the object being classified, and an assessment of whether the object is perceived to belong to a certain category or class (Bowker and Star, 1999, p. 62). It is claimed that we have a broad picture of an object in mind, a prototype, and make assessments as to whether another object is similar to this prototype and belongs in the same category. These two means of classifications are often used together, creating messiness and sometimes quite extreme consequences for those involved.

Because the two types of classification often conflate, the distinction between Aristotelian and prototypical classifications is not empirically very useful. But the distinction is theoretically useful and important because it helps us see what it is that classification mechanisms make visible. Classification systems, in an Aristotelian sense, make visible a set of characteristics or properties, that is, the norms, standards, and procedures used to classify individuals and groups. The systems do, however, also make visible a set of actors/organizations or groups of actors that are perceived as role models or prototypes for a certain group or class.

Classifications also have another feature that make their role in field and identity-forming processes salient; they divide things into groups and positions, and order things in hierarchies (cf. Shore and Wright, 2000). This provides a basis for comparison, and provides a structuring of individuals or units into distinct positions. Following Foucault, there are two such processes of partitioning: the development of an order through taxonomy (taxinomia), and the establishment of an order through measurement (mathesis) (Foucault, [1970] 2002, p. 79; Townley, 1993, p. 528). The former means an ordering into categories and a system of relations; the latter means a measurement (often numerical), ordering, and presentation of positions and things. This distinction illustrates that classifications can have different roles, both signalling what is to be associated with what and how things are placed in relation to each other. Foucault also discusses the effects of such classification systems, stating that 'The distribution according to ranks or grades has a double role; it marks the gaps, hierarchizes qualities, skills and aptitudes but it also punishes and rewards' (Foucault, 1977, p. 181). This way, measurement and classification mechanisms also constitute a normalizing process (Townley, 1993, p. 529), contributing to shaping the behaviour and actions of members of the field.

Rankings as Classifications

Highlighting the function of classifications in making visible, grouping and comparing certain practices, characteristics, or organizations, the role of class-ifications in forming fields and field boundaries and constituting an arena for field struggles becomes clear. The quote above from Foucault is particularly illustrative of the role of rankings and league tables, as these are clearly 'math-esis' forms of classifications relying on a hierarchical positioning of organiza-tions. The way such systems 'punish and reward' organizations for doing good or bad is one important driving force, as such lists are part of 'certification contests' between organizations, and thus part of the reputation building and image control of organizations (Elsbach and Kramer, 1996; Rao, 1994; Schulz et al., 2001). Rankings are part of struggles for status and reputation within fields (Rao et al., 2000). In a study of the early automobile industry, Rao (1994) show how certification contests generate status orderings in fields; victories in such contests contribute to a positive reputation of firms. The study indicates that cumulative victories in such contests increase the firm's access to resources and enhances the survival prospects for the winning firms (Rao, 1994, pp. 30–3).

Besides a general reflection of the belief that winning is better than losing, the enhanced reputation of a firm through certification contests is thus also linked to material rewards and resources (Rao, 1994). This is not just a fight for symbolic resources *per se*. The struggle for symbolic resources contributes to a status hierarchy in fields that is, in turn, part of the structuration process of fields (DiMaggio and Powell, 1983; Lounsbury, 2002). This way it contributes to determining the capital of fields and the distribution of that capital between members of the field (cf. Bourdieu, 1988). This struggle for symbolic resources, status positions, and reputation can be assumed to be particularly important in fields where the quality of 'products' are difficult to assess and where the goals of organizations are ambiguous (cf. Benjamin and Podolny, 1999; DiMaggio and Powell, 1983; Meyer and Rowan, 1977), as for instance, in education (Trow, 1998; Whitley, 1984).

The argument that there are material as well as symbolic benefits from participating in rankings and certification contests does not oppose the argument that rankings are arenas for field struggles and development. The definition and distribution of capital within fields, contributing to setting boundaries for how the field is defined, determines the bases for what is valued and exchanged in fields and the relative positions of actors in that field. In this sense, the definition and distribution of capital forms the ground rules for the field and clarifies the rules for subsequent distribution and competition for material resources. In line with both Bourdieu (1984) and Lamont (1992), the symbolic and the social worlds are inevitably interlinked.

Analytical Themes

The above theoretical discussion has established a view of rankings as classification mechanisms that serve as arenas for a continuous forming and structuring of fields and field boundaries. In an appendix about media rankings on 'intellectuals' and academics in France, Bourdieu (1988) suggests that rankings contribute to the construction and reconstruction of the field by influencing how legitimacy is created and which forms of capital are required for participation in field struggles. The above analysis has shown, however, that rankings as classification mechanisms can contribute more specifically to field formation and boundary-setting processes, by hosting struggles for what is valued and legitimate, but also by forming members' identities and perceptions of the group or category to which they belong. Rankings as arenas for such struggles thus help to create, protect or reform symbolic boundaries for the field – as perceptions of who is in, what is legitimate, which characteristics are valued, who compares to whom and so on.

The analysis that follows focuses around three main themes relating to the role of rankings in field formation and processes of boundary-work in fields. The first two themes are labelled 'templates' and 'positions'. These are interrelated and concern the function and construction of rankings as classification mechanisms, that is, what is measured, and how, and also the outcome in terms of the final ranking lists. The analysis of templates and positions links in turn to the overarching concern of rankings as arenas for boundary-work and field struggles and the 'autonomy' of the field, which is the third theme in the analysis. This theme, which is slightly different in character than the first two, and which concerns the authority of the rankings to evaluate and judge organizations in the field, depends on the first two themes: that is, on the ability of the rankings to create templates and positions. Let me clarify these themes and their relations to the theoretical arguments made above.

A template

The first theme refers to the forming and re-forming of a template for management education organizations. This relates to the conception of an Aristotelian classification, in which what is measured, and how, becomes important (Bowker and Star, 1999). The rankings are assumed to contribute to field struggles by defining characteristics and criteria for evaluating members of the field. The aspects and characteristics highlighted by classification mechanisms contribute to the struggle over field capital by determining the characteristics and qualities recognized as relevant and valuable in fields (cf. Bourdieu, 1988). These characteristics, and thus the template, need to be used and recognized in identity-formation processes of actors in the field. This is assumed to determine the boundaries of what claims are considered part of the field, and of what are legitimate activities of members in the field. In Gieryn's (1999) terms, this involves boundary-work against expansion of fields or groups.

Positions

The second theme, positions, is related to the actual ranking list. The rankings contribute to defining fields and field boundaries by presenting a list of field members that are considered part of the field and also of important organizations within the field (i.e., of those who 'count' within the field). This is connected to the recognition that classifications are also prototypical, both building on and constructing prototypes within the group (Bowker and Star, 1999). The field struggle, which is also about the distribution of capital between members of the field, determines who is considered part of the field as well as how organizations are ordered within the field (cf. Bourdieu, 1988). This struggle is assumed to determine the boundaries of who are included in the field and who are left outside, or assumed to concern boundary-work against expulsion, in Gieryn's (1999) terms.

Autonomy

The third theme, autonomy, is thus an extension of the first two and concerns the authority of rankings and classification mechanisms to evaluate and set criteria for organizations in the field. If rankings contribute to forming templates and positions, they are arenas for field struggles and for boundary-work on fields. As such, they compete with other mechanisms and arenas for the authority to judge members of the field, and they define the capital of the field. In Bourdieu (1988), the struggle of hierarchies of classifications implies such a struggle for authority, and because an increase in the number of authoritative judges may threaten the autonomy of the field (p. 269), the struggle corresponds to boundary-work conducted by members of the field to protect the autonomy of epistemic authority (Gieryn, 1999, p. 17). To distinguish this third form of boundary-work from the first two and to clarify its special character, Gieryn (1999, p. 17) refer to this as 'second-order' boundary-work.

These analytical themes will be used to analyse the development of rankings in Chapters 4 through 6. First, however, an empirical introduction to the field of European management education is needed.

3. A European business school field in the making

Management education is not a uniform concept. Management education programmes can take different shapes, and they can be run in various contexts and in different organizational settings. Forming an empirical background for the analysis of business school rankings and of the development of a European ranking system, this chapter will provide a view of the diversity of management education organizations in the European field. While illustrating diverse identities and organizational settings of business schools and other management education organizations, it will also show that a field is beginning to form around common perceptions of what makes up an international business school.

Presenting two organizational narratives of business schools in this field, this chapter links the identity-construction of individual business schools to the forming of a management education field. In keeping with the theoretical assumptions presented earlier, this field, like other intellectual fields, can be assumed to contain struggles for intellectual and other forms of symbolic and field-specific capital. This struggle is reflected and played out in the identities and in the identity-formation processes of individual business schools. The use of narratives in this chapter is linked to the theoretical use and understanding of the concept 'identity', as created and maintained through a process of narration (Czarniawska, 1997, p. 46). Narratives thus present a way of investigating, and of representing (from my perspective), the identities and the identity-formation processes of these business schools. The narratives will thus provide an understanding of the struggle for capital and different bases for legitimacy that can be found in European management education. The chapter begins with a brief look at the historical context of management education, and how the struggle for capital has characterized the development of business schools in both Europe and the United States. Then follows the presentation of the two narratives. The chapter ends with a concluding section linking these narrated field developments to the development of business school rankings.

A FRAGMENTED FIELD OF MANAGEMENT EDUCATION

The beginning of higher business education as we know it today dates back to the late nineteenth century and early twentieth century, when, in both Europe and the United States, new schools of commerce and business were set up inside established universities and as separate schools. In the United States, the Wharton School of Finance and Commerce was established at the University of Pennsylvania in 1881, followed in 1889 by initiatives at the University of California and the University of Chicago, in 1900 at Dartmouth College and New York University, and in 1908 at Columbia University and Harvard University. Among the early European initiatives we find, for instance, Ecole des Hautes Etudes Commerciales in Paris in 1881; the London School of Economics in 1895; St Gallen, Switzerland and Vienna, Austria in 1898; Bocconi University, Italy in 1902; Manchester University in 1904; and the Stockholm School of Economics, Sweden in 1909 (for a complete list of schools see Engwall and Zamagni, 1998, pp. 5, 8).

In the United States, higher business education expanded rapidly after the Second World War, and most of the approximately 2500 US institutions of higher education offered business education by the early 1970s (Engwall and Zamagni, 1998, p. 8).

Business studies developed as a separate faculty or school within universities, and was much more closely linked to business practice than were other related disciplines in the university, such as economics (Locke, 1989, p. 159). But Locke argues that with the expansion in business education after the war, the gap between the 'academic' university departments of economics and the 'practical' business schools narrowed, as a 'new paradigm' of management studies was introduced. This new paradigm established management studies as a science-based discipline, using methods and theories inspired by other social sciences and applying these to business problems (Locke, 1989, 159). Although all types of management education expanded after the war, the growth was most notable in graduate business studies, particularly in the United States. Harvard and Carnegie were established as graduate schools, but most business schools just added graduate studies as supplements to their undergraduate degrees (Locke, 1989, p. 162). Some previous undergraduate schools, such as UCLA, were transformed into graduate schools. A particular part of the development of graduate education was the MBA degree, a master's degree in business studies, which has expanded rapidly in the 1970s and the 1980s.

When talking about the development of management education in Europe, it is mostly discussed in terms of the adoption of, or resistance to, the 'American model'. Although the American higher education system is highly diverse, talk of an American model is very common, and often refers to a

model of a graduate business school offering MBA programmes and estab-
lished within a large American university (Locke, 1989; Engwall and
Zamagni, 1998). Model business schools are, for instance, Chicago, Harvard,
Northwestern, Stanford, and UCLA (Engwall and Zamagni, 1998, p. 10).

Even if it is questionable whether there really is one American model to
business education, this perception of American management education has
been important in forming many aspects of European management education
and in forming business schools in Europe. The interest in American business
schools and management education grew steadily in Europe after the war and
throughout the 1960s and the 1970s. Through study trips, training
programmes, and efforts to emulate the leading management schools in the
United States, the idea of the American-type business schools spread to
Europe (Engwall, 1992). The rebuilding of Europe after the war, with financial support from organizations such as the Ford Foundation, has also
supported the establishment of 'American-type' business schools in Europe
(Engwall and Zamagni, 1998).

Studies of European business education show, however, that such interest
has not been a straightforward adoption of the American business school
model. National contexts have helped shape the management education organizations and programmes in European countries, so there is no uniform adoption of the business school model. Just as there is no clear American model,
there is no clear European model for management education. Great Britain,
described by Engwall and Zamagni (1998) as a late adopter of the American
model, got their first university-based business schools in 1965 when the business schools in Manchester and London were established (Locke, 1989;
Tiratsoo, 1998). Other business schools have since been established within
British universities, and even such traditional universities as Cambridge and
Oxford started business schools in the 1990s. Locke (1989) points out,
however, that many of the British business schools, such as London,
Manchester, and Cranfield, are not normal university departments, but must,
unlike other departments, earn a large part of their funding from sources other
than governmental.

Other European countries have not so obviously adopted the business
school model. In France and Germany, for instance, where management
education has been established within the national university systems, the
business school model has largely been resisted (Engwall and Zamagni, 1998).
France has approximately 75 organizations offering MBA programmes
(Moon, 2002, p. 81), but management education has developed within the
'*grandes écoles*', in schools such as HEC and ESCP-EAP, rather than in the
university system. One exception is perhaps INSEAD, which is often thought
of as one of the most 'American' business schools in Europe but which is separate and independent from both the *grande écoles* system and the French

university system (Engwall and Zamagni, 1998, p. 12). INSEAD, founded in 1958, launched the first European MBA programme.

In Italy and Spain, on the other hand, business schools have developed alongside the traditional university systems, with the exception of SDA Bocconi, Italy's most famous business school established in the early 1970s, as it is part of Bocconi University (Gemelli, 1998). In the Scandinavian countries, management education has developed both inside traditional universities and as independent business schools, or as German-inspired *Handelshochschulen*, parallel to the university system (Engwall, 1992).

As seen, the adoption of business schools in Europe has been both inside and outside traditional universities, and always with adaptation to the national educational systems. Although the study of business has been established as a discipline, the organizational arrangement varies between countries and between educational organizations. Regardless of form and organizational set-up of these schools, in one form or another, the business school model as well as the MBA programme have become institutionalized parts of higher education systems in both the United States and Europe, and increasingly in the rest of the world as well (Moon, 2002, p. 21). Today there are approximately 700 MBA programmes offered in European-based business schools and universities.[1]

Whether we look in the United States or in Europe, the development of business schools and business studies as an academic subject was not without problems. All accounts of the expansion of business education tell that business and management studies met heavy criticism when introduced in the academic systems (Daniel, 1998; Engwall, 1992; Engwall and Zamagni, 1998; Locke, 1989). Economics professors in the United States as well as in the UK looked down upon their business school colleagues (Locke, 1989). In Germany, the struggle between what has been labelled the 'applied fields' and the 'pure fields' is perhaps most notable (Meyer, 1998, p. 29), in that the *Handelshochschulen* have progressed from trade schools to academic, research-oriented organizations (Kipping, 1998; Meyer, 1998). Engwall (1992) has described the struggles of management education to become an established university discipline as a process where 'Mercury meets Minerva', showing the struggle between the academic demands of universities and professors, and the interests of managers and companies. This has been described as a struggle between academic interests and pure research on the one hand and practical business knowledge and skills on the other.

Daniel (1998) claims that the academic status and profile of management education is also an ongoing debate concerning the MBA degree. The organizations providing MBA programmes are constantly drawn between the need and desire to satisfy the requirements and demands of the academic community, and, at the same time, the requirements to serve the business community with business skills and relevant research. Daniel (1998) claims that business schools are continuously criticized from both ends: for being either too practically oriented or for being of too little value for 'real-life businessmen' (Daniel, 1998, p. 287–9).

This conceptualization of the business school field thus shows various forms of organizations and organizational set-ups, and suggests an inherent struggle between academic values and business values in management education. The academic and the business values described above can be characterized as two ends of a perceived continuum of management education values – a 'business–academia' continuum. Although these are by no means the only values characterizing management education, they are historically derived as well as salient features in contemporary management education organizations, for instance evident in the debate about the role of the MBA programme.

The remainder of this chapter will describe two business schools with different identities and different organizational set-ups, illustrating different positions on this perceived continuum. Although not really representing any real forms, the ends of the continuum can be considered to identify two extreme or idealized forms of management education organizations, each to be represented by an example of the type. These should be understood in the Weberian sense of 'ideal-type', thus as prototypical abstract categories of things, rather than ideal in terms of representing desirability for what is good or proper (cf. Ragin, 1994, p. 70). For the purpose of the presentations of the narratives, the 'academic' end of this continuum is conceptualized as a business school with close links to a national university system, committed to academic values and to undergraduate as well as graduate education, and initiated and started within an established research university. The 'business' end, on the other hand, is conceptualized as a business school with no formal ties to a university system, oriented towards interests in businesses and corporations, and started by private initiatives or corporate interests. The identities and identity-formation of the two business schools presented in the following sections will illustrate the perceived continuum of business-school orientation, from academic to business, and will link this continuum to aspects of the capital of the field.

A BUSINESS SCHOOL IN A UNIVERSITY SETTING

The example of an academically oriented business school, hereafter referred to as the academic business school, is a relatively new business school in the field, formally started around 1990, but it has grown and developed rapidly with approximately ten professors and 60 research and teaching staff employed in 2002. The business school is part of a large and old university with a strong reputation both nationally and internationally. Being part of the university, the business school offers management education at all levels through several undergraduate and graduate programmes, one PhD programme, two MBA programmes, and a variety of executive education courses. The business school has over 300 students on its undergraduate, graduate (including the MBA programmes), and post-graduate courses every year and more than 600 participants in executive education courses. While research and the PhD programme are considered among the most important activities, the MBA and executive education courses grew considerably during the late 1990s, and are now part of the core strategy for the business school. As a latecomer in the MBA market, the school launched a full-time MBA programme in the late 1990s and currently admits between 100–125 MBA students every year.

The overall aim of the business school is to combine and balance teaching and research activities into a successful and highly regarded international business school. The expressed aim is for the school to be regarded as one of the leading international business schools, with strong links to the university and with a high academic standard:

> We see ourselves as a major business school, which has, . . . a very special opportunity but also a big challenge. The special opportunity is to grow a business school within this ancient, multi-faculty, inter-disciplinary university, which is worthy of the name of [the University], which will build on the strength of [the University] but not become so pulled back into an ossified, backward-facing departmental process that it can't compete with the major international business schools. So it is quite a challenge to do that, because the excellence of [the University] is in scholarship research and in some way in undergraduate as well as graduate teaching. (Director, 2001)

The quote above seems to suggest that this aim requires a balancing of two, perhaps quite different, identities: that of a university department and that of an international business school. It also seems to suggest that these two sides place different demands, restrictions, and expectations on the organization. As will be shown, these demands and expectations are reflected in the structure and activities of the organization as well as in the organizational narrative.

University Department

Stressing the strong link to the university, the aim for the business school is expressed as a wish to be ranked at the same level as other departments within the university:

> [The aim is,] ultimately, to be the equivalent of [the University] in the field of management and business. I think everybody here agrees [on that] even if they've got a diversity of views on other issues or on the details. But [the aim as described

above] is sort of what everyone agrees we are trying to do here; we are trying to be the management or business bit of [the University] (MBA admissions director, 2001)

In order to accomplish that aim, one of the main features is to keep the 'academic status' of the school high. Therefore, academic research and a PhD programme, as well as undergraduate and graduate teaching, are priorities within the business school.

> [... the excellence of the University is in scholarship research ...] We therefore have to make sure that we pay a lot of attention to our research, make sure that we publish in leading journals and that people have time to do research. So that that element of [the University] is very, very strongly represented. (Director, 2001)

The stated research aim is to have research output of the 'highest academic standard' and to provide 'relevance' to the needs of business and public policy. In order to facilitate research and encourage academic publishing, the school has a sabbatical system whereby all faculty members who work full time for two years get four months off to do research. Research record and analytical skills are also two of the important criteria when recruiting new faculty to the business school:

> We look for very high intellect in an analytical sort that will really advance knowledge in the subject. We look at the abilities to communicate, stand up and defend and work with very discerning graduate students. We look for good colleagues. But the first is a necessary condition. We do look for very bright people. (Director, 2001)

To live up to the expectations of being a part of the university, the business school sees as its main challenge to recruit and retain good faculty that are strong in both research and teaching, and to attract good, highly intellectual students. This, it is claimed, is one of the strengths that the university has lived and thrived on for many years (MBA director, 2001). The link to the university is also considered to require a strong focus on undergraduate teaching.

One of the important efforts, in order to recruit faculty and sustain the academic reputation, is creating a 'vibrant' environment for faculty to work in, and to secure the time and resources needed for faculty to do research. Faculty time is generally viewed as divided into three equally important parts: the faculty should notionally devote one-third of their time to each – research, teaching, and other professional activities within and outwith the business school. Compared to other departments within the university, the teaching load in the business school is believed to be relatively high, while it is considered to be low compared to many other business schools (Director, 2001). There are no set objectives for work that falls outside teaching and research and faculty are allowed to do private consulting work as long as it doesn't interfere with teaching and research obligations at the business school; there is no formal reporting or follow-up of consulting work within the business school. The director estimates that faculty spend about 25 days per year on outside activities.

The link to a large and resourceful university provides opportunities for students and staff to engage in multi-disciplinary work and exchange of ideas across subject areas. This feature of the university is another means of promoting the business school and linking it to the university's tradition. The possibility of doing multidisciplinary work and of drawing on the faculty and the competencies of many subject areas is also believed to be an 'opportunity', afforded to a department of a large research university:

> We also have the opportunity to build on the basis of links with other faculties, so that although we are quite small we can really get the benefit of the multi-faculty environment. . . . all these things mean that we are building on the basis of [the university] links, which although we are small means that our network of research and teaching associates can be very, very high. (Director, 2001)

Working across disciplines and faculties is a high priority in both research and teaching, as evidenced by a number of joint programmes, multi-disciplinary research projects, and research centres established at the business school.

An International Business School

If the focus on research and academic excellence is one part of the academic business school, another central character stressed in the school's narrative is the desire of that school to be seen as an international business school 'competing with other major international business schools'. This desire is about 'branding' the school as a business school in its own right, and has increased the importance of stressing the 'business school' features of the organization. To qualify as an international business school, the most important feature is considered to be that of having an MBA programme: 'In some sense if you want to be a serious management/business school, you have to have an MBA course, a really good MBA course, and ours fulfils in that sense the same kind of role that it would in most other schools.' (MBA admissions director, 2001). The MBA is considered important for the overall visibility and reputation of the business school, which helps to create an awareness of the business school name. Being an important feature of a 'true' business school, the MBA credential attracts interest among alumni, students, and other business schools, as well as corporate representatives all over the world: 'no other education qualification carries across borders like the MBA' (MBA director, 2001).

But incorporating this feature of a business school with the traditions of the university department is not without problems. One respondent indicated that the MBA programme has been considered slightly different from the other undergraduate and graduate courses offered at the academic business school, or a 'black sheep', mainly because it is the only programme where students pay a commercial fee rather than standard university tuition:

> With one proviso, [the MBA programme] is probably the single most important course that we run. And the proviso is that generally here [at the business school], there has been a desire not to allow the MBA to completely dominate everything that [we] do. It is not a case of saying that the MBA is important and implying that the other courses are not. There is sort of a desire for us to work hard at everything that we do. But we could describe it as the black sheep, and it has been described like that, and I suppose a lot of that is because of the financial input that it brings for the institute. (MBA admissions director, 2001)

The MBA fee, paid directly to the business school, provides revenue of which some can be used to support the development of the business school. The financial input that the MBA programme contributes is thus seen as a means for further growth. The aim of the MBA programme is thus to combine the requirements of a perceived MBA market with the demands and traditions of the business school as part of the university.

To create a closer link with corporations and partners is considered an important issue for the future growth and success of the MBA programme and the business school. The corporate connections are sustained for instance through an advisory board that includes 22 executives and directors from local and international companies. The school also has a corporate relations department that 'organizes and manages the relationships' with corporations (Director, 2001) – arranging, for instance, lecture series by business leaders and professors from around the world. Developing the executive education offerings is also considered to be an important part of strengthening the corporate connections: 'When I go and see chief executives in companies they always want to know what we do in executive education, they may not want to buy it, but they want to know that we've got people who can do it.' (Director, 2001).

One of the main reasons that the business school offers, and is now expanding, executive education is thus to enhance the school's 'reputation and credibility' among corporate partners and connections (Director, 2001). Executive education is also, however, believed to be important because it provides an opportunity for faculty to earn additional money. The business school is tied to the university's salary scales, and cannot offer salaries that are believed to be competitive with what other business schools can offer. Through the money earned in executive education, the business school can offer faculty members earnings that are outside that of their normal salary, and can hence be used to compensate them for the relatively low salaries offered by the university at standard salary scales. Thus, executive education is viewed as important in competing as an international business school both in terms of reputation and financial gains.

Comparisons and Competition

In its attempts to compete with other international business schools, the academic business school is continuously working to identify sources of competition for the school and its programmes. Among other things, it collects information about which schools their MBA applicants are applying to besides their own, and makes occasional surveys of applicants that reject an offered place on the MBA programme to find out which school they attended instead. Recently, the corporate relations officer composed and presented a competitor analysis for the business school, commissioned by the advisory board. This report presents an overview of the competitors and the competitive advantages of the business school in relation to other major business schools (Corporate relations officer, 2002). Using published ranking tables and their own MBA surveys, for instance, several business schools in Europe and the United States are identified as main competitors. Among these, we find business schools that are perceived as having the same kind of programme (one-year MBA) and the same institutional conditions in terms of links to a traditional university, strong academic reputation, and a fairly recently developed business school, but also schools that are very different in structure and character. These were mainly top-ranked European business schools. A few American schools were also mentioned as competitors, primarily high-ranked schools like MIT and Stanford, and to a lesser extent the business schools at Harvard and University of Chicago – mainly because these schools have connections to a strong research university.

THE BUSINESS OF A BUSINESS SCHOOL

As an example of a business school located at the business end of the proposed business–academia continuum, is a business school without ties to a university and established partly outside of the national university system. This school is very intent on trying to convey an image of a very different academic and management education organization: 'The one thing you really have to remember when you listen to us is that this is a dramatically different model than the classical model you will study' (President, 2000). This business school also came into being around 1990, through a merger between other business schools, both of which were established and run with the support of local or international corporations. Since the merger, the school has developed into an independent business school and it serves no single institution or corporation. The historical roots of the school have, however, given it a background in executive development rather than links to a traditional academic system.

This business-oriented business school focuses on executive education, and has several thousand participants in open and custom-made executive courses every year. The school only offers two degree-programmes, a full-time MBA and an Executive MBA programme, each relatively small, with an annual intake of less than 100 students in the full-time programme and around 50 in the EMBA.[2] This business school offers no undergraduate or PhD programmes. Like the academic business school, it has grown rapidly in the past few years and members emphasize that the school has grown financially and more than doubled its turnover between 1995 and 2000. The school has currently approximately 60 faculty members employed as teaching and research staff.

Executive Training and Development

When describing its programmes and activities in brochures, the business school stresses its focus on executive education and on working closely with partner corporations and businesses. Its programmes include a wide range of executive development courses as well as the MBA programmes. The full-time MBA programme was started in the early 1990s, while the executive MBA was started in the late 1990s. However, the delivery of between 30 and 40 custom-made corporate training programmes (every year) is considered the main teaching activity at the school. These programmes are designed and delivered in partnership with companies and corporations, with each being made to suit the needs and desires of the individual company. These partnership programmes, like the open executive courses with participants from different companies, vary from single two- to three-week courses to modular programmes of ten weeks or more. The businesses that take part in these partnership programmes are also part of a network of corporations and partners linked to the school, which pay an annual fee to take part in activities and services offered by the business school, such as seminars and research activities. In the presentation material, the business school also stressed research and development activities, which include the preparation of new learning material for courses.

This business-oriented business school thus describes itself as a business school with the focus of being a corporate learning centre, concentrating on executive development programmes for experienced executives and managers. The president also expressed this as a vision and a mission to serve client firms with executive development and learning:

Now we say that our mission is: how can we help our partner firms to attract, develop and keep their best people? So it is a mission that is received from the customer. . . . It is a different position for us than the typical university, where they kind of say that 'we know best'. We are in other words serving the client rather than imposing on the client. (President, 2000)

This quote illustrates the school's striving to be seen as international, as practical, and as having a client- or customer-serving attitude to education. The quote does also suggest that this is something that is 'different' from other schools and universities. The business school is very clear on the fact that they are not tied to a university, and that they differ from the 'standard' perception of business schools and university organizations. This distinction, or notion of being different, was pointed out to me in several of my interviews, and regarding many aspects of their activities: 'because we are an example of a top-notch school, by all criteria doing very well, having outstanding research, outstanding teaching, outstanding ratings but we are doing dramatically different than anybody else. And the interesting thing is that we are having just as good results' (President, 2000).

A Revenue Seeking Service Organization

The 'difference' relative to other business schools and management education organizations is reflected in many of the activities and discussions within the organization. The business school has taken three strategic decisions regarding the academic organization of the school that differentiate them from what is believed to be traditional business schools and universities. The first one is not to be organized in academic departments according to subject areas. The research and teaching faculty are organized as one single department, and no professor serves any specific subject area. This is done to encourage cooperation across subject areas and facilitate integrated work, and to avoid the creation of 'silos' (President, 2000). The faculty is instead organized around teaching programmes 'to work on value propositions vis-à-vis our clients that really make sense' (President, 2000). This is believed to enhance teamwork focused around certain programmes and/or certain research topics, which may involve many business issues and disciplines.

The second decision is to have no academic titles to avoid a loss of energy due to internal power and promotion struggles: 'We think either you are part of the team, or you are not. It makes no difference whether you are professor or this or that. We say that we refuse to spend energy and ideas about ranking each other' (President, 2000). The third decision has been to abolish the concept of tenure, which is based on the same argument about better serving the clients' needs and expectations, and not spending time on internal evaluations:

it is a feeling on our part that business schools typically spend too much of their energy in peer review processes, determining who is going to get tenure, who is going to get promotion. We'd rather get our energy focused on the customer, which is the corporations, rather than on the internal sort of things. (Dean of faculty, 2000)

This also implies, however, that the management team of the business school can ask faculty to leave if they are not considered to contribute to the organization or to the students and clients. It is considered an important ingredient in the efforts to create value for clients – a way of making sure that everybody contributes to bring revenue into the organization: 'we don't have life-time employment. Everybody will be asked to leave if they are not performing' (President, 2000).

Making sure that faculty contributes to the organization and performs well in teaching is also referred to as being billable. There is an internal matching procedure for the allocation of teaching assignments, where programme directors are responsible for staffing their own programmes, which creates a transparency of faculty performance: 'For our faculty that is probably the word we would use: are you billable? Billable meaning: are there programme directors who want to buy some of your time? If you don't have enough programme directors that want to buy some of your time, something is wrong' (Dean of faculty, 2000).

The importance of being billable is considered in the recruitment process as well, together with a strong focus on performance in the classroom.

When we bring people in, we go back to this notion that it has to be billable, potentially billable, so that we have to be able to see good promise, if it is a younger person, good promise that they will perform and can be trained to perform well in the classroom. If it is a more experienced person, it is demonstrated ability in classroom. So we are looking for people we know are exceptionally good teachers. Then we are looking for people that are innovative, self-starting, and entrepreneurial. The culture here is quite entrepreneurial, innovative in the sense that they have a good stream of idea generation. For older people we are looking at their research and development record, with younger people you are trying to assess their potential to do that. You are looking at the thesis work; how quickly they are moving at getting [ideas] out of that thesis into publication. (Dean of faculty, 2000)

Each faculty member has a contractual arrangement with the school that specifies the time spent on different activities, where the time ratios are identical for all faculty members. Approximately 60 per cent of the time is allocated to teaching (or 'classroom activities'); around 30 per cent to 'research and development' activities; and less than 10 per cent to 'citizenship'. Citizenship, which is administrative work and general support for the schools activities, includes handling corporate visits and representation lunches with corporate clients.

The contractual 60 per cent teaching load is considered to be high relative to other business schools, but the dean of faculty admits that faculty very often spends even more time on teaching activities. Some faculty members spend 80, 90, or even 100 per cent of their time on classroom activities, increasing the workload substantially. This extra activity brings in revenues for the business school, measured as a 'turnover' per faculty member:

> Our workload is relatively high, but we've learnt to live with that. It yields some tremendous productivity figures. . . . it is well over [500 thousand euros] per faculty member. I don't think there is any other business school worldwide that has that kind of ratio between revenue and faculty base. We are quite proud of that particular phenomenon. (Dean of faculty, 2000)

The additional workload is voluntary for faculty and is paid separately. This notion of buying back time from faculty is considered an important part of the faculty compensation and motivation schemes used at the business school. The management team has intentionally worked to get the board of the school to accept variable faculty compensation, including a merit based bonus system. The bonus system is modelled after those often used in consulting firms:

> I would say in terms of other intellectual providers we are in many ways rather similar to consulting firms like McKinsey, for instance we make sure that we make a profit which we then share with faculty members as bonuses. These are very strange things for normal academic institutions, but they are obvious in consulting firms. We can't see why our intellectual workers should not get paid like [them] . . . these people are very, very smart and they should be paid for it. The market should pay them for that. (President, 2000)

The bonus system is considered critical in attracting and retaining the best faculty, and faculty salaries are continuously benchmarked against competing European business schools and some of the leading US schools. The bonus system includes group incentives and individually based incentives, which weigh together an assessment of research, teaching and work with clients. The third part entails evaluation of a faculty member's ability to bring in consulting work or clients, and taking part in marketing activities for the school.

Research is considered to be an important part of the bonus system because the management team feels it is necessary to create some incentives for the faculty to spend time on research and to develop research and teaching materials. The management team meets with each faculty member twice a year to follow up on the research agenda, and to hold faculty members accountable for outputs:

> But we are making sure that every faculty member does have a research agenda and is held accountable at least twice a year, not so much inputs, but what is coming out.

> There is a process there that puts some pressure on faculty not to ignore that side of
> the activity. (Dean of faculty, 2000)

To further encourage research, the business school allows faculty to have short sabbaticals, planned ad hoc on a short-term basis, typically a few weeks.

The business school also supports faculty pursuing the 'third mission', interacting with the surrounding community. Consulting performance and faculty's ability to bring consulting work to the school is considered an important component of work, valued highly in the bonus system. Currently, faculty are also allowed approximately 50 days per year for conducting consulting activities outside of the business school. Consulting activities are considered a way for faculty to work closely with businesses and to learn about current business needs and practices.

Two important features are used to argue for the necessity of the above described strategic decisions and incentives structures of the school: (a) being 'closer to the market' than are other schools and (b) serving clients and customers in the best ways possible. These features are expressed as having 'a strong link between the market and the school' (President, 2000), where the clients can have an impact on the decisions. The president believes this link is ensured by only having private funding for the institution: 'Being sponsored by private funding really forces us to take the needs of our students and clients seriously. They are paying for something, and we have to make sure that what we teach is relevant for them, and that our research is relevant for them' (President, 2000).

Corporations are involved in both partnership programmes and other cooperative projects. The business school also has a business advisory council that meets twice a year, which is said to serve the purpose of collecting customer input and to ensure that the school remains close to the market and provides relevant programmes and courses.

Playing to the Academic Realm – Research and the MBA

Even though the identity of the business school is based on being different from traditional academic institutions, some activities are used to connect the school to the academic and 'traditional' business-school models. Research activities are one example. Research is promoted as important for the school in gaining and sustaining a reputation within the academic sphere, primarily through traditional, academic publishing, as elaborated by one of the researchers:

> So it is a very interesting piece of research, but the only way I could do that research
> here is by first of all giving individual companies reports on their survey data, doing

workshops with companies, so everything was groomed to serving the companies' needs, to improve their own internal practices and then, of course, I had the data. And from the data then I could do some very highbrow academic, number crunching, logic analysis etc. Companies don't care about that. So when it goes into an academic journal of that stature it has already become irrelevant. But it raises our calibre as an institution in terms of respect in the academic realm, so it is also relevant to that point of fact, because people want to go someplace that is also renowned for its reasons. But it all ties into being relevant to businesses. (Researcher, 2000)

Even though academic publishing is seen as important for the academic reputation of the school, for performance evaluations no distinction is made between, for instance, refereed journal articles and teaching cases or other forms of publishing. It is considered equally important that the research is practical and useful, and thus serving the corporate world with research results and new insights. This is also valued when allocating research and development support to faculty members:

when we look at the proposals [for research], the thing we are asking faculty to articulate is where these new ideas are quickly going to find a way into programmes. We would like to support that type of idea generation that is going to be relevant to the customers. (Dean of faculty, 2000)

The research carried out at the business school is also claimed to be practical and managerial oriented, and serves as a source of new learning material for courses and programmes at the school.

The two MBA programmes offered at the business schools also serve the purpose of connecting the school to the world of business schools and academic degree-awarding organizations. The MBA is considered a very small part of the school's business, both in terms of revenue and in absolute numbers (less than 100 students per year). But the programme is believed to yield credibility and visibility in the business school market, and attract attention to the school. The MBA programme is thus looked upon as a necessity, as an indispensable ingredient that is useful in promoting the schools other activities, yet slightly outside the focus on executive education:

we have no intention at this point of expanding the size of the MBA programme, although it is a very important programme in terms of external visibility, that that programme be rated highly and viewed highly on the outside. . . . so the MBA is essential to us. But our core business is really the executive education. (Dean of faculty, 2000)

The school claim to keep a small 'elite' MBA programme, which can be very selective in the intake of students, and which can provide students with a close interaction with faculty. One of the believed drawbacks of this strategy is that the school receives less visibility in the market, with fewer students and thus fewer alumni that can promote the school and the programmes. Despite this, the expressed strategy is to keep the MBA programme small, with no increase in the number of participants accepted to the programme.

Comparisons and Competition

Drawing on the many distinctions and differences from other academic organizations, the business-oriented business school claim that one of the important projects for the school is that of positioning itself as a business school and to create a brand with strong characteristics. Branding is talked about with great care, as something that is considered vital for the business school to survive. In 2001, the school launched a brand advertising campaign, with a series of advertisements in major international business newspapers and journals.

The business school compares and benchmarks with some of the top-ranked American business schools, primarily Harvard and Wharton, but also with Berkeley that ranks slightly lower. For the international profile of the school, the school also compares with Thunderbird, the Garvin School of International Management, in the United States. An essential part of the image is the networking strategy, to work closely with businesses and corporations, and here the Sloan School of Management at MIT in the United States has provided inspiration and comparisons in that MIT developed quite early the idea of forming partnerships and networks with businesses. The market orientation, or the 'market driven, high quality academic value creation', as the president describes the school's activities, is also inspired by schools from outside the specific management education field as well as with other 'intellectual providers' such as consulting firms (President, 2000). A few European schools are also mentioned as possible competitors, some with different characters and profiles, for instance large MBA programmes.

SIMILARITIES AND DIFFERENCES IN NARRATIVES AND IDENTITIES

The two narratives presented above show two business schools of about the same size, with approximately 60 teaching and research faculty, and they are both reasonably new entrants on the business school 'market'. Besides these common traits, however, the narratives show two distinctly different business schools with different backgrounds, institutional settings, and organizational solutions, and with different approaches to management education. The narratives thus illustrate some of the diversity in the management education field today, with European business schools having varying work procedures, activities, interests, and abilities as well as different identities.

One of the more notable differences between the two narratives is the construction of similarities and differences, where the business-oriented school's desire to be and to be seen as different from other management education institutions is most apparent. Differences compared to other business schools are often enhanced and elaborated in the narrative, and the school's distinctiveness is continuously underlined. For the academic business school the opposite is true, and the narrative supports a more traditional image in which similarities with other business schools and with a university department, and in which links to the traditions of the university, are continuously stressed.

The narratives, and their focus on distinctiveness and similarities as part of the identity and the identity-formation of the school, thus illustrate how the business schools continuously focus, shape, and frame their identities by the use of comparisons, labels, and words connected to academic as well as to business activities. The comparison of the two narratives show that although the words and expressions used to present the activities are sometimes similar or the same, there are underlying differences in the identities of the schools that make the interpretation of the activities quite different. The comparison supports the perceptions of the academia–business continuum drawn earlier, in that the identities of the two schools are very distinct and are formed around different core ideas. Let us review some of the similarities and differences pointed out in the narratives.

Faculty Motivation and the Role of Teaching and Research

Both schools claim that their research is at the highest academic level, and both promote research activities among their faculty members. The narratives show, however, that the research activities for the two business schools have very different roles. For the academic business school, research is considered a core activity to support the academic status of the business school as a part of the university. Creating a good research environment is also seen as an important precondition in order to recruit academic faculty, and a good research record is an important consideration in the recruitment process. At the business-oriented business school, on the other hand, research is considered important as a development activity, to give faculty opportunities to 'stay fresh in their thinking' (President, 2000) and to provide their clients with research results. This school stresses research that is possible to transform into teaching material, cases for instance, and does not distinguish between practitioner publishing and academic publishing in their evaluation of research results.

These differences in the role of research for the two schools illustrate how the concept of academic research can be used to promote different ideals, and how it can be stretched to mean different things. By not distinguishing between the production of cases, publication in practitioner journals, and publication in academic journals, such a concept of research includes activities that fit with the 'business' and teaching oriented activities that make up the identity of the business-oriented business school. Similarly, the role and function of faculty sabbaticals differs from the more traditional academic setting, in that the time allowed is shorter and the sabbatical leaves are conditioned on performance. Time for academic research has thus been devalued as a faculty motivation tool, and is instead used to argue that research is prioritized at the school.

The differences in the treatment of research in the two schools are also linked to the perceptions and views of teaching. For both schools, excellence in teaching is expressed as a main aim, although that implies mainly undergraduate and graduate teaching for the academic business school, and mainly executive teaching for the business-oriented business school. At the latter school, teaching is much more stressed than research when evaluating faculty in the recruitment process, and the teaching load for faculty is almost twice that at the academic school (60 per cent versus 33 per cent). In the narrative, the concept of teaching is described with a business terminology that supports the school's business identity and the core features of the school, using terms such as 'billable' and measuring 'revenues per faculty member', for instance. Also in line with this identity, the time allowed for outside consulting activity is almost double at the business oriented business school and is considered an essential part of faculty work. On the contrary, work with consulting activities and similar activities are not prioritized, and not regulated, in the academic business school.

These differences between the two schools, as the narratives point out, are linked to underlying assumptions about faculty motivations, and about academic evaluation and appraisal systems. In the case of the academic business school, the basic motivation for faculty and the primary evaluation base is considered to be academic research: creating a research environment, freeing time for research activities, both through regulated teaching loads and sabbatical systems, and using research record in the evaluation of new staff, signal the importance of research activities. This is claimed to be consistent with the academic traditions of the university. At the business-oriented business school, on the other hand, a quite distinct system of evaluation and appraisal of academic work has been built – modelled on systems used in consulting firms, and more generally, outside the management education field. The prime incentive here seems to be financial benefits, and the freeing up and allowing of time for outside consulting work. A quite detailed and large incentive system and variable payment structure has been created at the school, which requires extensive evaluations and reviews of faculty performances and publications every year. This stresses the school's business approach even more.

Similar Profiles – and Different Roles of the MBA

While many things are different, some are also similar between the two schools. In the narratives both schools stress a close relation to businesses and to the corporate world; both schools collaborate with both businesses and other business schools in networks and joint projects; both schools claim to provide students with practical management learning and a close interaction with business and companies; and both schools have established advisory boards and have corporate relations staff that work with creating and sustaining links to the business world.

One of the more striking similarities between the two schools is the description of their MBA programmes. Even for two schools with distinctly different backgrounds and focuses, the perceived strengths and particular characteristics of the MBA programmes are largely the same. As expressed in both interviews and written material, both schools claim to feature for their respective MBA-programmes (a) a global and international focus with an international mix of students and faculty, (b) a small programme that allows close interaction between faculty and students, (c) practical relevance of the programme, providing close interaction and networking opportunities with businesses, and (d) a strong focus on developing leadership skills and entrepreneurs. The words and descriptions of the two programmes are thus very much alike, despite the different identities of the two schools. As a word of caution in the interpretation of this observation, it is possible that only their descriptions might be alike, while the focus and content of the programmes and how they are taught may vary significantly.

These striking similarities in the MBA profiles exist despite the fact that the MBA programmes play different roles in the two organizations. At the business-oriented school the MBA is seen as somewhat of a sideshow existing next to executive education that is considered to be the main activity, and which brings in the financial assets to the business school. Although not contributing substantially in financial terms, the MBA is seen as providing academic reputation to the school and as a link to other business schools and to the academic field of management education. For this school, the MBA programme, together with research, is thus used to argue for and stress the link to academic institutions, and as a way to become more closely linked to other academic organizations and business schools. At the academic business school, however, the opposite is true. The MBA and executive education are used to promote a business school identity and link the school to other international business schools, thus somewhat of a counterbalance to a traditional academic and university-department profile. Furthermore, the MBA programme is considered an important source of financial resources, and is believed to make up an important part of the school's activities. For the academic school, the role of executive education is mainly to provide a link to business practice and to allow faculty to earn money outside their regular salary.

Identity Formation and a 'Business School' Field

The narratives from the two business schools illustrate the different forms of field capital involved in the struggle for authority in European management education. The identity of the academic school is built around the links to the university, and as a consequence, it pushes for a 'high academic standard' in all activities at the school. Narratives pertaining to courses and programmes advocate 'intellectual rigour', 'academic excellence', 'critical reflection', and the like, which characterize this identity feature and stress the importance of academic capital in the management education field. The identity of the business-oriented business school, on the other hand, is built around executive development and strong links to businesses. With historical roots in international corporations rather than any academic organization, the business school stresses corporate learning activities, with narratives advocating knowledge that is 'relevant' to companies, and stressing that the organization is 'customer-oriented' and 'close to the market', which also infixes the identity and which links to struggles for business capital in the field. A business attitude is also expressed in language and work practices at the school, as for instance, through talk about turnover, productivity, being billable, and financial incentives. This marks the two business schools as being very different organizations, and as relying on partly different capital bases – academic capital verses business capital.

The two narratives illustrate the continuous identity formation processes of these business schools, and how business schools form and reform their activities and the descriptions of themselves. Although their identities are different, both schools have an idea of what they are or should become as 'true' business schools. The processes of identity construction or formation are in both narratives driven by an abstract notion of what a true business school should be like and what its activities and characteristics should be. This is perhaps most clear in the academic business school narrative, where respondents continuously refer to a perceived model of the 'international business school', and frame changes in the business school as steps toward becoming more like a 'true' business school. The abstract notion of a traditional academic institution is also prevalent in the other business school narrative, but is here used most often as a negative model, that is something to be different from. While wanting to be different from this model, the school also want to be associated with a business school market and a business school profile.

The two narratives also illustrate that desires to become like this general and abstract 'model' of a business school stem from both ends of the perceived academic–business continuum. The academic business school argue that increasing the size of the full-time MBA programme and the executive education courses are necessary to become more like a business school, while the business-oriented school argues that the MBA programme and research is needed in order to be academic and accepted according to this abstract notion of what an international business school is (or should be). Thus, business schools on the academic side of the continuum seem to perceive the business school as needing to be more business-oriented, while business schools at the business end seem to perceive the business school as requiring a certain amount of academic strength and focus. It is thus not particularly clear what the business school 'model' really is.

But if there is no consensus on what a business school is, then a question arises. Is it a model for business schools, or is it in fact something else? Rather than a fixed model or very specific criteria of what a business school should be like, the schools make references to an abstract notion of what a business school should be, particularly what an international business school should be, and what they believe that a business school should be like. Thus, these business schools refer to a template, rather than to a ready-made model. The template consists of abstract notions and understandings of what a business school should contain, what activities and tasks it should undertake, and how it should carry them out. This abstract notion of an international leading business school seems to be somewhere in between the endpoints of the business–academia continuum.

The narratives thus tell us that these two business schools relate to the same field, a business-school field. Both link to this field in their identity-formation processes by referring to abstract notions of what a business school is and how it should work, and by forming their narratives to fit the template. Both business schools also link to the business school field by being members of networks and alliances with other business schools that are perceived to belong to the field, and that support their identities and identity-forming processes. Despite quite large differences identified in the two narratives and in the identities of the two schools, both business schools make efforts to belong to the international field of business schools as this field takes shape in Europe.

CONCLUSIONS

This chapter has provided an empirical background for the forthcoming discussion of the introduction and development of business school rankings in the field of European management education. It has shown the diversity of the management education field, with opposing values and very different characters of business schools in this field. The inherent struggle between academic and business capital is a historically recurring topic in management education, but also a contemporary characteristic of the European field of management education, as illustrated through the two narratives of business schools representing two ends of the perceived continuum of management education organizations. These narratives thus illustrate the struggle of fields and the competing forms of capital within the field of business and management education, and they also illustrate the identity-formation processes of the two individual business schools. These processes, in turn, show how the field is forming around perceptions of what a business school is and what it should do. Despite the different capital bases and identities of the two schools, they share enough features to be able to link to and identify with a common field, the business-school field. There is a template of an international business school around which these business schools unite. There is thus a European business school field in the making. The following chapter will investigate the role of rankings in forming and re-forming such a business school template, and hence contribute to the forming of the business school field.

NOTES

1. Information from the MBA info-guide at www.mbainfo.com (13 October 2003). It is an approximate count based on the information in the database. I have counted only those programmes that have a European country as origin, and a European-based business school/university as main referent (i.e. a European address).
2. Degrees are awarded through a local university because the business school lacks degree-awarding rights according to the national educational system.

4. The forming and re-forming of a business school template

The narratives in the previous chapter suggested that there is a template forming among management education organizations about what a business school is and what it should do, and that this template is important for the forming of the business school and management education field. The aim of this chapter is to discuss the features of this template, and particularly investigate the role of rankings in shaping and spreading this template among organizations in this field. The ability of the rankings to create and diffuse the template is one of the reasons they have become so widely spread around the world.

The claim in this chapter is thus that rankings contribute to forming, re-forming, and diffusing a template of an international business school in the field of European management education. The theoretical chapter argued that measuring and classification mechanisms, such as rankings, contribute to setting criteria for how to evaluate organizations or units, in this case business schools and their programmes, which in turn makes certain characteristics and properties of the evaluated units visible (Bowker and Star, 1999; Townley, 1993) and making others invisible. Classification mechanisms use a variety of techniques for measuring and classifying, which contribute to the standards set and the properties and abilities made visible and comparable. The specific techniques and criteria used for classification also contribute to setting norms and standards through the programmatic or normative element that such techniques carry (Miller, 1994; Power, 1997). This way, the criteria set by measurement techniques such as rankings contribute to diffusing norms, standards, and ideas about business schools and programmes.

The argument in this chapter, however, is that we need to be more specific about what is being diffused through these techniques, and that rankings contribute to creating and diffusing a template for international business schools. The concept of template is both more general and more specific than the common reference to, for example, norms, values, and models in institutional theory, although it is clearly related to these concepts. The concept of template is more general in the sense that it does not refer to very specific procedures, models, or practices, as for instance, quality management as a practice (Røvik, 2002; Walgenbach and Beck, 2002) or the multidivisional form (Fligstein, 1985). Ideas and models that diffuse in institutional fields are often formulated like 'recipes' for certain aspects of organizations, such as various models for organizational structures (Røvik, 1998, 2002). A 'business school model', for instance, has been used to refer to specific financial or governance structures for business schools (Borum and Westenholz, 1995). The concept of template, however, suggests very few specific characteristics, properties, or recipe structures for business schools. On the other hand, the concept of template is not so general as to allude to all kinds of norms, standards, and ideas that diffuse in fields. Strang and Meyer (1993) argue that specific recipes require the institutionalization of certain underlying norms and values in order to spread, for instance, notions of what 'organizations' are. Such references to norms, logics, or rationalized notions of organizations in general are too broad, and do not cover any specific aspects of the organization or the idea.

The concept of template refers to something between recipes or specific models, and the more general underlying norms or value systems. An abstract notion or a template shares more similarities with the 'generalized other' specified by Mead (1934) than with popular models of how organizations work and are structured. A template is conceptually a generalized other, a picture not only of characteristics of another unit, but an understanding of the role of that other unit in relation to all other roles and actors in the 'game' (Mead, 1934). A template thus provides a picture of the entire social system, not just a specific model of organizing. In this way, the concept of template is not just normative but also cognitive in character, and relates to aspects of organizational identity, as noted in the previous chapter. A template includes cognitive processes of actors and an understanding of what business schools are and what the business school template is. Thus template refers to a particular aspect of the logics or norms prevailing in the field, as an abstract notion of what a business school is and should do.

In this chapter I will investigate how the rankings contribute to forming and diffusing a template for business schools, what this template contains, and how business schools have reacted to the template created by the rankings. I will show that the rankings both build on an already existing template, as well as set their own criteria that contribute to the forming and re-forming of that template. By doing so, the rankings also contribute to setting boundaries for the field in terms of what is considered legitimate activities for business schools in this field.

RANKINGS AND A BUSINESS SCHOOL TEMPLATE

Business school rankings are part of an ongoing struggle within the emerging field of management education about what higher management education is, whom it should serve, and how performance is defined. By setting criteria to evaluate the performance of business schools and their programmes, rankings take part in the discussion of what makes success in management education, and what makes a good business school. Daniel (1998) shows that the early American rankings showed diversity in the way they measured the performance of business schools. The rankings had different criteria and asked different people about their opinion of management education, for instance deans or students. Since there was no consensus on the criteria for the rankings, there was no consensus of what was actually the outcome of management education and thus there was uncertainty as to whether high ranks in academic circles or good job opportunities for graduates was the prime target for business schools (Daniel, 1998, p. 217). In this section I will investigate the criteria used in the current international rankings and the way the different rankers assess the performance of business schools, which contributes to our understanding of what is valued in management education and how performance is evaluated.

An International Business School Template?

The introductory chapter noted that although rankings are not new to management education, the recent rankings launched in the international business press have included a new group of schools in the rankings game. These so-called 'international' rankings claim to be global in character and to compare and assess schools from across the world. Although several rankers have noted the difficulty of finding criteria that are able to bridge differences between countries and regions, all of the claimed international rankings build on assumptions of similarity and universality. They assume that business schools and programmes are the same across countries, or at least similar enough to be comparable.

As the MBA label has diffused throughout the world, this programme is now most often used as the 'standard' that makes schools comparable in rankings. The full-time MBA programme is ranked by all five rankers reviewed here, while both executive MBA and other executive education programmes are ranked by the *Financial Times* and *Business Week*. Although the rankings focus their measurements on specific programmes, these are often marketed as rankings of business schools, for instance *Business Week* with its headline 'The top Global Business Schools' in their 2002 edition of rankings (*Business Week*, 21 October 2002). Rankings thus appear to centre on the concept of a business school, and of what is believed to be standards for what a good business school is.

The claimed global focus of the rankings is not always evident, however. Table 4.1 shows an overview of the characteristics of the major international rankings, and provides guidance on how the rankings attempt to assess business schools and create criteria for comparing schools internationally. The table shows that although the rankings claim to be international, most of the business schools featured in the rankings are still American and European. But the international rankings do, to an increasing extent, include schools from all continents. The first *Financial Times* ranking of full-time MBA programmes, published in 1999, included three Canadian and 16 European schools in a top-50 ranking, while the 2003 ranking featured eight Canadian schools, two Australian schools, and three schools each from Asia and South America along with the European and American schools. *The Economist* ranking includes the largest share of non-US schools and the largest share of European schools as well, and is, together with the *Financial Times*, the only ranking with a significant share of international schools. The *Wall Street Journal* ranking features only two schools outside North America and Europe, and *Business Week*, none. The template created in the ranking thus claims to cover schools internationally, but North American and European business schools dominate.

One of the reasons the rankings are still dominated by North American and European business schools could be the way they select business schools and programmes to be included in the rankings. One important factor in deciding who are featured in a given ranking is the selection mechanism that the ranking uses to define the population of schools to survey and assess. Table 4.1 shows that several of the rankings use accreditation as a screening mechanism, primarily the American AACSB, the European EQUIS, and the British AMBA accreditation systems. These three accreditation systems currently accredit schools internationally, but the majority of business schools accredited by each organization are still from their own region (Hedmo, 2002). The *Wall Street Journal* ranking, one that does not use accreditation to select the international schools in their rankings, claims that the universe of international schools selected for inclusion 'was the result of meetings and discussions with experts in the field of MBA recruiting, including business-school deans, business-school associations, recruiters, and career-services directors' (*Wall Street Journal*, 30 April 2001, p. 33).

These screening mechanisms reveal that already in the selection process there are tendencies to favour some US schools (AASCB accreditation) and large and well-known schools that are considered 'good' by other standards. In this sense, the population of management education organizations that are ranked or are eligible to be ranked is quite limited and is, to an extent, based on an already existing understanding of what a good business school is. Furthermore, small or newly established schools are often denied entrance in the rankings by the minimum requirements for inclusion in the final lists: for instance, minimum requirements concerning size, age, or turnover (see Table 4.1). Together, selection mechanisms and minimum requirements secure a

Table 4.1 *Characteristics of international rankings*

	Financial Times			Business Week			WSJ	EIU	Forbes
	MBA	EMBA	Executive education	MBA	EMBA	Executive education	MBA	MBA	MBA
No. of schools	100	75	45/50*	30+10	35	20	50	100	75
US schools (%)	56	56	42/40*	75	83	75	82	41	84
European schools (%)	28	28	35/44*	15	9	25	10	41	12
Selection criteria	EQUIS, AACSB, AMBA	EQUIS, AACSB, AMBA	EQUIS, AACSB, AMBA	Not available	EQUIS AACSB	Schools named by company directors	AACSB for US schools. 'Reputation' for non-US schools	Not available	Not available
Minimum requirement	20% responses >3 grad. classes	20% responses >3 grad. classes	$2M turnover in each area	Not available	4 years running >25 students	Not available	>50 MBA graduates >20 recruiter ratings	>10 survey responses or 25%	>15% alumni responses

Note: * For open and custom-made executive programmes respectively.

Sources: *Financial Times*, 20 January 2003; 19 May 2003; 20 October 2003; www.ft.com, 9 November 2003; *Business Week* 21 October 2002; www.businessweek.com, 27 February 2004; www.wsj.com, 22 September 2003; http://mba.eiu.com, 22 September 2003; www.forbes.com, 4 September 2003.

certain form of stability in the rankings and keep the results reasonably in line
with other perceptions of what constitutes good business schools.

A Customer Approach

Even though the rankings seem to rely on an existing template of business
schools, the rankings don't just reflect perceptions of good business schools;
they also construct their own criteria for measuring and evaluating management education organizations. The introduction of rankings in the international
business press has meant that management education reaches a partly new
audience, and is subject to an increasing scrutiny by various media outlets. By
introducing rankings, newspapers and media have decided to not merely report
on quality discussions and on issues surrounding business schools and MBA
programmes, but to actively contribute to the construction of criteria for judging management education and to provide guidance on the respective quality
of schools. Business education entering the media and the public sphere thus
means the introduction of a partly new means of comparing, evaluating and
reporting on what is assumed to be the quality of business schools.

An issue raised in my interviews with business school representatives was
that of an increasing student pressure on business schools and their
programmes. One dean illustrated this with a story of students claiming to be,
and acting as if they were, 'customers' of business schools:

> I had students come in lately and said, 'we are customers, and we have rights'. I
> don't think that argument takes them very far, because, as I said to them, I don't
> think Microsoft's customers have very many rights vis-à-vis Microsoft! And I said
> we live in a world where customers actually don't have very many rights, so you
> might have more rights as a student than you have as a customer. So they never
> really thought about it, they just thought because they are paying a lot of money, so
> they are customers, and as customers they have more rights. The world of business
> doesn't give very many rights to customers. (Director of business school, 2001)

One of the features of the rankings is that they attempt to define and display
such notions of customers of business education, thus building on market
logics and assumptions of market demand and supply. Although the different
rankers have taken varying approaches to the ranking of business schools, all
rankings rely to a greater or lesser extent on surveys, and thus rely on reputation measures of business school performance. Elsbach and Kramer (1996)
note that this was one of the major features that made the *Business Week* ranking very popular when it was launched. The ranking was framed as an objective measure because it was based on large-scale consumer surveys and thus
provided 'proof' of market opinion (Elsbach and Kramer, 1996, p. 445). By
attempting to define and appoint customers in business education, rankings

both build on and contribute to forming a notion of a 'market' for management education in general, and for MBAs in particular.

The current international rankings show diversity in the way business school performance is assessed and measured, and in who are considered customers of management education. Four of the rankers investigated here use some form of reputation measure in their rankings and aim to define customers of management education (*Financial Times, Business Week*, the *Wall Street Journal* and *The Economist*) although the weight given to reputation in the final ranking varies.[1] The identified customer groups also vary between the different rankings.

Business Week has taken the most pronounced customer approach and argue for the importance of representing the 'customer's voice' in management education:

> Let the customer speak. That's the philosophy behind *Business Week*'s ranking of the best business schools. We think b-schools have two customers: the graduates, who trade their suits for backpacks; and recruiters, who seek out the best and brightest from among the business schools' ranks. The frank views we receive from both groups have made *Business Week*'s ranking a crucial source of information on business schools since it was first undertaken a decade ago. (*Business Week*, 19 October 1998, p. 70)

Business Week's full-time MBA ranking is based on two surveys: a survey of students graduating from the MBA programme and a survey of corporate recruiters hiring MBA graduates. Together, the results of these surveys (although weighted with the results from previous years' polls) make up as much as 90 per cent of the final ranking of the school. This ranking thus has a very strong commitment to a reputation- and customer-oriented view of education that identifies both students and recruiters as the main interest groups. The *Wall Street Journal* also relies strongly on reputation allowing 80 per cent of the rank to be determined on a recruiter survey, and hence considers corporations to be the main customers of business education. This survey assesses the satisfaction of recruiters with particular schools and with the students they have recruited from each school.

In comparison, the *Financial Times* and the Economist Intelligence Unit rely much less on customer satisfaction polls for their full-time MBA ranking (55 and 20 per cent respectively). The *Financial Times* has chosen to survey a slightly different group of customers, namely, the alumni of schools rather than students currently in the programme or those just graduating. This survey asks alumni to assess their MBA experiences three years after graduating from the programme, focusing more on career progress and employment aspects than the perception of teaching, for instance.

The customers identified in the executive education rankings are slightly different from the ones in the full-time MBA rankings. Here the main customers are considered to be the person in the client companies that takes the decision to buy executive education courses for their employees. This represents a move away from the participants of programmes, to personnel directors, leadership-development directors, HR managers, and the like in companies, although the focus is still on the notion of customers. A more notable choice of survey respondents is the EMBA directors that *Business Week* surveys for the Executive MBA ranking (making up 50 per cent of the rank, while the remaining 50 per cent is determined by a student survey). This choice breaks with the customer approach prominent in the other rankings, and asks EMBA directors at business schools to rank ten schools, other than their own, that they consider provide the highest quality programmes. This is the only ranking, among these international rankings, that targets members of other business schools to evaluate management education programmes.

Taken together, the international rankings thus identify various customer groups of management education: students, corporations, and recruiters. Relying on surveys, albeit of different kinds, underscores an accountability argument, stating that the surveys are representing 'market opinion', and are therefore very difficult to ignore. This accountability discourse, which has been brought into higher education with a series of audit activities, includes a series of terms and practices, including 'quality assurance', 'accreditation', 'transparency', 'benchmarking', and 'visibility' (Shore and Wright, 2000, p. 60). From this discourse, it follows that business schools, like other organizations, should be held responsible and accountable for their performances (Trow, 1998).

The Employability of Graduates

How the rankings assess performance and what customer groups are identified are two important considerations because the answers to those two questions signal what education is believed to be and what is considered important in the business school template. Besides identifying customers, the rankings specify criteria that are used to construct the final ordering and list of business schools and programmes. To illustrate what ranking measures and what criteria the various rankings use, a compilation of their criteria has been made. This compilation is presented in two-dimensional matrices (Table 4.2 through Table 4.5) below.

Whether opinion-based or more factual criteria are to be used in rankings has been debated since the beginning of rankings (Daniel, 1998). For the first dimension, I will thus distinguish 'reputation' criteria from 'feature' criteria. 'Reputation' encompasses all criteria that business school deans and directors, students, recruiters or professors are asked for, when soliciting their subjective opinions about their experiences with the programme or school; whereas 'feature' encompasses those criteria that assess features or characteristics of schools, students or programmes, as for instance, the number of published articles, starting salaries for graduates, and so on. This data can be supplied from outside sources: for example, from published statistics, or from the schools or students themselves, primarily through questionnaires.

The second dimension of the matrix classifies the information according to what the criteria measure. Scott identifies three types of indicators used for assessments: those based on outcomes, on processes, and on structures ([1981] 1998, pp. 354–9). Outcome measures relate to the effects of work procedures, and the 'output'of organizational efforts, as for example, changes in the knowledge or attitudes of students in educational organizations. Process measures, on the other hand, assess efforts rather than effects. Process measures thus focus on the quantity or quality of the activities carried out, which in educational organizations relate to assessments of teaching, research, and other activities carried out by the school. Structural measures, the third type of measure, index not the work performed but the capability of organizational structures to perform work effectively. These indicators focus on inputs of the organization and on specific features of the participants: for instance, features of the student body, faculty, and facilities. I have chosen to label this category 'inputs'.

A specific compilation of the criteria used in the various rankings is provided in Tables 4.2 to 4.5.[2] This compilation shows that the various rankings have quite different criteria for ranking business schools and MBA programmes. Generally, there are very few process criteria in the rankings that assess the educational experience and the actual content of the MBA programmes. The *Business Week* ranking is perhaps an exception, because it has quite a large number of criteria aimed at assessing the quality of teaching, teachers, and teaching material, and at measuring the students' satisfaction with the MBA programme compared to other rankings. Input measures that assess the diversity of class and faculty, the characteristics of the class, the percentage of faculty with PhDs, and so forth are most prominent in the Economist Intelligence Unit and the *Financial Times* rankings, but are also present in the other two rankings. Important features of both the *Business Week* and the *Financial Times* rankings are their measures of research, or 'intellectual capital' as it is labelled in the *Business Week* ranking. These are the only two rankings that include measures of research publications.

One of the major features of the rankings is a strong focus on output measures, which attempt to measure the students' success after the programme in terms of salaries, employment, and job offers, for instance. This is consistent with the customer approach discussed above, in which students and corporations are considered the main target groups for educational efforts. The

Table 4.2   Profile of the Business Week *full-time MBA ranking*

	Feature criteria	Reputation criteria
Input		Calibre of class Technological tools (*3)
Process	Research publication Popular publication	Expectations fulfilled Teaching, teachers and teaching material (*9) Skills stressed (*2) Work load
Output		Contacts with business community Usefulness of skills (*2) Value for money Usefulness of networks (*3) Recruiting and job-info (*2) Recruiters' experience with graduates

Note: * indicates the number of criteria relating to a particular aspect that have been used in the ranking.

Source: www.businessweek.com, 12 November 2000 (revised from Wedlin, 2004).

Table 4.3   Profile of the Financial Times *full-time MBA ranking*

	Feature criteria	Reputation criteria
Input	Diversity of faculty (*2) Diversity of class (*2) Diversity of board (*2) Languages required PhD rating (*2)	
Process	Research publication Internationality (*2)	
Output	Salary (*3) Value for money Employment and recruitment (*2)	Career progress Aims achieved Alumni recommendation

Note: * indicates the number of criteria relating to a particular aspect that have been used in the ranking.

Source: *Financial Times*, 20 January 2003 (revised from Wedlin, 2004).

Table 4.4 Profile of the Wall Street Journal *full-time MBA ranking*

	Feature criteria	Reputation criteria
Input		Career service office
		Faculty expertise
		Student characteristics (*2)
		General like or dislike of school
Process		Curriculum content
		International perspective
Output		Recruitment experience (*4)
		Value for money of recruiting effort
		Skills and abilities of graduates (*10)
		General like/dislike for student
		Awareness of corporate citizenship
		Overall satisfaction with school
		Likelihood of returning to school for further recruiting

Note: * indicates the number of criteria relating to a particular aspect that have been used in the ranking.

Source: www.wsj.com, 21 November 2002.

criteria used to measure output also reflects a focus on the employability of graduates as an important measure of business-school and MBA success, which accentuates the focus on strong relations with the corporations that recruit MBAs and attend management education programmes (see also Wedlin, 2004).

Surveying graduates three years out, the *Financial Times* has focused the survey on the career progress and the employment opportunities for graduates, particularly salary measures: 'At the heart of the ranking is the value each MBA programme commands for its graduates in the market today, based on the salaries earned by alumni who graduated in 1995' (*Financial Times*, 25 January 1999, p. I). By surveying only recruiters, the *Wall Street Journal* has an even more pronounced focus on output and the 'employability' of MBA students. A particularly interesting aspect of this employability focus of the rankings is various criteria for assessing the 'value' of education. 'Value-for-money' is included in two of the rankings, and is also the sole criteria for the *Forbes* rankings. These value criteria are measures of how much the salary increases after the MBA, minus the costs of tuition and forgone earnings.

Table 4.5   Profile of the Economist Intelligence Unit full-time MBA ranking

	Feature criteria	Reputation criteria
Input	Faculty/student ratio Percentage faculty with PhD Incoming class characteristics (*2) Diversity students (*2) Alumni efforts (*)	Faculty rating Rating of culture and class Assessment of alumni network
Process	Overseas exchange programmes Languages on offer	Programme content and electives Facilities and services
Output	Diversity of recruiters Employment and job offers (*2) Recruitment Salary (*2)	Career service

Note: * indicates the number of criteria relating to a particular aspect that have been used in the ranking.

Source: http://mba.eiu.com, 12 September 2002.

Value measures also reflect and strengthen the impression that education is aimed at satisfying the demands of students and corporations to provide them with education that is 'valuable', perhaps primarily in a financial sense.

The Forming of a Template

The various rankings evidently set different criteria for assessing business schools and programmes and use different methodologies. However we can conclude this far that the rankings share a customer view of education, and that most rankings focus on the outcome of education rather than on aspects of the content and form of teaching, for instance. Furthermore, very few criteria, and in most rankings none, actually measure the content or form of the MBA programmes or other management education programmes. Rather, the rankings focus on measures of reputation and on measures that assess the outcome of educational efforts in terms of financial gains and employment opportunities, and also on measures of class and faculty characteristics and diversity. In line with the findings of Segev et al. (1999, p. 562), who concluded that there is no one model, or 'best' structure, of an MBA programme that determines the ranking of schools, there are very few features in the rankings that would promote specific structural characteristics of schools. Quite simply, the criteria valued and used by the rankings are not those that would propose the teaching of specific topics or areas, or that would recommend a particular structure for management education organizations. Rather than promoting a particular model of business schools, or rather than judge what the education should contain and how it should be structured, the rankings promote general notions of what it means to be a 'good' business school in the field. This way, rankings contribute to the creation of a general template for management education organizations.

To summarize, the rankings promote ideas about what a business school should do, what the output of educational programmes should be, and who the customers of management education should be. Even though the rankings claim to rank specific programmes, they often infer the results to the business schools in general and many criteria are school features rather than programme features: for instance, criteria that measure facilities, the research output of schools, the diversity of the board and the faculty. This suggests that rankings are taking part in forming and diffusing the business school template, both by building on and confirming already existing systems of evaluation, and by constructing new measures for success in management education.

IDENTIFICATION WITH A BUSINESS SCHOOL TEMPLATE

The rankings take part in forming and re-forming the template of an international business school, together with many other mechanisms and regulations in the field. The strength of this template in contemporary management education is significant. In the survey conducted among European business school deans I asked them to describe and characterize their institution.[3] The results show that the majority of management education organizations (55 per cent) in the surveyed population consider themselves to be 'business schools', either independent or related to a university. The remaining schools consider themselves to be 'university departments', 'executive education institution' or 'other'. The business school concept is thus important while not entirely dominating the field.

Looking at the distribution for the ranked and the non-ranked schools separately, however, we find that the number of schools that consider themselves to be business schools is much higher among the ranked schools than among the non-ranked schools, see Figure 4.1. Among the ranked schools, 70 per cent of the deans consider their schools to be business schools, either independent or

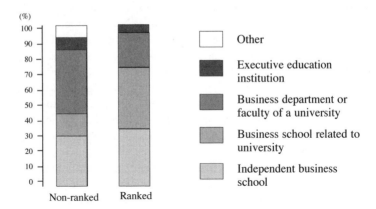

Figure 4.1   Types of organizations, categorized by the deans

related to a university, compared to 43 per cent of the deans of non-ranked schools. These data suggest that the business-school concept is much stronger, and the template of an international business school more dominant, among ranked schools than among non-ranked schools.

These findings can be interpreted in two ways: (a) the schools that are ranked are those that, to start with, identify with the business school template, or (b) being ranked implies a stronger identification with the business school template. Both interpretations are valid, following the suggestion above that the rankings both confirm an existing template and contribute to the creation of this template. Furthermore, a comment during my survey shows how not fitting into the business school template is perceived of as keeping many schools out of the rankings: 'It is not a matter of indifference to us [that we are not ranked], but we do not fit in any of the standard perceptions of business schools'.

As the review of the ranking criteria suggested there are few characteristics or structures of schools and programmes recommended through the rankings, and there are no clear perceptions of what makes up a standard business school. An important question then becomes: What makes a school 'fit in' and identify with this template? How is the template used in identity-formation processes? The following examples from three different business schools highlight the insecurities about identities faced by business schools, and how these insecurities drive the identity formation processes of schools. The prominence of the business school template in driving changes in business school activities and profiles is stressed. The last two examples, referring to the business school narratives in Chapter 3, particularly show what the business school template is not, and illustrate how both schools try to dissociate themselves from other forms of management education training. Thus when business schools accept and adhere to one specific template, they simultaneously repudiate other templates and models produced in the field. This way the identity formation of business schools contributes to draw boundaries for the field.

A 'Fully-fledged' Graduate School of Business

One aspect appears to be more important than others in the template, and it is to have an MBA programme that can be compared with other programmes internationally. The business school narratives in the last chapter pointed to the role of the MBA in the identity-forming processes of the two business schools, and to how the MBA provided a link between business schools at the two ends of the proposed business–academia continuum. In the survey, about one fifth (22 per cent) of the non-ranked schools (i.e., accredited schools that would be eligible for participation in the rankings) state that they have chosen not to participate in the international business schools rankings.[4] The main reason is said to be that the rankings don't rank the specific national-type programmes that the school specializes in, and that the school cannot, or wants not to, offer MBA-type or executive education programmes that are measured and assessed in the rankings.

The rankings thus reflect the strong position of the MBA programme in international management education (cf. Moon, 2002), and contribute to an even greater focus of the business school template on this type of programme. The business school representatives that I interviewed confirmed this prominent role of the MBA, particularly that of the full-time MBA, for being considered a hallmark of a 'true' business school and for conforming to the business school template. While some denounce the focus on the MBA, most deans have accepted it as an important feature of a business school and work to form their activities to conform to this aspect of the template. Efforts at a Scandinavian school provide an illustrative example of the importance of the MBA programme in order to be considered part of the 'club' and a true business school, and how the school tries to form their identity around this business school template.

The school is an independent business school that provides teaching and research in primarily business studies and economics. The school focuses on undergraduate and PhD education, and on research, but the school also provides executive education through a fully-owned subsidiary company. In the early 2000s the school is also setting up an entirely new, full-time MBA programme with the expressed aim of competing internationally with business schools around Europe as well as in the United States. The decision to start a full-time MBA programme at this Scandinavian school is described as a way to create 'a fully-fledged graduate school of business' (Assisting dean, 2002). This full-time MBA programme is started at a time when competing Scandinavian schools are also developing full-time MBA programmes.

Ultimately, the development of this new MBA programme is seen as a way of creating a true business school, and of qualifying as a member of the top group of European schools. The start of the MBA programme is also believed to create a pressure to participate in the rankings and to compare well with other international business schools. With the new programme, the school recognizes that it will need to play to a more international audience and that business school rankings will be a part of that.

> the main reason for starting the MBA is not to be ranked. But we know that we cannot play football in [Scandinavia] and claim that we are better than others in Europe without proving it. We have to play in the Champions' League, the European Cup, and the World Cup [to prove it], and it is the same for us. We cannot say that we have a special model and that we play . . . [games] with our own rules; we must play in the international arena. (Assisting dean, 2002. My translation)

This indicates that desires to conform to the template and start an MBA programme also creates desires to participate in the rankings. The business school rankings, and the aspects of management education enhanced through the rankings, are thus closely linked to the business school template.

Business School Versus University Department

Participating in the rankings and identifying with the template is not always easy and straightforward, and may lead to contradicting demands. As suggested in the narrative in the previous chapter, the academic business school identifies with the strong links to the university as well as to what is perceived as the international business school market. The narrative also suggested that there are two sides to running a business school within a university: a business school side and a university side. My respondents indicated that these two sides do not always push in the same direction, and that there was a perceived tension between the two:

> The [university] is relatively the best known name in the world, and therefore one of the crucial ways in which people come through to us, the way MBA applicants come through to us, is that they know of the [university] and they discover that the [business school] is the business school within [this university]. So in that sense I think [the link to the university] is absolutely crucial. That of course brings a potential tension about what we do here, and whether what we do is consistent with the university's aims. Because sometimes, particularly in the modern world of business schools, what seems the right thing to do isn't necessarily consistent with

the historical aims of a traditional university. And there are tensions [one can find] there, tensions that we have. So, although it is absolutely crucial that we remain very much a part of this university, and hope that we remain true to its aims, there are pressures and tensions that push you away from that. (MBA admissions director, 2001)

These contradicting demands were played out in a number of discussions about the profile and aim of the school, and the size and content of the MBA programme. Being an important part of the business school template, the issue of the size and focus of the MBA and what principles should be guiding the development of the programme was particularly sensitive.

An increase in the size of the MBA programme, from approximately 80 students to 130, was claimed to be of vital importance for the continued development of the business school and to increase the visibility of the programme in the MBA and business school markets. The revenue enjoyed from the programme was also an important argument in this debate. Some even argued that the MBA programme needed to grow to accept 240 or, eventually 300, students every year in order to compete as an international business school. The main arguments against an expansion of the programme, on the other hand, were concerns that an increase in the intake of students might compromise the university tradition of small classes and a close and interactive relationship between faculty and students, and that it would threaten the quality of accepted students. Thus, an increase in the number of students in the MBA programme was perceived as, possibly, threatening some of the central characteristics of the business school as a university department, if specific care was not taken. Ultimately the decision was made to increase the programme with up to 50 per cent in the early 2000s, counting on approximately 130 students each year.

A similar example of the tensions and contradicting interests between the business school template and what is perceived as the university model was a discussion about the profile and the guiding principles for further development of the MBA programme. A discussion about the content and form of the MBA programme reflects a perceived tension between MBA career ambitions and academic pursuits of the programme:

There is another tension, another example of this, which is that MBA students, having come from possibly several years working for commercial organizations, may well be very, very interested in what this course [will] do for their career. Some aren't, but most are. There is a slight tension between that and the academic performance of this [business school] as a part of the university. Sometimes they coincide, but sometimes they don't. (MBA admissions director, 2001)

Decisions about content and form of teaching in the MBA programme at the academic business school was claimed to be guided by a number of academic aims and pursuits, and by the interests of individual faculty members. These aims and pursuits were believed to contradict the demands and expectations of incoming MBA students, whose career ambitions and job expectations exert pressures for more practical, business relevant, and hands-on experiences.

A more general tension and problem in the organization was an experienced contradiction of teaching and research. Research time and teaching time were believed to be in competition sometimes, as when faculty members plan their time and their activities:

> So of course there are tensions because our greatest resource is the academics, and the academics are their brains and their hearts and their minds, so where are they going to put their emphasis, where are they going to put those spare ten hours a week? Are they going to put them to ensure that their programme is absolutely top shape, or are they going to use it to publish a paper? And at the end of the week, those ten hours are where you make the marginal choices. And what I want is academics who make marginal choices in a balanced way, and to understand that they have to be absolutely brilliant in the classroom, but their being brilliant in the classroom will not secure their academic development and therefore our academic development so they must also pay attention to the research side. . . . There are tensions that are played out institutionally and are played out right at the heart in all of us as individuals, and one has to get a balance between them. (Director, 2001)

For the business school, the tensions that have been described here were perceived to add up to an ultimate tension between the perceptions of a traditional university 'model' and an international business school 'model'. The strong template of a business school again influences the perceptions of the identity of the school. The template, which is creating insecurity about the identity of the school, is used inadvertently to argue for changes and adaptations in the activities and the profile of the school and its programmes. Respondents at the business school believed that the school must conform to both the traditional academic 'model' and the business school template in order to be successful:

> I started right in the beginning saying we are an academic department of the [university] and we are an international business school, and if you can make these two things work, then we have enormous strengths in both areas. And I don't see it that we have a choice, I think we have got to do both. (Director, 2001)

Business School Versus Executive Training Institution

Discussions similar to those illustrated above regarding the size of the MBA programme took place at the business-oriented business school, that is, discussions about increasing the programme to 160 or 200 students, in the beginning of the 2000s. Mainly the same arguments in favour of the enlargement were used here as well (i.e., to take advantage of the cash flow and the increasing visibility in the market that such an increase would yield). This school took the opposite route, however, and decided not to increase the size of the MBA programme. The proposal was turned down because it was not considered to fit within the school's overall programme portfolio and thus not consistent with the focus on executive education of the business school. Members of the school expressed a perceived risk that a large MBA programme would alter the strategic direction of the school, and add 'MBA specialists' to the faculty that would not fit in with the general executive teaching team.

While this issue was common to the two business schools, the concerns and problems that were raised in the interviews at the business oriented school about their activities and the role of their business school were generally of a slightly different character than those portrayed at the academic business school. Being on the business end of the continuum, the business-oriented school's activities are close to those of many corporate learning centres, with a lot of activities aimed at consulting and at serving corporate partners. The problems faced by this business school also reflected insecurity about the identity of the school, but the contradiction here stems not so much from an academic model as from consulting and other management education activities.

One potential problem or area of concern raised in my interviews with members of the business-oriented business school was that of setting boundaries for the organization and of clearly distinguishing the activities of the business school from other organizations' offerings. A first example of such an issue is the definition of faculty consulting activities. With programme development and delivery often being tightly linked to individual businesses and with faculty conducting consulting and research activities in cooperation with its business partners, the dividing line between business school activity and private consulting work of individual faculty members was unclear. To handle this issue, the management team of the school set strict rules for what and how much consulting activities faculty members were allowed to perform outside the business school. The consulting activities, which had to be reported, were reviewed twice a year and the school reserved the right to refuse individual faculty work for any of the business partners or clients if the school felt it interrupted school activities.

A second example of the difficulty of distinguishing the activities of the business school from other offerings was brought about by an increase, witnessed recently, in the number of corporate universities and other forms of management training organizations. The most immediate perceived threat of these organizations, which was also raised in my interviews, was considered to be that the corporate universities and other institutions cherry-pick the best professors from business schools to teach in-company programmes. As with the issue of outside consulting for faculty members, finding the boundaries for school activity and private work is difficult when handling relations with corporate universities; rules were set up to handle this issue.

Besides setting very strict rules for faculty activities outside the school, the business school has also tackled this recently experienced 'new' competition from corporate universities and other training organizations by widening its own scope of activities, and by adding corporate universities as a new customer base.

> I think we've spent a couple of years trying to understand if corporate universities would be a new source of competition for us, and I think the outcome of all that anguished thinking has been no. In fact that would be if anything an opportunity. (Partnership programmes director, 2000)

Thus rather than competition, the business school considered corporate universities to be a new and opening market for them, offering several possibilities for expanding their current activities, such as providing consulting services, but also for developing new activities. Corporate universities were considered potential buyers of existing executive development courses at the school, but can also be useful in generating new courses and, more importantly, new ways of making money, for instance by providing advisory services to their partner companies on how to design internal programmes and how to structure their corporate universities.

Identity Formation and Boundary-work

These discussions from the three business school examples show how insecurity about identities of business education organizations spurs identity formation processes within them, constituting a form of boundary-work. The identity formation of schools is clearly influenced by the general template of an international business school. All three schools exemplified above relate to this template when forming and reforming their activities and identities. The identity formation processes are also a continuous form of boundary-work, as particularly the latter two organizations have been shown to struggle to dissociate from other forms of management education and to conform to the template. The narratives of the academic and the business oriented business schools thus illustrated that it is not only important what belongs in the template, and what aspects are highlighted and enhanced in order to conform to the template, it is also important to repudiate other templates and perceived models of organizing. This struggle to form identities contributes to setting boundaries that determine which activities are considered to be inside, or left outside, the field of management education. This struggle thus shows how the template of an international business school guides the identity formation of schools, and contributes to the definition of boundaries for the field.

The extracts from the two business school narratives, the academic and the business oriented schools, thus illustrate processes of boundary-work, where schools, in their efforts to secure a stable identity, continuously redefine the activities and roles of the business school. Insecurity about the identity of school thus also drives these instances of boundary-work. But because a template rather than a model drives this boundary-work, diversity and change is allowed. Although the two schools share some important features of the template (for instance MBA and executive education programmes), I have shown that they are distinctly different. The different characters of the two organizations are evidently important for the kind of boundary-work being conducted. In the case of the academic business school, the boundary-work is primarily about finding the balance between academic demands and the demands from what is perceived to be a competitive, international MBA and business school market. For the business-oriented school on the other hand, boundary-work is mainly about finding and defining a dividing line between business school activities and that of other management education providers, such as consultancies and corporate universities. These processes of boundary-work imply that the field, and the boundaries for legitimate activity within that field, are constantly in motion, changing through the continuous identity formation of individual schools.

The two narratives thus suggest that there is a struggle between the business school template and business values in management education, as well as a struggle between the template and academic values. The template has thus a stake in the struggle over capital of the field and in the discussions about the character of management education as an intellectual field in the academic system. The struggle between the business school template and business values is perhaps mostly discussed in the literature (for instance, Daniel, 1998; Locke, 1989), whereas the struggle between a business school template and academic values is less often described as problematic. But the narrative of the academic business school provides an intriguing example that shows how important it is for the business school within a large and well-reputed university to both associate with the university and simultaneously dissociate from the perceptions of a very strict university and academic setting.

The European template of business schools that is forming thus places the business school outside the university systems, or at least questions the obvious relation between the university system and business schools. The often referred to 'American model' of business schools includes the business school in a university setting, but this does not hold true for the European field where the relation of business schools to universities is not self-evident (Engwall and Zamagni, 1998). The template that is forming in the European field seems to suggest that the business school is something between a freestanding organization and an academic university department. This grey area dictated by the template allows for all kinds of organizational set-ups (i.e., independent business schools as well as university departments, see previous section). Hence, adhering to the values prescribed by the business school template, rather than adopting specific organizational set-ups, is important.

BOUNDARY-WORK AND RANKING CRITERIA

Thus far, we have seen how the template is contributing to the identity-formation of business schools, and hence how the identity processes of individual schools contribute to the boundary-work of the field. Identity formation and boundary-work are also exercised in direct response to the rankings through debates about the criteria that the rankings set for the template. The rankings both confirm and relate to the identity features of the organizations, and constitute an arena for discussing and influencing the template. Thus, rankings are arenas for actors to conduct boundary-work in fields.

The two narratives can be used again here to illustrate how different identities and approaches to the business school template relate directly to the rankings, suggesting that the rankings are met in relation to the schools' perceived focuses and their identities. The business-oriented business school, for instance, scores high for several criteria in the rankings: management positions and responsibilities; value-for-money and salary of graduates; international mobility; and composition of the board, faculty, and student body with respect to international representation. For these criteria, the school has no objection. The school does object, however, to other criteria used in the rankings, such as the focus on a doctoral programme and academic research:

> So on five or six dimensions we were number one or number two worldwide, and then on some dimensions we were last: in terms of women on our board, in terms of having a doctoral programme, in terms of academic, pure academic research. Because this is not the game we are playing! . . . So do you want to be an average, or do you want to lead in a number of dimensions? So we have chosen our strategy. And I guess our job is to try to influence the *FT* and try to educate them that these are the kinds of dimensions you should look at. (MBA director, 2000)

This quote illustrates that the rankings are enhancing several of the features that the business school consider to be their core values and their main strengths and strategies, which supports their profile and their reputation in these areas. The MBA director also pointed to three criteria in the *Financial Times* ranking which he believed are poor measures of the quality of an MBA programme, which are also the criteria that school scores low on: the number of women on the board, the number of academic papers published by faculty, and whether the school has a doctoral programme. His explanation was that these measures do not reflect the needs of the MBA students. He argued that board representation and having a doctoral programme has no influence on the content of the MBA programme, nor on the way the MBA programme is taught. The number of published academic articles was said to have no influence on actual management practices, and therefore of no importance to the MBA students.

Similarly, in the narrative of the academic business school, some criteria were criticized in the organization for not reflecting the strength of the school, or for not reflecting the important features of a good business school or MBA programme. Some of the diversity criteria, such as number of females in classes or on the board, were viewed with scepticism, not because they were considered unimportant, but because the immediate impact of these criteria on the quality of the programmes offered was questioned. Other criteria, such as research and the international diversity of the student body, were considered important reflections of school and programme quality, and were valued highly. Particularly the research rating was considered important because it played to their identity of being part of a well-known research university:

> I am pleased with the *FT* that the research reputation, or research quality, is in there because I think it is very fundamental for a university like us, with the kind of top academic standard. It is nice to see that in there, so it is not just about commercial organizations and making money. So that is reassuring. (MBA admissions director, 2001)

The rankings thus confirm some of the identity features of the schools, while also highlighting some that do not fit with the perceived perceptions of school identities. The reactions to the rankings thus seem to be different according to the different identities or profiles of the schools. The quote from the first MBA director illustrates, however, that the business-oriented business school perceive their role to be that of influencing the rankings criteria and the *Financial Times*, and to educate them on the kinds of aspects that are important for measuring business-school success. This can be interpreted as an effort to influence the template and to use the rankings to do so, and thereby change the perceptions of business school activity. This way the rankings can be perceived as arenas for business schools to do boundary-work, and to influence the template that the rankings create and diffuse. Let's investigate this suggestion a bit farther.

Debating Ranking Criteria

The criteria in the rankings have been subject to continuous boundary-work by members of the business school field. Business schools have discussed criteria with the rankers, particularly the *Financial Times*. Although the business schools perceive their influence on the rankings to be very limited, my survey results show that approximately half of the ranked schools do actually claim that they have had some influence on the *Financial Times* rankings and on the way they measure performance of schools.[5] Fifteen business schools consider that they have had no influence at all on the *Financial Times* ranking (rating 1), while 14 schools consider their influence to be low or moderate (rating 2 or 3), and one school considers its influence to be quite high (rating 4). The European schools only feel that they have had an influence on the *Financial Times* rankings, not on *Business Week* or the *Wall Street Journal* rankings. Only one of the non-ranked business schools indicated that they believed that they have had an influence on the rankings, although rating the extent of influence as low for each of the rankings (rating of 2).

An example of how the business schools have been involved in the development of criteria, and how they use rankings for boundary-work against expansion, is a debate about the role of research criteria in the rankings. The lack of research criteria in the *Business Week* ranking has been notable for many years. The founder of the *Business Week* survey claimed that the rankings contained no research criteria, and that this was an explicit attempt to move away from research criteria in the evaluation of management education programmes. As we saw earlier (see Chapter 1), he criticized the research focus of many schools, claiming it threatened the teaching quality that students received. With the rankings, *Business Week* thus wanted to actively contribute to forming standards for management education that did not include the usual research focus. When asked if he believes the rankings have had an impact on management education, particularly a negative impact on research, he continues:

> Thankfully, it [the *BW* ranking] has had a somewhat negative impact on research, but not negative enough. I wish it had a far more aggressive negative impact because I feel there is still way too much negative research that goes on that is a total and complete waste of time for the professors, the schools, and I know for the corporations and the students. Total waste of time. The stuff that is being done is garbage today – not nearly as much as was done in the 80's, but a tremendous amount of waste and a lot of stupidity out there. And I wish that there was a way for us to more aggressively get at it and ridicule it and force it out of the system because it is a detriment to everyone. (Selections Interview 3, *Business Week*, p. 7)

The rankers are thus interested in setting boundaries that serve the public, which in this case means leaving research criteria out of the evaluation of business schools. As the overview of the rankings criteria showed, rankings are to a large extent focused on criteria that measure the satisfaction of students and customers, aspects that are not related to research criteria. In 2000, however, *Business Week* included a measure of 'intellectual capital' in their rankings, intended to measure 'a school's ability to shape current management thinking through faculty publication' (*Business Week*, 2 October 2000, p. 78). This makes up 10 per cent of a school's rank. In the 2002 edition of the ranking, this included publications in 18 chosen academic journals as well as the number of book reviews in the *Business Week*, the *New York Times*, and the *Wall Street Journal* (*Business Week*, 21 October 2002, p. 50).

The research criteria, which have been subject to discussion also in the *Financial Times* ranking, is one of the criteria that have been included because of suggestions from business school deans (Selections interview 2, *Financial Times*, p. 3). Business schools have actively influenced the process of setting criteria and giving advice on how to design the rankings throughout the process of constructing the *Financial Times* rankings.

The research criteria in the rankings, having been given more weight over the years, have changed direction slightly. In 1999 the research rating was based on three criteria: a peer-review evaluation by a committee of deans and senior faculty members; an 'impact' rating measuring the number of articles in *Harvard Business Review*, *Sloan Management Review*, and *California Management Review*; and the number of case studies sold. This research rating together with criteria for the number of faculty with a doctorate and a PhD graduate rating made up 16 per cent of the final rank (*Financial Times*, 25 January 1999). In the 2000 ranking, the peer-review assessment was abandoned. Instead, the research rating was based on the number of publications in a selection of 33 academic and five practitioner journals for the past three years. In the 2000 list, the research rating, together with criteria for the number of faculty members with doctorates and a PhD graduate rating, made up 25 per cent of the final rank (*Financial Times*, 24 January 2000). In 2001 the list of journals was adjusted (based on journal recommendations from schools) and the way faculty publications were counted was altered to measure the ability of schools to attract faculty members with a good research record (Business education correspondent, *FT*, 2001). The list of journals was again amended in 2002, and in 2003, to include 40 journals.

Varying Perceptions of Ranking Criteria

Ranking criteria other than that of research are discussed and debated in the business school community. Perceptions of most of the ranking criteria vary. Some are liked and some are disliked.

> [The rankings] are causing a situation where (*weak*) deans have abandoned their academic strategy simply to improve their ranking. For example, *if* I lowered my average age to 23, all female and all U.S. citizens, stopped entrepreneurship and ended my civil servant contract, fixed my advisory council and replaced with only females from the Falkland Islands (!), *then my ranking would improve by 40*

positions. The *Financial Times* methodology is *wrong*!!! (Survey comment, business school dean)

It seems the rankings, and their way to measure and assess business schools, evoke strong feelings and views among schools. Based on the survey results, this section will discuss how business schools view the rankings and the criteria rankers use to evaluate and measure school performance, to investigate further the rankings as an arena for influencing the template and for conducting boundary-work.

European business school deans were asked to rate the relevance of each ranking criterion in the *Financial Times* rankings. Table 4.6 shows the average ratings, and the highest and lowest rated criteria.[6] On the 5-grade scale, 1 represents 'irrelevant', and 5, 'most relevant'. The least liked criteria in the rankings are the ones that measure the number of programmes that the business school runs in other countries and the food and accommodation offered for executive courses. Other disliked criteria include 'whether more than one language is required in the programme' (which is a measure of internationality) and 'the number of females on the board of the school'. Among the criteria found to be most relevant are those that measure the output of education, such as employment opportunities, career progress, and placement success, and those that measure internationality. Research output and the number of faculty with doctorates are also highly valued.

Since the number of criteria is large, finding clear patterns for which criteria are liked and which are disliked is difficult. Grouping the criteria into factors is thus useful. A factor analysis was used to identify groups of criteria that are related and that measure the same aspects (see Appendix B for a complete discussion on the factor analysis and results). The factor analysis of the ranking criteria identified seven factors, each associated with a group of variables used in the rankings, and each given an indicative name: experience, gender diversity, international diversity, employability, academic orientation, financial gain, and other. The factor 'experience' measures the experiences of students during the time spent at the business school in terms of programme features, languages, international experience, and business school features. 'Gender diversity' and 'international diversity' measures the share of students, faculty and advisory board members that are female and international, respectively. International diversity also includes a measure of the international mobility of alumni. The 'employability' factor includes measures for the employment opportunities and placement success of graduates, whereas the factor 'academic orientation' measures academic performance through for instance faculty publication measures. 'Financial gain' refers to the salaries and salary increases enjoyed by graduates. The 'other' factor contains a mix of school feature criteria and programme feature criteria, and includes food and

Table 4.6 Deans' ratings of ranking criteria

	n	Mean	Median
Employment opportunities	53	4.3	4
Research output	53	4.2	4
Career progress	53	4.1	4
Usefulness of skills	53	4.1	4
Value-for-money	51	3.9	4
Placement success	51	3.9	4
International students	53	3.8	4
International faculty	53	3.8	4
Faculty with doctorates	52	3.8	4
International mobility of students	53	3.7	4
Facilities	48	3.3	3.5
International experience	52	3.4	3
Salary and salary increase	53	3.3	3
Firms recruiting on campus	53	3.2	3
International board members	53	3.0	3
Female students	53	3.0	3
PhD programme	53	3.0	3
Female faculty	53	2.9	3
Joint programmes with other schools	52	2.7	3
Joint programmes with corporations	52	2.7	3
Female board members	52	2.5	2.5
Languages required	53	2.8	2
Food and accommodation	52	2.4	2
Programmes run in other countries	52	2.3	2

accommodation, facilities, and skills taught in the programme. Table 4.7 shows the mean values of each factor as rated by the deans in the survey. The table shows that no single factor (i.e., group of ranking variables) is either very liked or very disliked by the respondents. The employability of graduates is the most liked factor used in the rankings, while experience and gender diversity are the least liked factors.

There are no significant differences between the ranked and the non-ranked group of schools in their evaluation of the variables used in rankings, although the ranked group of schools seem to like academic orientation, international diversity, and financial gain as factors for ranking slightly more than did the

Table 4.7   Composite measures of ranking criteria, mean values

	Ranked	Non-ranked	Total
Employability	3.8	3.8	3.8
Academic orientation	3.8	3.5	3.6
International diversity	3.6	3.5	3.6
Financial gain	3.6	3.4	3.5
Other	3.2	3.2	3.2
Gender diversity	2.8	2.8	2.8
Experience	2.7	2.9	2.8

non-ranked schools. The non-ranked schools, on the other hand, rated experience as a factor slightly higher than did the ranked group of schools.

As was illustrated in the quote in the beginning of this section, there are quite strong views about the rankings and the criteria among the European deans, and this seems to be particularly true among the deans of ranked schools. Three deans of non-ranked schools and fifteen deans of ranked schools volunteered additional comments on the ranking system and the ranking criteria, besides rating the different criteria. The two criteria that several deans would like to see included in the rankings were measures of school size (e.g., turn-over and national market shares) and that some indicators of the performance of schools should be related to aspects of 'contribution to society', which values, for instance, training students for the public sector and civil servant jobs. This was explained as a way of counterbalancing the focus on salary and financial gains of students after going through the programme, because several respondents also complained about the focus on salaries in the *Financial Times* ranking. More measures of process was also asked for, such as aspects of programme content, development of management competencies, and the quality of teaching. A few deans also recognized, however, problems in measuring such criteria.

The major overall concerns about the rankings were issues of comparability across countries, and of the weighting of the criteria: for instance, a few deans asked for more criteria and higher weight given to European factors. I will return to this issue of comparability in Chapter 6.

Rankings Criteria and the Capital of Business Schools

Because it is unclear from the above presentation that some criteria are considerably more liked than others, we need to investigate further how schools reacted to the criteria set by the rankings and by the template formed in the business school field. In trying to categorize the business schools according to their activities and focus, or their respective forms of capital (Bourdieu, 1988), as discussed in previous chapters, business schools were asked to rate the significance of certain activities and programmes.[7] This data was also put into a factor analysis in order to find groups of variables that describe the same or similar aspects of business school activities. The factor analysis compiled three aspects of business schools, or groups of variables, that have an influence on the profile of the schools: academic focus, business focus, and the MBA programme (see Appendix C for factor analysis results). The fact that the MBA programme became a separate factor in the analysis is interesting, and shows that the MBA is neither a measure of academic performance, nor a measure of a business orientation. Rather, the MBA programme holds the specific position of being a bridge between the two capital bases.

Two factors have thus been used to construct a measure for the business–academia spectrum representing the capital of the field: the academic focus and the business focus. These can be seen as opposing values on the business–academia continuum (discussed in Chapter 3), and can be used to investigate whether there are criteria in the rankings that appeal to specific types of business schools. These values have been correlated with the opinions of the ranking criteria (grouped according to the previous section). High correlations would indicate that there are certain criteria in the rankings that appeal to certain types of business schools, thus supporting the suggestion made above that business schools only like the criteria that favour their own schools. These statistics can also reveal if there are groups of criteria in the rankings that are more liked because they appeal to specific business school profiles. Correlation statistics are shown in Appendix D.

The results show that the academically oriented business schools rate the ranking criteria that measure academic performance high. This is perhaps not surprising, as these schools have influenced the rankers to include research performance evaluations in their rankings as shown in the previous section. The data also show that business oriented business schools tend to rate criteria for salary and employability of graduates high, as there is a correlation (at the 0.05 level of significance) for these factors. There is, interestingly, no group of ranking variables that correlate with a high rating of the MBA programme. This could be a reflection of the fact that many criteria in the rankings do not just refer to the specifics of the MBA programme; they also measure the overall profile and character of the business school, as for instance, (a) criteria for faculty, student, and board diversity, (b) academic orientation, (c) experience, and (d) the aspects included in the 'other' category.

These results show that the academic criteria in the rankings are most highly rated by the academically oriented business schools and that some business features are rated higher by business oriented business schools, suggesting that the rankings criteria do not favour a particular end of the business–academia continuum. Rather, both forms of capital appear to be valued in the rankings. Furthermore, for several groups of criteria there are no correlations between the rating of ranking criteria and the academic or business capital of business schools. This indicates that the rankings promote abstract notions of business school characteristics, which can be applied, without significant opposition, to both academically and business oriented business schools. Most ranking criteria are thus general in character, and represent no specific model or form of management education organization.

These data thus seem to contradict the results of the interviews presented above, where a clear difference was noted between the two business schools in their reaction to the rankings and to the rankings criteria. This may have several explanations. One interpretation of this discrepancy is that the two business schools are in fact representing two rather extreme points on the continuum, where their views are very different on the rankings and the criteria. A reasonable assumption is that most business schools are somewhere in between these two 'extremes', and thus differ much less in their opinions of the rankings. Relating to this, another explanation is that the measurement used to capture the differences in business school profiles and activities is not fine-tuned enough to reflect differences among schools. Thus, although the evidence is not conclusive and entirely consistent on this point, these survey results are not necessarily contradictory to the interview results presented above. The results do support, however, the suggestion made above that the research criteria are very important for the academically oriented business schools, so much that they have lobbied to get research criteria included in the rankings. There is also support for the argument that some criteria are more liked by the business oriented schools. Overall, however, these results support the claim that it is a template rather than a specific model, or a set of specific characteristics of business schools, that are constructed and diffused in the rankings. The template is abstract and general and can be applied to business schools with varying profiles, structures, and activities.

CONCLUSION

A fundamental question concerning published rankings of business schools was discussed and examined theoretically and empirically in this chapter: How do the rankings provide an arena for boundary-work of fields by contributing to the forming and reforming of a template for European business schools? The rankings contribute to the creation, evolution, and dispersion of an existing template because they build on and use existing measures and assumptions about business schools, as for instance, accreditation and the notion of business schools and MBA programmes. The rankings also contribute to forming and shaping this template by setting new criteria and new means of evaluating business schools, largely resting on assumptions of customer surveys and the employability of graduates as measures of performance. The rankings also contribute to shaping perceptions of an international market for higher business education. The template that is forming and diffusing in the field is an abstract notion of a business school, and does not relate to a specific model or form of management education organization. This chapter has shown that the template is a collection of aspects and perceptions of what a business school is, varying between, for instance, aspects of teaching quality, the gender diversity of faculty and students, and the salaries earned by alumni after the programme. The template thus allows for diversity within the field. Some business schools were shown to consider themselves to have an impact on the way the rankings are created, and have thus recognized the rankings as an arena for boundary-work and an arena to influence the template that is diffusing in the field. This issue will be discussed in more detail in Chapter 6.

NOTES

1. *Forbes* surveys business school alumni for salary data but does not ask for opinions about business schools. It is therefore not included as a reputation measure here. The target for surveys (approximate weighting in parentheses) in the other rankings are: *Financial Times* MBA and EMBA: alumni three years out (55 per cent); *Financial Times* executive education: company representatives (80 per cent); *Business Week* MBA: students (45 per cent) and recruiters (45 per cent); *Business Week* EMBA: students (50 per cent) and EMBA directors (50 per cent); *Wall Street Journal* MBA: recruiters (80 per cent); Economist Intelligence Unit MBA, students/graduates (20 per cent).
2. This categorical attempt illustrates the major features of the rankings and is not an exact description of the criteria. It is based on the information published by the rankers describing the 'methods' of the rankings and additional information provided in articles about the rankings. These methods change slightly over the years, but the main profile and approach of the different rankings have remained the same.
3. The question asked was: 'How would you characterize your institution?' (Five alternatives and one open-ended alternative were given): Independent business school; business school related to a university; business department or faculty within a university; independent college; executive education institution; and other. No school answered 'independent college'.
4. The question asked was:
   International ranking lists of MBA and executive education providers appearing, for instance, in the *Financial Times*, *Business Week* and the *Wall Street Journal*, have become popular. Your school has not yet appeared in any such ranking. What is your view of that?
   – It is a matter of indifference to us.
   – We do not wish to participate in these rankings because: ....
   – We would like to participate in the rankings because: (ten statements, to be rated from 1 to 5, where 1 = Strongly disagree and 5 = Strongly agree) It is a necessary marketing tool for our programmes; It is essential for the schools' academic reputation; It is essential for international recognition; It is essential for external visibility; It stimulates quality developments; It is essential for quality control; It distinguishes us as an elite institution; It is

demanded by our students; It is demanded by our corporate clients; It is necessary because our competitors participate.

From the survey, one cannot know whether these schools have been asked to participate in the rankings and declined, or whether they have not been asked and have decided that they do not wish to participate.

5. The question asked was: 'Has it been possible for you, as an institution, to influence the way in which the following rankings measure business school performance? *Business Week*; *Financial Times*, *Wall Street Journal*, National ranking (please specify)' (Each rated on a five-graded scale where 1 = Not at all, 5 = Very much).

6. The question asked was: 'In your opinion, how relevant are the following criteria in measuring business school performance? (Please note that we do not ask you to evaluate the methods used to measure each criteria, but only the relevance of each criteria)'. Rated on a five-graded scale, where 1 = Irrelevant and 5 = Most relevant.

7. The question asked was: 'For each activity selected in question 15a [programmes and activities available at your school], please indicate your estimation as to the relative significance of that activity for the business school. Academic research; applied research; custom executive programmes; open executive programmes; Executive MBA programme; full-time MBA programme; PhD programme; Undergraduate programme.' Rated on a five-graded scale where 1 = Insignificant and 5 = Highly significant.

5. The creation and re-creation of positions

The argument in this chapter is that rankings contribute to the creation and re-creation of positions of business schools within the European field. Rankings as a classification mechanism produce a list of schools that are considered good and a hierarchical order of their respective positions. The list of schools that the rankings present has been shown to threaten the perceived positions of schools, particularly their respective standings compared to other business schools, and thus the list threatens the identities of business schools (Elsbach and Kramer, 1996). The forming of positions also involves boundary-work on fields, in that struggles to create and defend positions are part of setting boundaries for who are (and who are not) included in the field.

In studies of cultural fields (Bourdieu, 1984, 1988; DiMaggio, 1987) as well as institutional and organizational fields (DiMaggio and Powell, 1983), field members are often assumed to have specific positions, and their actions and understandings are assumed to vary according to those positions. For instance, neo-institutional theory stipulates that organizations in the field imitate those organizations that are perceived to be leading and successful, creating, in turn, mimetic isomorphism (DiMaggio and Powell, 1983; Sahlin-Andersson and Sevón, 2003). Illustrating different positions, organizations and actors have been dichotomized as, for instance, leaders–followers, central–peripheral actors, role models–imitators (DiMaggio and Powell, 1983; Greenwood et al., 2002; Sahlin-Andersson and Sevón, 2003). Bourdieu (1984, 1988) refers to dominant and dominated actors, claiming that positions are formed according to the amount of specific cultural capital that organizations acquire in field struggles. When and how such positions are created, maintained, and reformed is not discussed, however.

Bowker and Star (1999) argue that classifications and classification mechanisms are often based on both discrete and distinctive categories, labelled Aristotelian classifications, and on prototypes that represent different categories, or prototypical classifications. Such prototypical classifications are thus based on perceptions of similarity and differences that are formed not just around specific characteristics and values, but also around specific organizations perceived as 'ideals' or prototypes (Bowker and Star, 1999).

Classification mechanisms are thus partly shaped by perceptions of prototypes and model organizations, but can also be assumed to contribute to the creation and diffusion of such prototypes in fields that in turn can be used in mimetic processes and in the forming of fields. Hence the forming of prototypes and prototypical classifications can be assumed to foster mimetic isomorphism, and to be shaped by perceptions of organizations as such prototypes.

In this chapter I will discuss the role of rankings in creating positions and prototypes of the field of management education. I will investigate how the rankings create and re-create positions for individual schools, and, by doing so, contribute to setting boundaries for inclusion in the field and in the group of business schools. The chapter will show that the rankings contribute to the forming of an elite group of business schools, and to constructing and confirming specific positions within that group. By doing so, rankings contribute to the boundary-work in fields in two distinct ways: determining who are to be included, and determining who are prominent members of the field. This includes a discussion of rankings not only as Aristotelian classifications, that is, which criteria and template they set for organizations in fields, but also the forming and functioning of ranking lists as prototypical classifications that promote specific organizations as prototypes for that template.

BUSINESS SCHOOL RANKINGS AND THE POSITION OF SCHOOLS

The five ranking lists that are presented as international rankings provide slightly different pictures of the relative positions of business schools around the world, particularly those in the United States and Europe. Table 5.1 shows the top 30 positions in each of the five ranking lists for rankings published in 2002 and 2003.[1] A first observation from this overview is that the perceived dominance of US schools in international management education is also reflected in most of the rankings, as we expect from the review of the selection mechanisms in the previous chapter. Several well-known American business schools, such as those at the universities of Chicago, Columbia, Harvard, Northwestern, Pennsylvania, and Yale as well as Dartmouth College, are featured in the top 15 of all the five rankings. Business schools at Stanford University and Virginia (Darden) are ranked in the top 15 by four rankings. Thus despite significant differences in methodological approaches identified in the previous chapter, the rankings place several of the same business schools in the top positions. The ranking lists differ more for the remaining positions. In all, 30 schools are featured in the top 15 positions of the five rankings, while the number of schools is 47 for positions between 16 and 30.

Table 5.1   The top 30 positions in five international rankings

	Financial Times 2003	Wall Street Journal 2002	EIU Which MBA? 2002	Business Week 2002	Forbes 2003
1	U. of Pennsylvania: Wharton	Dartmouth College: Tuck	Northwestern: Kellogg	Northwestern: Kellogg	Harvard BS
2	Harvard BS	U. of Michigan	Dartmouth College: Tuck	U. of Chicago: GSB	INSEAD
3	Columbia BS	Carnegie Mellon	Duke: Fuqua	Harvard BS	Columbia BS
4	Stanford: GSB	Northwestern: Kellogg	U. of Chicago: GSB	Stanford: GSB	U. of Chicago: GSB
5	U. of Chicago: GSB	U. of Pennsylvania: Wharton	Stanford: GSB	U. of Pennsylvania: Wharton	Dartmouth College: Tuck
6	INSEAD	U. of Chicago: GSB	Columbia BS	MIT: Sloan	Yale
7	London BS	U. of Texas at Austin	UCLA: Anderson	Columbia BS	IMD
8	NYU: Stern	Yale	IMD	U. of Michigan	U. of Pennsylvania: Wharton
9	Northwestern: Kellogg	Harvard BS	U. of Virginia: Darden	Duke: Fuqua	Stanford: GSB
10	MIT: Sloan	Columbia BS	Yale	Dartmouth College: Tuck	U. of North Carolina: Kenan-Flagler
11	Dartmouth College: Tuck	Purdue: Krannert	Henley MC	Cornell: Johnson	Cambridge: Judge
12	Yale	U. of North Carolina: Kenan-Flagler	Harvard BS	U. of Virginia: Darden	Northwestern: Kellogg
13	IMD	Michigan State U.	Cranfield	UC Berkeley: Haas	Oxford: Saïd
14	U. of Virginia: Darden	U. of Indiana: Kelley	U. of Pennsylvania: Wharton	Yale	U. of Virginia: Darden
15	Duke: Fuqua	UC Berkeley: Haas	Cornell: Johnson	NYU: Stern	Cornell: Johnson

Table 5.1 (continued)

	Financial Times 2003	Wall Street Journal 2002	EIU Which MBA? 2002	Business Week 2002	Forbes 2003
16	UC Berkeley: Haas	U. of Maryland: Smith	Instituto de Empresa (Madrid)	UCLA: Anderson	Washington U. (St Louis): Olin
17	Georgetown: McDonough	Emory: Goizueta	York: Schulich	USC: Marshall	NYU: Stern
18	IESE (Barcelona)	Ohio State: Fisher	U. of Notre Dame: Mendoza	U. of North Carolina: Kenan-Flagler	UCLA: Anderson
19	Cornell: Johnson	Cornell: Johnson	U. of Michigan	Carnegie Mellon	MIT: Sloan
20	UCLA: Anderson	U. of Virginia: Darden	UC Berkeley: Haas	U. of Indiana: Kelley	London BS
21	U. of Toronto: Rotman	IMD	MIT: Sloan	U. of Texas at Austin	U. of Texas at Austin
22	U. of Western Ontario: Ivey	U. of Rochester: Simon	HEC (Paris)	Emory: Goizueta	Brigham Young U.
23	Carnegie Mellon	Wake Forest: Babcock	London BS	Michigan State U.	Emory: Goizueta
24	U. of North Carolina: Kenan-Flagler	NYU: Stern	U. of Minnesota: Carlson	Washington U. (St. Louis): Olin	Carnegie Mellon
25	U. of Michigan	Duke: Fuqua	Emory: Goizueta	U. of Maryland: Smith	York: Schulich
26	Instituto de Empresa (Madrid)	Vanderbilt: Owen	Carnegie Mellon	Purdue: Krannert	U. of Michigan
27	York: Schulich	ITESM, Monterrey, Mexico	Washington U. (St. Louis): Olin	U. of Rochester: Simon	UC Berkeley: Haas
28	Rotterdam	IPADE, Mexico	U. of Illinois at Urbana-Champaign	Vanderbilt: Owen	Duke: Fuqua
29	Emory: Goizueta	Southern Methodist: Cox	U. of Edinburgh	U. of Notre Dame: Mendoza	SDA Bocconi
30	Cambridge: Judge	MIT: Sloan	Manchester BS	Georgetown: McDonough	College of William and Mary

Source: Financial Times 20 January 2003; Wall Street Journal 9 September 2002; EIU http://mba.eiu.com, 12 September 2002, Business Week, 21 October 2002; Forbes, www.forbes.com, 4 September 2003.

The rankings thus reflect the prominence of the US business schools, and place many of the large and well-known schools in the top. Mainly the large university-affiliated American business schools are placed in the top positions; six of the seven business schools ranked in the top 15 by all rankings are university-based business schools. The only exception is Dartmouth College. This supports the perception of the 'U.S. business school model' (Engwall and Zamagni, 1998; Locke, 1989) with the business school as an integrated part of a large and well-known American university.

Looking at the positions of European schools in the rankings, the picture becomes very different. First, the positions of European schools vary more than their US counterparts. Table 5.2 shows that while only four European schools are ranked by all four rankings, their positions in the rankings vary considerably between the different ranking lists.[2] As Table 5.2 also illustrates, the majority of European schools are featured in only one or two of the rankings, and that the positions can vary considerably (up to 50 positions) between the different lists. Because of this variation, which of the European business schools are considered prominent by the main international rankings is unclear.

A compilation of only the top European business schools from the five rankings, however, shows a clearer picture of how the rankings assign the top European positions. Table 5.3 shows the respective positions of the top European business schools in international rankings. As with the table of US schools, it is clear that a few business schools stand out in the top ranks. IMD, INSEAD and LBS are ranked in the top in several of the rankings, while a few other schools (e.g., Cranfield, Rotterdam, IESE, and Instituto de Empresa), each ranks high in two or three of the rankings but are not featured in the others.

While the rankings thus give the top international, and US, positions to the large and university-based business schools in the United States, they give the top European positions to mainly independent, non-university affiliated business schools such as INSEAD, IMD, LBS and Instituto de Empresa. Cranfield, although a university today, has an almost exclusively graduate and post-graduate focus as does the IESE business school in Spain (affiliated to the University of Navarra). The business schools more closely related to undergraduate and graduate universities are found further down the rankings, business schools at universities such as Cambridge, Warwick, Oxford, Bocconi, Manchester, and Edinburgh. The exception is perhaps the *Forbes* rankings, which rates the business schools at Cambridge and Oxford in the top 15. Relating back to the discussion of template, these results indicate that the rankings promote very different aspects of business schools in the United States and Europe; business schools can be either university-based, and promoting US business schools, or independent and hence promoting European business schools. Having reviewed the

*Table 5.2   The position of European business schools in international
             rankings*

	Financial Times 2003	Wall Street Journal 2002	EIU Which MBA? 2002	Forbes 2003
Ashridge	95		63	
Aston Business School			45	
Bradford University School of Management	85			
Canterbury Business School			100	
City University Business School	68		90	
Cranfield School of Management	54		13	52
Edinburgh University	73		29	
EM Lyon			36	
ENPC	92		98	
Erasmus University, Rotterdam School of Management	28		71	54
ESADE	83	33	52	78
ESCP-EAP	82		83	
HEC	62		22	75
Helsinki School of Economics	78		94	
Henley Management College			11	
IESE Business School	18		65	38
IMD	13	21	8	7
Imperial College	78		61	
INSEAD	6	37	33	2
Institut d'Etudes Politiques de Paris			68	
Instituto de Empresa	26	43	16	
Judge Institute of Management	30		74	11
Lancaster University			64	
London Business School	7	45	23	20
Manchester Business School	44		30	77
NIMBAS			79	
Norwegian School of Management, BI			99	
Nottingham			78	
Nyenrode University	73		41	
Saïd Business School	35		72	13

Financial	Wall Street Times 2003	EIU Which Journal 2002	Forbes MBA? 2002	2003
SDA Bocconi	43		57	29
Sheffield University Management School			48	
Solvay BS Université Libre de Bruxelles			95	
Strathclyde Business School	98		85	
Theseus International Management Institute			93	
Trinity College Dublin	86		92	
University College Dublin	89		86	
University of Bath	91		88	
University of Birmingham			44	
University of Durham	95		55	
University of Glasgow			37	
University of London			81	
Warwick Business School	34		69	

Sources: *Financial Times* 20 January 2003; *Wall Street Journal* 9 September 2002; EIU http://mba.eiu.com, 12 September 2002; *Forbes*, www.forbes.com, 4 September 2003.

positions in these rankings briefly, it is appropriate to begin the analysis of why the rankings look like they do, and whether the positions assigned by rankings matter.

CONFIRMING BELONGING TO A BUSINESS SCHOOL ELITE

The suggestion in this section is that the results of the rankings, or the actual lists, are important because they signal which schools are considered good and proper business schools in the management education field. Business schools are not indifferent to the fact that they are ranked by international rankings, but rather seem to want to participate in the rankings. Because the rankings are based on voluntary participation and rely on business schools to supply data and information, all ranked business schools have agreed to participate in them. According to my survey, 65 per cent of the non-ranked schools would like to participate in rankings in the future. A dean of a non-ranked school expressed surprise over this fact that business schools agree to participate in business school rankings, and even seem to wish to do so:

Table 5.3 Top European business schools in international rankings

	Financial Times 2003	Wall Street Journal 2002	EIU Which MBA? 2002	Business Week 2002	Forbes 2003
1	INSEAD	IMD	IMD	INSEAD	INSEAD
2	LBS	ESADE	Henley	IMD	IMD
3	IMD	INSEAD	Cranfield	LBS	Judge Inst. of M.
4	IESE	Instituto de Empresa	Instituto de Empresa	Rotterdam	Saïd BS
5	Instituto de Empresa	LBS	HEC	IESE	LBS
6	Rotterdam		LBS	HEC	SDA Bocconi
7	Judge Inst. of M.		U. of Edinburgh		IESE
8	Warwick		Manchester BS		Cranfield
9	Saïd BS		INSEAD		Rotterdam
10	SDA Bocconi		EM Lyon		Manchester

Sources: Financial Times 20 January 2003; Wall Street Journal 9 September 2002; EIU http://mba.eiu.com, 12 September 2002; Business Week 21 October 2002; Forbes, www.forbes.com, 4 September 2003.

It's difficult to understand why business schools and universities are still going into the ranking business. Nothing will change in the marketplace if there are no rankings. The participants are the ones that need to choose the most convenient business school and programme. Each business school is different; different value, faculty, methodological approach etc. How will somebody rank apples and bananas? The rankings are the business of the *Financial Times*, *Business Week* etcetera and the business schools are stupid enough to follow this race. (Survey comment, business school dean)

Why, then, do business schools participate in the rankings? Common answers to that question that we often find in newspapers and interviews with business school representatives, is that there are strong student pressures to participate in rankings, and that they are a good and efficient marketing tool for the MBA programme. When asked about possible effects of not being in the rankings yet and why the business school would like to be included, an MBA director pointed to the student pressure that is supposedly very strong: 'We have applicants asking every time [we interview for the programme . . .] Certainly also because [our competitor] was in and we were not.' (MBA director, 2001). Perhaps slightly less frequently, it is also argued that rankings are quality tools for business schools to keep track of their performance: 'They [rankings] are an external monitor to help you move towards excellence. They are a quality checkpoint' (Dean of the Kellogg School at Northwestern University, in the *Financial Times*, 20 January 2003, p. VIII).

Investigating these assumptions in more detail, my survey asked business school deans what motivates their participation, or desire to participate, in the rankings.[3] Table 5.4 shows the respondents' ratings of different reasons for participating in international rankings. The results suggest that the most important reasons for business schools to participate is that the rankings are believed to contribute to international recognition for the business schools, and to confirm belonging to an elite league of business schools internationally. For the ranked schools, the highest rated reason is that their rankings are considered to be essential for their 'international recognition'. Hence, they believe that the rankings are important for their schools' abilities to become known internationally and to be compared to schools outside their regional and national areas. Closely connected to this, although rated slightly lower by the schools, are aspects of 'external visibility' in general and a perception that the rankings distinguish a school as being an 'elite institution'. The rankings are also considered a 'marketing tool' for programmes, or a way to attract students and other resources to their programmes.

All four of these variables suggest that the rankings are part of marketing efforts of business schools, both to create awareness of their programmes but also to create a general visibility and international recognition of their schools. This is somewhat in line with the assumptions above. However, what is also

Table 5.4 Reasons and experienced pressures to participate in rankings

	Ranked schools			Non-ranked schools			Total		
	n	Mean	Median	n	Mean	Median	n	Mean	Median
International recognition	30	4.4	5	15	4.4	4	45	4.4	5
Competitors participate	30	4.3	4.5	15	3.7	4	45	4.1	4
External visibility	30	4.1	4	15	4.1	4	45	4.1	4
Distinction elite inst.	30	4.0	4	15	3.9	4	45	4.0	4
Marketing tool, programmes	30	4.0	4	15	3.8	4	45	3.9	4
Demanded by students	30	3.7	4	15	3.5	3	45	3.6	4
Academic reputation	30	3.3	3	15	3.0	3	45	3.2	3
Demanded by corporate clients	30	3.2	3	15	2.7	3	45	3.0	3
Quality development	30	2.8	3	15	2.8	3	45	2.8	3
Quality control	30	2.3	2	15	2.1	2	45	2.3	2

clear from these results is that this is not primarily about recognition in the academic sphere, and reputation as an academic institution. Academic reputation is rated lower than the four aspects of marketing and recognition. The responses rather indicate that participating in rankings is more about putting oneself in a group, and perhaps even in a new and international group. This suggests that the rankings are a particular kind of marketing effort that promotes a particular aspect of the school, which is not related directly to academic reputation and academic performance. Rather the rankings signal belonging to a top group of schools internationally, and recognition as an 'elite institution', and hence signal distinction from other schools. These aspects are rated higher (or as highly as) the general marketing reasons suggested in the questionnaire. Furthermore, rankings are not believed to be important as quality tools by European business school deans.

The results show that competition also compels participation in the rankings. The statement that participation is 'necessary because our competitors participate' is rated the second most important reason overall for business schools to participate, rated higher than experienced pressure from both students and corporations, which leads us to slightly revise the assumptions about the strong student pressure to participate in rankings. Instead, this finding strengthens the perception that rankings are about belonging to a group, and defining a group of schools, to which you compare and are compared, rather than just a matter of accommodating demands from students or other interest groups. It is because of the fact that the rankings are considered to define a group, an elite group, that participation in that group becomes import-ant. If competing schools, and hence schools to which you compare your own school, are in that group, your school is suddenly outside if it does not partici-pate. And, as expressed by one of my interviewees, 'you then have to explain why you are not in [the rankings]', and hence also why your school is not in the top group. Supporting this, the ranked schools also experience a stronger competitive pressure to participate than do non-ranked schools.

Rankings and Accreditation

Rankings are not the only mechanisms in fields that can create the feeling of belonging to a top group and that can enhance the international reputation of schools. There are other mechanisms for creating a group and showing that you belong to the top league. Business schools participate in, for instance, networks and alliances to build reputations and make comparisons within the group. Business schools continuously compare and 'benchmark' themselves against other business schools in the field, and link up in professional organizations that spread ideas about legitimate business activities. Respondents of

Table 5.5 Reputation influences

	Ranked schools			Non-ranked schools			Total		
	n	Mean	Median	n	Mean	Median	n	Mean	Median
International rankings	30	4.0	4	23	2.4	2	53	3.3	3
International accreditation	30	3.8	4	21	3.5	4	51	3.7	4
Alliances companies	30	3.5	3.5	23	3.3	3	53	3.4	3
Professional networks	30	3.3	3	23	3.4	3	53	3.3	3
Alliances business schools	30	3.2	3	22	3.1	3	52	3.2	3
National rankings	27	3.0	3	23	3.0	3	50	3.0	3
National accreditation	26	2.9	3	23	3.5	4	49	3.2	3

my survey were asked to rate the importance of different grouping mechanisms for the overall reputation of their schools.[4] Reputation has been asked for here to cover both the internal identification, and the externally driven aspects of identities (see Chapter 2).

In comparing different ways of creating a reputation and means of comparison within groups, accreditation and ranking stand out as important mechanisms for this kind of identity formation and identification (see Table 5.5). For the entire group of accredited schools, international accreditation is considered the most important driver for reputation among the alternatives listed. This is not surprising, and may be a result of the fact that international accreditation is one of the things that all schools in the sample experienced in that they were selected because of their participation in international accreditation.

The picture becomes slightly different, however, if we analyse the results for the ranked and the non-ranked schools separately. For the non-ranked group of schools, both national and international accreditation is more important than other grouping mechanisms. For the ranked schools, international rankings take a prominent position next to international accreditation, while national accreditation is rated lower than for the non-ranked schools. These results point to the overall importance of accreditation for this entire group of schools, specifically international accreditation, accompanied by international rankings by the ranked group of business schools.

National rankings have a separate standing, however, because they are not available in all countries, and therefore these figures need to be interpreted carefully. British and French schools, primarily, have mentioned the importance of national rankings: in mentioning *The Times* and *The Guardian*, for instance, and the *Nouvel Economiste*, *Challenges*, and *Le Figaro* as important rankers. One Dutch school has pointed to the Dutch weekly magazine *Intermediare*'s as an important ranker; and one Polish school, to *Polityka*. A Spanish school has mentioned favourably the ranking by *AméricaEconomica*, as a local and regional ranking that lists Latin American and Spanish speaking schools.

A comparison of the stated reasons to participate in both accreditation and rankings illustrates some of the similarities and differences in the two classification mechanisms.[5] Table 5.6 show for the ranked schools, the scores (mean and median) for the reasons they have chosen to participate in accreditation and rankings and for the pressures they have experienced to do so. These statistics are for the ranked schools only, because these schools participate in both systems. These results suggest differences on six variables, and a statistical comparison (reported in Appendix E) between the reasons for participating in rankings versus accreditation confirms significant differences on four of these variables: academic reputation, quality development, quality control, and competition. Differences on the variables 'international recognition' and

Table 5.6   Reasons and experienced pressures to participate in rankings and accreditation

	Rankings			Accreditation		
	n	Mean	Median	*n*	Mean	Median
International recognition	30	4.4	5	29	4.2	4
External visibility	30	4.1	4	29	3.9	4
Distinction elite institution	30	4.0	4	29	3.8	4
Marketing tool	30	4.0	4	29	4.0	4
Academic reputation	30	3.3	3	29	3.8	4
Quality developments	30	2.8	3	30	3.9	4
Quality control	30	2.3	2	30	3.4	4
Competition	30	4.3	4.5	29	3.7	4
Demanded by students	30	3.7	4	29	3.2	3
Demanded by corp. clients	30	3.2	3	29	2.8	3

'demanded by students' are not statistically significant.

These results indicate, not surprisingly, that accreditation is more closely linked to the academic reputation of business schools than are rankings, as well as more closely linked to aspects of quality development and quality control. Accreditation, as opposed to rankings, are launched as systems to secure and create quality and quality standards in management education, and are hence more tightly linked to a quality discussion and discourse (Hedmo, 2002). The comparison also suggests that the deans feel a stronger competitive pressure to participate in rankings than in accreditation, in that there is a significant difference between accreditation and rankings on the variable 'competition'. This suggests that the rankings are slightly more important as a competitive grouping mechanism than are accreditation mechanisms, although there are no great and statistically significant differences concerning pressures from either students or corporate clients.

Confirming Conformity with the Business School Template

The results presented above show, overall, that for business schools, both rankings and accreditation are considered important tools for creating a reputation and for placing oneself in comparison groups. Both international rankings and accreditation are considered important for international recognition and for providing evidence of being in an 'elite' group of schools internationally. The prominence of both accreditation and rankings in confirming inclusion in a top group is important, and perhaps needs more extensive investigation. Why are these mechanisms more prominent than others, such as networks of schools and professional associations? A survey comment, which summarizes the importance of these grouping mechanisms, provides a clue: 'Rankings and accreditations, etc. are problematic; but without recognition like these, you are nobody, and not really a part of the international business school community.' (Survey comment, business school dean).

This quote suggests that the importance of international rankings and accreditation lies primarily in their ability not just to define a group, but to acknowledge conformity to a business school template, that is, to qualify as an international business school and to be part of the 'business school community'. Besides providing credentials for participating notably in the management education field and for belonging to a top group of schools, rankings and accreditation thus provide evidence of conformance to the business school template.

Illustrating that the phenomenon of rankings and of belonging to this top group are linked to processes of identity creation and formation in business schools, the narratives of the two business schools further strengthen the suggestion that rankings are important to support the identification with the business school template. For the academic business school, rankings are considered important not primarily to show its excellence as a university department but rather to prove its claim that it is also a 'world-leading' business school. The rankings are thus not just important for being compared to a group, any group, but are primarily related to the specific template of the leading international business school. As part of this business school template, the rankings are considered important for the MBA profile of the school; staying outside the rankings is not considered an option, at least not 'if you want to run a major MBA school in the international market' (Director, 2001). This view is further explained as follows:

> If we weren't running an MBA, if you look at somewhere like [X,] they don't have an MBA, they don't have pretensions as an internationally leading business school in the sense that we do; they have a number of specialist masters programmes; so they are playing more to the academic side . . . But they don't run an MBA so they are less interested in [rankings].
> . . .
> What it is tied to is competing in a high-priced international competitive market. . . . It is a combination of things, but nonetheless, faculty and applicants are making choices on the basis of evidence, and if you are in the MBA and executive business school market, some of the evidence they use is rankings. (Director, 2001)

The rankings thus signal conformity to the business school template and contribute to the identity-formation of the academic department as a business school.

This would suggest that it is only pressures from the perceived business school market, and desires to be seen as a true business school, that induces schools to participate in the rankings. My interviews at the academic business school suggest, however, that there are also pressures from the 'academic side', the university, to participate and do well in the media rankings. Once the business school was featured in the rankings, the university expressed expectations that the business school should perform well in the rankings. Because of its links to the university, there are expectations that the school should be highly regarded and should achieve high status internationally, and that it should rank high to be comparable to the status of the university overall.

> what [the university] wouldn't like is to see its business school being very poorly ranked. If it is well ranked, or they don't know about it, that is fine. It would be very difficult if we weren't highly ranked, because [the university] has very, very high expectations of all its departments. They expect all their departments to be world class. (Director, 2001)

Desires and pressures to participate in rankings are thus tied to beliefs about a business school and the MBA market, and to beliefs that rankings are a prerequisite for being considered a proper and good business school in the field. To sum up the arguments in these sections, the claim that business school rankings define the boundaries of fields, by signalling which schools are included and which are not, needs to be slightly revised. The data suggest that rankings and accreditation not only signal belonging to a top group of schools, internationally, but in doing so, they define the boundaries of an elite group of schools in the management education field, rather than boundaries for the whole field. The boundary for this elite group is also the boundary that defines an international business school community, or the boundary for which organizations are considered to conform to the template of an international business school. This increases the importance of the template (discussed in the previous chapter) and again points to the importance of rankings for creating and diffusing this template within the business school community.

CREATING DISTINCTION AND DISTINCTIVE POSITIONS

Classification mechanisms such as rankings and accreditation have been shown to be important because they signal belonging to a top group of schools, and to the business school community. Such mechanisms are thus important for the identity formation of schools, because it puts them in specific groups and categories, and it forms the identification with other members of the field (Sahlin-Andersson and Sevón, 2003). But theory also tells us that organizations strive toward distinction, to distinguish their specific character from other members of the field (Alvesson and Willmott, 2002; Bourdieu, 1988; Czarniawska, 2004). This kind of distinction also assumes distinct positions within the field. Despite the identified similarities between rankings and accreditation as grouping mechanisms, the rankings have one important feature that separates it from accreditation and that make business schools participate in both accreditation and rankings. That feature is the 'mathesis' of rankings (Foucault, [1970] 2002), and the limited number of positions in the rankings. The limited number of positions means that when including some business schools, rankings will simultaneously exclude others. In this respect, rankings are more distinguishing than accreditation. Rankings thus contribute to boundary-work by defining and redefining distinctive positions of business schools in the field, besides creating belonging to an elite league.

The deans of my two ideal-type business schools both express this need for distinction as scepticism towards the usefulness of accreditation for their own schools. Neither of the two deans considers accreditation as a grouping mechanism to be very important for their school in terms of reputation and recognition. For both schools, participation in the European accreditation program EQUIS was seen more as a basic confirmation of belonging, or an 'insurance policy', rather than an important driver for reputation and status. Similarly, the business oriented business school interest in the European accreditation programme is primarily explained as a way to foster a strong European profile for business education, and to create a basic status or quality level of the European schools. The president considers this European accreditation programme important to create a stronger market with less fragmentation, and fewer 'fly-by-night' schools, regulated by the schools themselves rather than by any governmental body.

> I find that for [this school] it's important that the European level of competence, and professionalism and standards is at the highest possible level. . . . we feel it is important that the European playing field is somehow disciplined and you don't have all these fly-by-night schools, you know, fragmentation. So in that sense it is very important for us, but for us as a school per se, I have to say that I don't think we got major insights out of the accreditation process. Nobody asks whether we are accredited or not, it's our reputation which is strong and drives it for us. (President, 2000)

This quote illustrates again that the basic function of accreditation is to create a group, and provide confirmation of belonging to a group, but also that the school desires something more. Both schools imply that accreditation is important for setting the basic standard, and for creating a group in which business schools fit, but in which others, such as corporate training institutes, do not 'qualify'. Enough schools do qualify, however, so the self-appointed top schools do not consider accreditation, as a measure, good enough to distinguish themselves from competitors. An MBA director at a European business school voices this even more vigorously, claiming accreditation only provides belonging to a good league: 'Who needs the EQUIS blessing? The top school? EQUIS, to be totally honest, is good for less well-known schools who want to be promoted into the good league' (MBA director, 2000). Some of these perceived 'top' schools thus demand a better, more distinguishing classification mechanism.

It is in this context that the importance of rankings can be understood. Because rankings provide distinction and differentiation between schools in a way that accreditation does not, business schools have demanded rankings to supplement other grouping mechanisms, primarily accreditation. The specificity and numerical detail of the ranking lists has thus spurred their development, because the identity-formation processes of business schools have created needs to secure specific and prominent positions in the field. The rankings make the inclusion in the elite league very clear, and appoint relative positions to schools inside this group. In Foucault's ([1970] 2000) terms, the taxonomic measuring system that accreditation represents needs to be supplemented with more specificity, or a mathesis, which also provides distinction and distinctive positions to members of the field.

However, at the same time as this precision and detail is a driving force of rankings, it is also a source of frustration for many business schools: 'Rankings, in general, are a source of frustration in that their attempt to quantify many qualitative parameters often falls short of conveying a true picture. They are, nevertheless, a "necessary evil" ' (Survey comment, business school dean). The specificity and the detail of the rankings thus create uncertainty and insecurity for business schools, calling for continuous efforts to secure a position and an identity in the field. Because the rankings are volatile and change over time, business schools feel anxious and uncertain about the outcome:

> I am slightly bothered and worried about the rankings because I think we are in a zone of the ranking where there is very little separating the different schools. I think we can easily fall, as other schools are trying to improve their score, and I think the rankings are potentially quite volatile. And so as we have done well in the first round, if we fall in the second, then that will have consequences. (Business school dean, 2001)

This paradoxical relation between certainty and uncertainty thus drives instances of boundary-work and identity-formation processes in business schools.

MBA Rankings Influence Perceived Positions

It is thus argued here that rankings provide distinction by creating and recreating positions of schools in the business school field. This suggestion needs more investigation, however: do the rankings define positions within the field? Do business schools care about the positions assigned by rankings? A very simple measure of the usefulness of rankings for defining positions is the extent to which the rankings and the perceived position of business schools are the same. The perceived positions of business schools, expressed by the business school deans in the survey, were compared with the actual ranking, or non-ranking, in the most recent *Financial Times* rankings.[6] In Table 5.7, the perceived current position internationally has thus been cross-tabulated with the current ranking of the school in the *Financial Times* full-time MBA ranking 2002. The full-time MBA ranking has been used because it covers the largest number of business schools.

The results seem to suggest a relation between the perceived position of business school deans and the MBA ranking of the schools, although the sample is too small to make a conclusive argument. Table 5.7 shows that no school ranked itself lower than the ranking in the *Financial Times*, although several schools ranked themselves higher. For the majority of the ranked schools, the perceived position is in line with their MBA rankings, with some exceptions: three out of four schools consider themselves to belong in the top 30 group, a position that is higher than their rankings. While the results for the ranked schools thus are fairly coherent, the spread of the responses is larger among the schools not ranked in this ranking. A considerable number of non-ranked schools rank themselves higher, or much higher, than their non-ranking suggests, with 12 schools perceiving themselves to be in the top 50. One school that is not ranked even suggested a top 10 position. This suggests that the rankings are related to the perceptions of business school positions. Among the 12 schools from the ranked group that did not make the 2002 full-time MBA ranking list, a comparison between these schools perceived position and the actual position in the other *Financial Times* rankings show that the perceived position of five of these schools corresponds to ranking positions in the part-time MBA or executive education rankings, while four schools rank themselves higher and three schools believe their position to be lower than their actual rankings.

This data tells us that a large part of the perceived perceptions of European business schools' positions are in line with the *Financial Times* rankings, and deviations may to some extent be explained by the fact that there are different rankings to choose from. But the fact that the perceived current positions of business schools are consistent with ranking positions does not necessarily mean that rankings are used to construct positions in the field. The data can be interpreted in one of two ways: (1) the relation between ranking and perceived

Table 5.7 MBA rankings and stated current position of business schools

	2002 *Financial Times* full-time MBA rank by category						
	Top 5	Top 10	Top 30	Top 50	Top 100	>100	Not ranked*
Stated Current Position Internationally — Top 5			1				
Top 10		1				1	
Top 30			3	3		3	4
Top 50				1	4	2	2
Top 100					5	6	6
>100							8
Total		1	4	4	9	12	20

Note *The distinction between >100 and non-ranked schools is as follows: The column marked '>100' represents those schools that belong to the ranked category of schools, but which have not been featured in the 2002 full-time MBA ranking (i.e., they are either ranked in the EMBA, or in the Executive education rankings, or in the 2000 or 2001 full-time MBA ranking). The column marked 'not ranked' represents the schools in the non-ranked group.

position reflects that business schools make use of the rankings to define their position or (2) the rankings just reflect the previously perceived positions of business schools in the field. The following two sections will elaborate on these two explanations, and propose that both are valid: rankings are constructed to confirm existing positions, but they also contribute to the creation of new positions in the field.

Confirming Existing Positions in the Field

The first section of this chapter showed that there were mainly large, well-known American business schools in the top positions of the rankings. Also, largely the same schools were in the top 10–15 positions in the different rankings, despite quite large differences in methodological approaches between rankings (identified in the previous chapter). The top positions of the rankings are therefore not surprising, and seem to reflect mainly the 'expected' positions of business schools in the top group – suggesting that rankings reflect perceived positions in the field. Returning for a moment to the development of the *Financial Times* ranking, it becomes clear that this is primarily a result of how the rankings are constructed.

When introducing business school rankings in the late 1990s, the *Financial Times* stressed the need to create a ranking list that would be authoritative in the market, and that would compete well with the previous rankings in the field. But they discovered that developing a business school ranking that would have the necessary authority had problems. The first ranking produced by the *Financial Times* was published in 1998, and featured only European schools (*Financial Times*, 19 January 1998, p. 2). This ranking attempt was associated with a lot of unrest among business schools and management education organizations, so the ranking was altered shortly before publication (Crainer and Dearlove, 1999, p. 177). They had intended the ranking to be based on a survey of MBA recruiters, but the response rate from companies was considered too low, so the rating was dropped. Instead, the ranking published in 1998 was based on a listing of the salaries enjoyed by European business school graduates.

One interpretation of this failed ranking attempt is that business schools did not accept the poor methodology of the ranking, and therefore protested. Although this is probably part of the story, another explanation is that the rankings did not reflect the existing perceptions of the relative positions and standings of business schools in the field, and were therefore denounced. The argument is thus that, in order to be accepted, a ranking must fit (at least partially) the pre-existing perceptions of school quality and the relative standing of schools. Support for this proposition is found in a quote from the business education correspondent at the *Financial Times*:

When we looked at the data, it just didn't look right. . . . If we had done the recruiter response [ranking], what we would have found was that all the British schools would have come top, because we got huge responses from British companies, and all the Spanish schools would have come second because they were also quite good there. (Business education correspondent, *FT*, 2001).

This quote thus suggests that the rankings depended mostly on pre-existing perceptions of reputation in the field. Thus, the rankings build on, and must confirm, many of the positions already in place. The evolving methods for ranking are hence reactions to existing templates and positions within the field, and would not be considered right and accepted if they did not (at least to a certain extent) reflect perceptions of the field. Rankings cannot set positions entirely on their own; they need to be both accepted and recognized by others.

With this experience of the somewhat failed attempt to survey MBA recruiters, the *Financial Times* decided to further develop their ranking for the subsequent year and to put more effort and resources into finding suitable criteria and methods for collecting data for the ranking. To secure legitimacy and support from the business school community, the *Financial Times* created an advisory committee with representatives from eight leading business schools around the world to help decide on the criteria to be used in subsequent rankings. This advisory committee consisted of deans and senior faculty members from business schools in the United States and Europe, four from each region: INSEAD, IESE, Oxford University, and London Business School in Europe, and in the United States, Yale, Stanford, Northwestern (Kellogg), and Harvard University (Business education correspondent, *FT*, 2001). The committee was asked to put forward suggestions for the rankings criteria and the areas of importance (Selections interview 2, *Financial Times*, p. 3).

To be able to reflect pre-existing conceptions of reputation and positions, and hence construct a ranking that is considered a reasonably fair picture of the relative standing of schools, the ranking system depends therefore upon the participation of the majority of the leading schools:

It is very sensitive. You can't have Harvard saying 'we aren't going to participate'. Then you haven't got a ranking, have you? It is all right for small schools in Asia to say that they are not participating, because nobody notices. But if we upset the big schools, we are really in trouble. It is very, very sensitive. (Business education correspondent, *FT*, 2001)

Hence, having the 'right' schools in the rankings is as important as setting legitimate criteria for management education organizations. This suggests that, following Bowker and Star (1999), business school rankings are not just constructed as an Aristotelian classification: that is, setting criteria that are perceived to reflect important and legitimate aspects of management education. Rankings are also a prototypical classification, meaning that they are modelled around existing prototypes. This also means adapting the rankings criteria and methods to reflect an already existing template and the prototypes of that template.

Survey responses also support this suggestion that the rankings, to some extent, confirm existing positions within the field. Respondents were asked to rate the extent to which the ranking of their school was consistent with their expectations (before the rankings), with 1 representing 'not at all' and 5 'very much'.[7] Figure 5.1 shows that the responses were quite diverse, and that the results differ between ranking lists. Particularly for the full-time MBA programme, the responses varied. The number of schools that felt their positions in the rankings were much (or very much) in line with their prior expectations (categories 4 or 5) were almost equal to the number that felt their positions were not at all (or only slightly) in line with their prior expectations (categories 1 or 2). Responses for the EMBA and executive education rankings show a greater consistency with expectations than the full-time MBA ranking. No respondents indicated that the EMBA and the executive rankings were 'not at all' consistent with expectations (category 1). For the executive education rankings, the majority of respondents claimed their positions in the ranking were much or very much in line with their expectations. One explanation for the finding that the EMBA and executive rankings are more in line with previous perceptions is that the market for these programmes is smaller and perhaps more local, making it easier for schools to define their positions in those areas.

These results suggest that business school rankings reflect existing and expected positions in the field, at least partially; they also explain why the rankings look quite similar at first glance and why they have largely the same group of business schools in the top group.

Creating Positions

The conclusion that rankings confirm existing positions only explains, however, part of the results above. The same data could be used to argue the opposite: that rankings also create positions in the field. For the full-time MBA ranking, almost 50 per cent of the respondents also claim that their positions in the rankings were not consistent with their prior expectations and perceptions of positions. This share, which is lower for the other ranking lists, suggests the opposite conclusion; that rankings also seem to create positions and to contribute to reforming the respective positions within fields. We now investigate this suggestion.

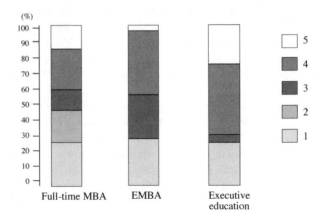

Figure 5.1   Rankings consistent with expectations

Survey respondents representing ranked schools were asked to rate the extent to which the rankings have changed their perception of the school's position.[8] For this question, 25 of the 30 business school deans admit to having changed their own perception of the position of the school at least slightly because of business school rankings (rated 2 or higher). A more balanced picture of the changes, however, is that approximately half of the schools (16 of 30) have rated the extent to which the rankings have changed their position as 1 or 2, that is, rather small changes or no changes at all. But at the same time, seven schools have rated the changes high or very high (4 or 5), and another seven have rated them as moderate (3). These results indicate that the rankings have changed the perceived position of business schools moderately or quite a lot in almost half of the cases. There are no indications in the data that only the lower ranked schools have changed perception of positions, or the opposite.

To illustrate what it may mean for business schools to have changed their own perception of position within the field, let's review a few brief examples from business schools in different contexts. After the school's first appearance in the *Financial Times* executive education rankings, a member of a Scandinavian business school wrote an article in the *Financial Times*, explaining how the school believes they are 'now officially In Competition' and continues to describe the changes that took place in the school after the rankings were out: 'It was an interesting organisational apotheosis, along the lines of Sally Fields' infamous Oscar acceptance speech. "You like me! You really, really LIKE me!" ' (*Financial Times*, 4 June 2001, p. VIII).

Although perhaps a rhetorical exaggeration, this quote expresses an experienced importance of the rankings and the creation and reformation of positions that the rankings provide. Expressing this experience more clearly, a member of the business school explains how the perspective of the school changed from a local to an international outlook:

> And everybody was stunned. Nobody thought we'd be ranked. And the administrator who had put together the information was very conscientious and did this faithfully without thinking that it would really happen. Suddenly, there we were in the paper. It revolutionized how this organization saw itself. We stopped being a local player, and in our own minds we started thinking more broadly. (Executive education administrator, 2002)

The impact of actually making it into the ranking list was thus larger than anticipated. This example suggests a linkage between the identity of schools and business school rankings other than the one proposed above. Rather than the rankings influencing the template, and in that way creating identity changes, as was shown in Chapter 4, this case illustrates how the rankings can also change a school's identity by changing the perceived position of schools. By changing perceived positions, the need and desire to conform to the template is created.

The examples in this and the previous chapter thus suggest that the rankings influence both the template and the perceived positions of schools that fall inside this template. The influences on schools' identities and identity-forming processes are thus twofold: (1) the rankings influence the template which may lead schools to make changes in priorities and activities, which ultimately changes identities, and (2) the rankings influence perceived positions (causing identities to change) and spur desires to make changes in activities and priorities. Caution is needed in attributing causality to these two processes – the processes are closely related and interlinked, and most likely reinforces each other. These processes do make it even more clear, however, that the rankings provide 'proof' of belonging to a group and to the template, and that the rankings, both indirectly through the template and directly through positions, influence schools to change, for instance, MBA offerings and executive education courses.

BENCHMARKS AND PROTOTYPES

We have thus far concluded that the rankings contribute to forming as well as confirming positions within the field. Specifically, the rankings confirm the centrality of some business schools as has been discussed throughout this chapter. But simply by looking at the rankings we do not know if the business schools taking the lead in the lists are also those schools used as prototypes or benchmarks by other members of the field. We only know that schools themselves use

Table 5.8   Referenced European business schools

	Total number of references	References by non-ranked schools	References by ranked schools
Ranked business schools			
Warwick Business School	19	10	9
London Business School	11	3	8
IMD	10	3	7
Cranfield School of Management	9	2	7
INSEAD	8	1	7
Erasmus University Rotterdam	7	1	6
Manchester Business School	6	2	4
Stockholm School of Economics	5	3	2
Lancaster University	4	3	1
Ashridge	3	2	1
Norwegian School of Management, BI	3	3	0
Durham Business School	3	3	0
ESADE Business School	3	1	2
HEC	3	2	1
Imperial College London	3	1	2
University of Nottingham Business School	3	2	1
University of Bath, School of Management	2	2	0
University of Edinburgh	2	1	1
E.M. Lyon	2	2	0
Essec Business School	2	2	0
IESE Business School	2	0	2
Judge Institute of Management	2	0	2
SDA Bocconi	2	0	2

	Total number of references	References by non-ranked schools	References by ranked schools
University of Strathclyde, Graduate School of Business	2	2	0
City University Business School	1	1	0
ESCP-EAP	1	1	0
Henley Management College	1	1	0
Saïd Business School	1	0	1
Non-ranked business schools			
Aston Business School	3	3	0
Brunel University	1	1	0
Copenhagen Business School	1	1	0
University of Exeter	1	1	0
Loughborough University	1	1	0
Manchester Metropolitan University	1	1	0
Norwegian School of Economics and Business Adm., NHH	1	0	1
WHU-Koblenz	1	1	0

rankings to create and confirm positions. Thus, we need to look at the benchmarks used in the European field of management education.

The survey asked business school deans to name three other business schools that they consider as benchmarks for their school.[9] This provides a picture of which schools are used as references and benchmarks for other schools, and thus are considered important players in the field. Table 5.8 shows the referenced business schools and the number of references to each. A first observation is that there are a large number of schools, 36, referenced at least once, indicating that there are no very clear benchmarks in the field. From this table it is evident that only one ranked business school has referenced a non-ranked school as a benchmark, and the majority of business schools used as benchmarks are ranked. This data thus suggest that the ranked business schools are more central than are the non-ranked schools.

Using the software program UCINET 6.0 (Borgatti et al., 2002), the pattern of referencing was turned into a social network graph presented in Figure 5.2. This graph reveals many things about the use of prototypes in the European field of management education and about the business schools used as benchmarks in this field. It appears from the graph that ranked schools (represented by triangles) are more central than are non-ranked, but accredited, business schools (represented by squares).

Most clearly from the graph, however, we can identify seven nodes representing the schools that are more referenced than the others. The single most referenced school is Warwick Business School in the United Kingdom. The other nodes are LBS, Cranfield, IMD, INSEAD, and Rotterdam. The seventh most referenced school is Manchester Business School, which takes a central place in the graph as well. We thus find that the business schools identified in the beginning of the chapter as leading European business schools are also considered benchmarks by other business schools in the field and are among the most referenced business schools. Primarily LBS, INSEAD, and IMD are considered central in the rankings, and are used as benchmarks in the field. To some extent the same is true even for Cranfield and Rotterdam, although their respective positions in the rankings vary more than the three previously mentioned schools. These schools are what I have earlier referred to as inde-

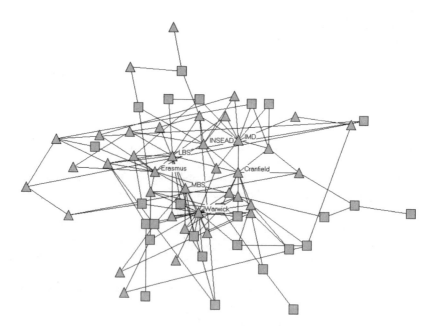

Figure 5.2   European business school benchmarks

pendent business schools, or business schools with mainly graduate activities (i.e., Cranfield), with the exception of Rotterdam, which is university-based.

The most interesting result from the social network graph is therefore Warwick, which does not hold a very distinguished position in the rankings, but is the most referenced business school in the field. Unlike the five other business schools mentioned above, Warwick is a business school linked to a large university. It is difficult to explain why Warwick is so much more referenced than other business schools, but it is possible to see from the graph that Warwick receives ties from a varied set of schools, both ranked and non-ranked schools, as well as schools both central and less central in the graph. Perhaps Warwick represents a middle alternative, a business school in a large university setting but one that has become known to be progressive and innovative and thus attract interest from a wide set of schools? Clark (1998) uses Warwick University as an example of an 'entrepreneurial university' that has developed to become a popular and very highly respected research university, while being innovative regarding sources of funding, organizational decentralization, and so forth. Such attributes separate the school from many other universities. One reason for the prominence of Warwick could thus be that it appeals to both university-based business schools and to independent business schools with a different organizational set-up. Another explanation for the prominence of Warwick as a benchmark for business schools in the field is that it is one of few European schools that are accredited by all three accreditation organizations, and thus is very active and prominent in professional organizations, and in the field in general.

Although not fully explaining the prominence of Warwick, one can conclude that most of the business schools assigned prominent positions in the rankings are also used as benchmarks in the European field of management education. Although an organization that is used as a benchmark is not necessarily also a prototype for the field, one can argue that the business schools that are referenced, are prominent in rankings and are used as benchmarks by several business schools in the field are more visible and thus more likely to serve as prototypes for field members. These findings thus suggest that rankings not only confirm elite schools, but also contribute to creating prototypes for the template.

It is important to keep in mind that such prototypes and benchmarks are not only created and identified through rankings but are also created through other means and other arenas, as the example of Warwick suggests. In light of this, the identity-forming processes of the 'elite' schools described in the previous section become even more interesting, and make it even easier to understand how these identity-forming processes influence the template of business school activities. As these schools form their identities and redefine activities and concepts to create that identity, they also serve as prototypes for other schools, and hence influence the perceptions that others have of them and of the field. The boundaries are thus redrawn not just for activities at individual schools, but also for perceptions of legitimate activities of prototypes or of the 'elite' business schools. This boundary-work also shapes the template that is diffused in the field.

CONCLUSION

This chapter has discussed the importance of rankings as an arena for boundary-work by contributing to the creation and re-creation of distinctive positions within fields. Rankings, like other classification mechanisms, enable belonging to a group and identification with a group that is important for the identity formation of schools. Business school rankings and accreditation are, however, specifically important, because they not only give rise to the status of belonging to a top group of management education organizations internationally, they also confirm adherence to the business school template that is diffused in the field. Another attribute, one just as important as that of belonging to a group, is distinction from other members of that group. The rankings have been shown to be particularly important because of their ability to create distinction and distinctive positions within fields. Business school rankings are thus important because they create very specific positions for business schools in the field; and these positions, in turn, contribute to defining benchmarks and prototypes in the field. In conclusion, business school rankings are important for their ability to set boundaries for an elite group of business schools and to define distinct positions within that group. Together, different forms of classification mechanisms discussed here contribute to setting boundaries for which schools are included in the field of management education organizations and to providing the attribute of belonging to a group, whereas the specific contribution of rankings is limited to setting boundaries for membership in what is perceived to be a top or elite group.

NOTES

1. These rankings have been used to get a group of rankings that are published reasonably close in time, all published within a few months in the fall of 2002 and the spring of 2003. Furthermore, these rankings were produced and published at the time when I conducted my survey, thus reflecting the standing of the field as business schools perceived it at that time. Although the positions in the rankings change over time, the general argument presented here is still valid. The only major change in the rankings is the *Wall Street Journal* ranking, which have a revised methodology for the 2004 ranking that has significantly elevated the standing of European schools. IMD, LBS, ESADE and HEC now hold in the top four positions of the ranking.

2. Note that the rankings of the fifth ranker, *Business Week*, cannot be used for comparison because it does not provide an integrated international ranking.

3. The question was phrased as a number of statements and the respondents were asked to rate the extent to which they agreed or disagreed, where 1 = Strongly disagree and 5 = Strongly agree. The statements were: 'We participate in rankings because/we would like to participate in rankings because: it is a necessary marketing tool for our programmes; it is essential for the school's academic reputation; it is essential for international recognition; it is essential for external visibility; it stimulates quality developments; it is essential for quality control; it distinguishes us as an elite institution; it is demanded by our students; it is demanded by our corporate clients; it is necessary because our competitors participate'.

4. Respondents were asked to rate statements from 1 to 5, where 1 = Not at all and 5 = Very much. These were: 'To what extent has the overall reputation of your school been influenced by: national accreditation; international accreditation; national ranking lists, international ranking lists; membership in professional networks; alliances with other business schools; alliances with companies?'

5. The questions were phrased as a number of statements to which the respondents were asked to rate the extent to which they agreed or disagreed, where 1 = Strongly disagree and 5 = Strongly agree. 'We participate in rankings because/we chose to apply for accreditation because: it is a necessary marketing tool for our programmes; it is essential for the school's academic reputation; it is essential for international recognition; it is essential for external visibility; it stimulates quality developments; it is essential for quality control; it distinguishes us as an elite institution; it is demanded by our students; it is demanded by our corporate clients; it is necessary because our competitors participate.'

6. The question was: 'In your opinion, what is the current position of your business school as a whole in relation to other schools domestically? And /internationally?' The alternatives given were: no. 1; top 5; top 10; top 30; top 50; top 100; >100. Twenty non-ranked and 30 ranked schools answered this question.

7. Respondents were asked about their reactions to the full-time MBA, executive MBA and executive education rankings respectively. The question was: 'To what extent was the position of your school in the most recent ranking consistent with your prior expectations?' Respondents were asked to rate their reactions from 1 to 5, where 1 = Not at all and 5 = Very much. The number of respondents were: n = 27 for full-time MBA rankings, n = 16 for EMBA, and n = 19 for executive education.

8. The question was: 'To what extent have the rankings changed your perception of your schools' position relative to other business schools?' Rated changes from 1 to 5, where 1 = Not at all and 5 = Very much.

9. The question was: 'Please name three business schools that you would regard as benchmarks for your own school (open question)'. These data were also supplemented with an e-mail (2004–01) to non-responding business schools, asking them to answer this question only, which yielded an additional seven responses. This section is thus based on the responses of 60 European business schools.

6. Business school rankings and the autonomy of the field

The previous chapters have shown how business school rankings contribute to forming and diffusing a template for international business schools, and how they both confirm and create positions within the field of management education. This way, the rankings constitute a mechanism that contributes to boundary setting for fields in two ways: setting criteria for evaluating management education and assigning positions of business schools in the field. Rankings signal both belonging to a top group and distinction within that group. Furthermore, rankings indicate how extensively the template is used and which business schools follow or use the template. Because the rankings contribute to these kinds of field processes and boundary-work, and because field members take part in these processes, rankings can also be conceptualized as arenas for field struggles. The concept of arena has been used in institutional theories of fields to conceptualize and localize processes of change (Greenwood et al., 2002; Rao, 1998), and by Gieryn (1999) to locate credibility contests and instances of boundary-work. Such arenas are however often taken for granted in studies of fields and field formation, stressing stability and conformity more often than incremental change and non-conformity of members in fields.

Because templates and positions of fields are continuously formed and reformed, we need to explicitly investigate the arenas where field struggles take place. In this sense, the concept of arena depicts not just a meeting place, or a place where discussions take place, but also describes a whole set of interactions, debates, and activities that take place and that contribute to forming and re-forming the field. This arena comprises interactions with members of the field: the template is used, and positions are accepted (or refused) and used in identity-formation processes of business schools. The concept of arena thus makes it possible to capture the mutual influences of such processes: that is, how members of the field are both influenced by and influence the forming of fields and their boundaries. This opens for an understanding of how various actors and mechanisms participate and contribute to field formation processes.

The rankings as arenas for field struggles contribute to the third kind of boundary-work and to the drawing of the third kind of boundary for fields, namely, that of which actors and which mechanisms are accepted and recognized as 'evaluators' or judges of management education. The introduction of new judges in the field is not directly a threat to existing means of evaluation, in that fields may contain multiple classification mechanisms (Bourdieu, 1988) that may place inconsistent or even conflicting demands on organizations (D'Aunno et al., 1991; Meyer and Rowan, 1977). This means, however, that classifications compete for authority and legitimacy in boundary-work. The introduction of new, or of more, judges of performance, or new means of gaining legitimacy in the field, may threaten the autonomy of the field and thus the ability of members to set standards for their own performance (Bourdieu, 1988; Gieryn, 1999).

This chapter will more explicitly discuss rankings as arenas for forming and diffusing templates and positions, and thus forming and shaping the field of business education. As such an arena, rankings compete with other classification mechanisms and means of setting boundaries, just as they compete with each other for authority as rankers. This chapter will further investigate the development of the *Financial Times* ranking, and the reactions that this and other rankings have met in the field of European management education. In this chapter I will show how the development of a European-based ranking was driven by a demand for an arena for boundary-work in the field of European higher management education, as well as discuss the influence of this arena on European business schools and the extent to which this arena is shaping management education in Europe.

AN ARENA FOR CREATING A EUROPEAN PERSPECTIVE ON MANAGEMENT EDUCATION

Contrary to a common perception of rankings as imposed on the business school field (Elsbach and Kramer, 1996; Segev et al., 1999), this section will argue that business school rankings as arenas for boundary-work have been driven by media competition as well as by demands from the European management education field for new arenas within which to conduct boundary-work. The rankings have developed because of demands for an arena that would create a template for international business schools that would better fit the European context, and to create new and better positions for European schools within the international management education field. The rankings, as such arenas for field struggles, both build on and compete with other such arenas for defining and redefining fields. Such struggles may threaten the autonomy of the field by including more and new judges and evaluators of performance in the field.

To illustrate the demand for new arenas for boundary-work, let me again return to the development of the *Financial Times* rankings. When the *Financial Times* started to rank business schools in the United States and Europe in 1999, the explicit intent was to provide a ranking that compared business schools in these different regions and assessed the relative standing of these schools. The *Financial Times* claim that there was a demand from European business schools to define and diffuse a template of an international business school and to create an international ranking that would feature the leading business schools outside the United States. The *Financial Times* felt a pressure primarily from three European business schools, INSEAD, IMD, and LBS, to produce an international ranking that would set criteria for business schools internationally and would include the European schools. This demand was a reaction to the American *Business Week* and *US News & World Report* that had produced rankings of US schools for a long time. These European schools feared being left out, as the dominating American rankings gained increasing attention:

> one of the things I can tell you is that business schools hate rankings, but in fact we started producing them because we were under pressure from some of the big business schools in Europe to produce rankings. . . . What they said was that all rankings are U.S. based . . . and if *Business Week* only produces rankings of U.S. schools then that looks as if that is the world ranking and not just a U.S. ranking. So we were under pressure from these schools because they wanted to see a proper international ranking. . . . They wanted an international ranking that had them in it, which is of course what they got. Then they didn't like it because they didn't like where they were! (Business education correspondent, *FT*, 2001)

The starting of the *Financial Times* ranking was thus driven by a demand for a ranking that would provide a different picture of the field of management education; a picture perceived to be more international than American and that would provide a basis for European schools to be part of the international management education field.

This experienced demand for an international ranking and for new ways to define the field of management education partly throws aside assumptions that rankings are imposed on the business school field by the media, and that business schools are left feeling both powerless and trapped. Rather, business schools and their willingness to participate have also driven the rankings. Among the European schools currently ranked by the *Financial Times*, my survey shows that 20 per cent of the ranked schools report that they themselves have taken an active approach to be included in one or more of the rankings.[1] This finding supports the suggestion that the development of rankings is spurred also by the involvement of schools and their eagerness to participate. This finding also seems to suggest that the schools find that being in the rankings is important and worthwhile. This was also shown in the previous chapter, where the reasons for schools to participate were examined; desires to be included in an international group and to market programmes and to create visibility for the business schools were stronger than the perceived 'pressures' from students and corporations to participate.

An Authoritative European Arena

Before contemplating farther the reasons for this demand for a new arena, the relative authority of the different rankings in the field must be investigated. So far, the different rankings have been treated as one unit, and some common features of the rankings have been discussed, such as a focus on MBA programmes and the hierarchical ordering of schools into positions. But as pointed out above, the rankings also have a lot of differences: they identify different customer groups, have different methodologies and different criteria, and create slightly different positions for schools. The rankers thus compete with each other, and their ranking systems compete for authority and legitimacy as classification mechanisms and as means of presenting a trustworthy representation of the field. This continuous struggle for the rankings to be credible and for the rankers to gain legitimacy, authority, and acceptance for their presentations of the business education field illustrates the reality of competition between classification systems.

If this competition is taken seriously, the rankers and rankings can enjoy different 'statuses' and be given different degrees of authority in the field. Who is in the lead is not obvious: 'I had this wild idea that was undoubtedly born out of me working really long hours on this stuff, that it would really be [fun] if all business schools got together and ranked the guys who rank us!' (External relations officer, 2002). This was expressed, not without slight frustration, by one of my interviewees; the idea was quite serious. Although this particular effort did not materialise, European business schools have been given their chance: my survey asked European business school deans to rate and rank the rankers and the different ranking lists that feature European business schools, to capture some of the dynamics of the competition for authority as rankers.

European business school deans were asked to rate how well or poorly they believe that various rankers measure performance in their rankings.[2] The results, presented in Table 6.1, suggest that the *Financial Times* is considered to provide the 'best' international measure of business school performance by the European deans, and it is the most authoritative of the international rankers asked for here. The *Financial Times* ranking also has the highest response rate both in the sense of actual responses, but also in the sense that fewer people have responded 'no opinion' when asked to rate them.[3] Fewer deans have responded to questions about the *Business Week* and the *Wall Street Journal* rankings than about the *Financial Times*.

The data in Table 6.1 also show that there are no great differences between the ranked and the non-ranked group of schools in how they rate the different international rankers. There is only one significant difference between the two groups: the ranked group of schools rank national rankings much higher than the non-ranked group, and the national rankers are rated even higher than any of the international rankers by these schools. The interpretation of these results needs caution, however, because 18 schools have declared that national rankings don't apply to them, and 13 have offered 'no opinion'. The sample is thus very small. These data could suggest that many of the internationally ranked business schools are prominent in their national context and in the national rankings, thus having a greater influence (in terms of being benchmarks or prototypes) on the national rankings than any of the non-ranked schools. This does not explain, however, why the non-ranked schools rank the national rankings much lower than the international rankings. The results suggest, however, that the ranked and the non-ranked group of business schools have similar perceptions of the international rankings, thus indicating that the rating of the different rankers is not directly dependent on participation in the rankings.

Business school deans were also asked to rank the three specific ranking lists that they consider to be most important for their school.[4] In this data also, the *Financial Times* stands out as the most important ranker; two of the *Financial Times* ranking lists are rated higher than any other ranking (see Table 6.2). The results also confirm the standing of the full-time MBA rankings – as most prominent and important of the different ranking lists. This is particularly true for the *Financial Times* full-time MBA ranking. This data confirms the prominent position of the *Financial Times* as an important ranker for the European field of management education.

One possible explanation for this difference in 'authority' between the rankings could be the different methodological approaches chosen by the rankers. Recall from Chapter 4 that the *Financial Times* surveys alumni for the full-time MBA, *Business Week* surveys students and graduates in their full-time MBA ranking, and surveys business school deans for their EMBA programmes; and the *Wall Street Journal* surveys employers. Thus, one can argue that the different approaches taken may have an impact on the relative standings of the rankers.

However, among the respondents of the survey, there is strong consensus that alumni satisfaction, graduates' evaluation, and employers' evaluation of programmes are all relevant criteria for judging business school performance (see Table 6.3). Thus, all three of the current full-time MBA rankings approaches are rated high, and are thus considered relevant measures of performance by the European deans. However, Table 6.3 also provides evidence that other deans' evaluation of programmes is not rated as highly as the other approaches, and thus is considered less appropriate as a measure of

Table 6.1 Perceptions of performance measures in the different rankings

	Ranked schools			Non-ranked schools			Total			
	n^*	Mean	Median	n^*	Mean	Median	n^*	Mean	Median	No opinion
National	10	3.7	4	8	2.1	1.5	18	3.0	3.5	13
Financial Times	28	3.1	3	15	2.9	3	43	3.0	3	7
Business Week	23	2.6	2	12	2.4	2	35	2.5	2	14
Wall Street Journal	23	2.3	2	13	2.4	2	36	2.3	2	13

Note: In the table, 'n' does not include the respondents who have answered 'no opinion'. Including these gives total $n = 31$ for national rankings; $n = 50$ for the Financial Times; $n = 49$ for Business Week and the Wall Street Journal.

Table 6.2   Ranking the rankings

	Number of ranks	Rank 1
Financial Times MBA	42	31
Financial Times EMBA	25	10
Business Week MBA	20	3
Financial Times Exec. ed.	19	7
National ranking	12	4
Wall Street Journal MBA	7	0
Business Week EMBA	4	1
Business Week Exec. ed.	3	1

performance. These results thus suggest that there is no one predominant model and technique that is more accepted than another, although it is clear that other deans' ratings of business schools and programmes are considered less relevant than the three aforementioned approaches. Differences are only small between the ranked and the non-ranked group of schools in these ratings of the various methodological approaches.

These results clearly indicate that the *Financial Times* rankings have become an important arena for European schools, as a supplement to *Business Week* and other rankers and rankings. These results also suggest that the MBA ranking is considered the most important of the ranking lists, but with a caveat: only a handful of European schools are ranked by more than the *Financial Times* ranking lists, and hence have dealt with the other rankings close by. There is a risk that the *Financial Times* is overrated simply because its rankings feature a larger number of the European schools. Contradicting that, the data do not seem to indicate that schools only rank the lists that they themselves are featured in. The *Financial Times* rankings are rated high by both ranked and non-ranked schools; and among the schools rating the *Business Week* rankings high, we find schools that have been ranked by these rankings and those that have not. Similarly, mainly non-ranked schools have rated the *Wall Street Journal* ranking high.[5]

The finding that it is primarily alumni, graduate, and employer evaluations of management education that are considered appropriate methods for the rankings suggest that these are different from the more traditional peer-review evaluations of educational organizations and programmes, where academics evaluate and assess each other and each other's organizations. This is how, for instance, the academic publishing industry works, and also other evaluations and classifications, such as the British Research Assessment Exercise, and

Table 6.3 Evaluation of interest groups identified in the rankings

	Ranked schools			Non-ranked schools			Total		
	n	Mean	Median	n	Mean	Median	n	Mean	Median
Alumni evaluation	30	4.7	5	23	4.6	5	53	4.6	5
Graduates' evaluation	30	4.5	5	23	4.4	4	53	4.4	5
Employers' evaluation	30	4.3	4	23	4.5	5	53	4.4	5
Deans' evaluation	30	2.8	3	23	3.0	3	53	2.9	3

even national and international accreditation programmes. Therefore, the results showing that surveying members of the business school community is not considered a legitimate way of evaluation is quite contradictory, in that such an approach to rankings would protect some of the peer-review thinking, but under a new form. Rather, however, the rankings promote other approaches that are considered more legitimate by the business education community.

Business school rankings have therefore introduced not only new measures, but also a different way to approach educational evaluation. Although rankings coexist with other measures and with peer-review processes, the introduction of more and different measures of performance is ultimately a threat to the autonomy of the field because those measures compete for attention and authority in the field. Moving away from traditional peer-review processes, such competition might imply that members of the business school community consequently lose some control over the processes through which they are evaluated.

Need for a European Arena

Having established that the *Financial Times* rankings are the most authoritative in the European field, we move back to the initial claim that the rankings have been driven by a demand for an arena that promotes European business schools and allows them to do boundary-work on the field. One argument would be that the *Financial Times* rankings, in being European-based, has become important because they have promoted a European perspective on business school rankings and management education, and have promoted what are perceived to be European criteria in the rankings. Another argument is that the *Financial Times* rankings promote European schools by including them, and that they are important because they constitute an arena for European schools to do boundary-work and protect the autonomy of the field. For the interviews and the questionnaire, several respondents suggested that the *Financial Times* promotes European criteria and values, at least more than other rankers do. Although this evidence is not entirely conclusive, one dean notes that: 'International media tend to use Anglo-Saxon criteria. With their inclusion of European schools and universities they have found it indispensable to alter their criteria in order to take into account the specific characteristics of other education systems.' (Survey comment, business school dean).

Returning briefly to the criteria in the rankings and business schools' reactions to the *Financial Times* rankings criteria, it is easy to apply a new interpretation to the survey results in light of this. Some of the differences between liked and disliked criteria indicate the split between what are considered

'American' criteria and criteria perceived to be more adapted to the European context. European deans generally liked the measures of employability of graduates, for instance, while they disliked measures of salaries and salary increases that are perceived to favour the American schools. One respondent commented saying that the *Financial Times* places 'undue emphasis on salaries, consequently the U.S. model dominates.' The evaluation of internationality measures, which are generally considered to favour European schools, are mixed: international student and faculty bodies are liked, while the languages required and the number of programmes run abroad are disliked. For other criteria that are disliked, for instance the share of females among students, among faculty, and among persons on the board, it is not clear that these are perceived to disfavour European schools.

The popularity of the *Financial Times* has thus to do with the fact that they have redefined positions in the field and have included European schools in the rankings to an extent that other rankers have not, but also the fact that the *Financial Times* has at least partly included criteria that are perceived to favour European schools, and thus have reformulated aspects of the business school template to better fit the characteristics of European schools. But despite the fact that these rankings have included more European schools and more 'European' criteria, an opinion seems to persist that rankings in general promote and continue to support an 'American model' of education:

> It is questionable whether rankings can be based on criteria uniformly applied to all schools irrespective of their strategy and philosophy. The current rankings rely on a very specific (North American) model of what and how business schools should be set up to do. This model itself is very questionable. (Survey comment, business school dean)

In line with this, one of the persisting criticisms of the *Financial Times* rankings is the way it measures research output. Although research and academic criteria are highly rated by European business schools and regarded as very important criteria, there are still debates and criticisms of the way they are measured, particularly the journals selected for the evaluation of research: 'Another point is related to the types of economic journals selected for the rankings and for evaluation of the quality of research: too many of them are edited in the U.S. and do not reflect the perspective of a real global way of thinking' (Survey comment, business school dean).

The list of 40 journals used in the assessment of research consists of mainly American based journals, with only four journals edited in Europe in 2003. This is what has upset many European business school representatives and deans. One European business school dean expresses his dilemma with the research criteria:

I have for a long time been very passionate within Europe about trying to persuade my colleagues in Europe, and my own staff, to publish in European journals and to not be sucked in to having to publish in North American journals. I have to say now, that in two years of being the director of the school, I am now puzzled about what I should be asking my staff to do, given the impact it is having on the ranking system. (Euram conference panel of deans, 2001)

The *Financial Times*, on the other hand, claim that both sides have their own perception of how this criterion is to be measured. European and American schools each have their definitions of a fair representation of the research criteria, and of which journals should be included:

We admit immediately that this is a very difficult thing to measure. But as a proxy, it is a fairly accurate measure. It is also a measure that, as far as we can see, the majority of business schools are happy with although there may be questions about the selection of journals. The Americans say it is pro-European, and the Europeans say it is pro-American. So, we kind of feel like we are between a rock and a hard place. (Selections interview 2, *Financial Times*, p. 4)

Although most objections seem to be towards criteria that favour American schools, and towards an 'American model' of education, a comment made by the dean of a south European school suggests that there are also other issues of debate when evaluating the rankings criteria. There is not only a struggle between United States and Europe, but also between groups of business schools and specific interests within Europe: 'International rankings do not take care of the diversity in different countries, so they are too much oriented to U.S. and UK criteria and way of thinking about education. They also have an unbalanced weight of internationalization [versus] contribution to the management development in each country' (Survey comment, business school dean).

This dean thus turns not just towards the United States, but also to the United Kingdom, and claims that the criteria reflect a UK way of thinking rather than a European or international perspective. One of the concerns raised by these schools is that measuring only contributions to international journals favour English-speaking countries, and disfavours countries with strong national publications and research perspectives. For instance Spanish and Italian schools with strong traditions of publishing in their native languages feel threatened by the Anglo-Saxon focus of the rankings. These schools thus ask for criteria that take into account also the contributions made to national research and management development taking national contexts into account. This illustrates even further the importance of rankings for debating the template and the positions in the field, and for arenas by which business schools influence the formation of the field.

Competition in an International Field

The introduction of international measures in the rankings is interesting, and provides evidence of attempts to create an international field of business education that includes business education organizations in the United States and Europe, and that eventually becomes a global inclusion of such organizations. It is also evidence of attempts to expand the template of business schools to include European schools and European criteria. The introduction of rankings in the *Financial Times* is thus not only a stake in the media competition, but more importantly, also a stake in efforts to construct an international field of management education. With criteria intended to bridge regional differences, the rankings attempt to create a uniform and coherent field of business education, thus extending the boundaries of the field beyond national and even continental borders.

The rankings are thus driven by desires to redraw boundaries for the field and hence create an international field of business education. At first glance, this way of setting the boundaries for business education runs contrary to other efforts to draw boundaries for the field of higher business education, as for instance, those pursued by the Efmd in developing a European accreditation scheme (cf. Hedmo, 2002). The development of EQUIS can be described as an effort of European business school representatives to create a 'European approach' to management education, and to create assessment criteria that account for specific regional characteristics of management education programmes and institutions (Hedmo, 2002). These efforts can hence be interpreted as attempts to create a distinct European field of management education. But a closer look taken here suggests, however, that the original driving forces of the *Financial Times* ranking efforts are very much in line with the efforts of the European approach: to establish criteria that better assesses the strength of European schools and provides positions for European schools in the international business school community. The accreditation and ranking systems are thus both competing and serving the same purpose.

Accreditation and rankings are also connected more directly to each other, and they are highly interdependent. Several of the rankings use accreditation as a screening mechanism for their rankings, that is, they target for their surveys and information gathering only schools that are accredited, as was noted in Chapter 4. Furthermore, the *Financial Times* has an unwritten rule that they don't write about business schools that are not accredited by any of the three international accreditation institutions (the Efmd, the AMBA, and the AACSB International). The rankings thus build on and use the boundaries set by accreditation in their own boundary-work. Rankings are dependent on other arenas for boundary-work and need to take into account both the boundaries that are currently drawn by other rankings and by other mechanisms, as well as those previously established.

Illustrating further the interconnectedness of rankings with other forms of evaluations, assessments, and classification efforts, the *Financial Times* has since 2002 incorporated an audit function into the full-time MBA rankings (*Financial Times*, 21 January 2002, p. V). A commercial audit firm audits some of the schools each year to make sure that the data going into the rankings are measured in the same way and that they are accurate. This auditing is linked to demands for comparable data and reporting systems, and for a way to make rankings trustworthier. Ten pioneering business schools were audited in 2002. In 2004, 60 of the 100 ranked business schools had been through the audit.

This effort by the *Financial Times* to audit ranking information is closely related to efforts by the Graduate Management Admissions Council, GMAC, in the United States to standardize information going into the rankings. This organization has developed 'MBA Reporting Criteria', with the intention of setting norms for how ranking information is to be reported, and providing access to such information through the GMAC web site. All information submitted for publication on the web site is subject to an audit, securing the accuracy and consistency of the data. The GMAC initiative was launched in 2000 and, as of November 2003, 129 schools had signed it (www.gmac.com, 27 November 2003). This setting of standards links rankings to other efforts to structure the field and the information in the field, and illustrates how one form of scrutiny and regulation often leads to further efforts to scrutinize and audit (cf. Power, 1997), and to more regulations (cf. Hedmo et al., forthcoming).

The result of the processes described in this section is a threat to the autonomy of the European field of management education in two distinct ways. The media rankings have become important and authoritative judges of management education organizations, competing with other means of classification and evaluations such as accreditation and peer-review processes. The rankings are distinctly different from these more traditional peer-review assessments of education, suggesting that business schools and members of business schools get less influence and need to adapt to criteria set by other organizations, such as the media. This reduced influence on the criteria used to evaluate the discipline thus threatens the autonomy of the field by introducing more judges and competing, and sometimes conflicting, logics or modes of evaluation.

The introduction of rankings has also more specifically threatened the autonomy of the European management education field, such that the rankings create a power dilemma for European business schools. European business schools feel that they are being evaluated on the bases of American criteria, although the *Financial Times* ranking has been demanded and promoted as a counterforce to that. In being considered important to promoting the standings of European business schools, the rankings are, at the same time, also considered to promote an American focus and perspective on management education even further. For European management education organizations, media rankings thus provide both an opportunity and a threat to the protection of what is perceived to be a European approach to management education, and to the standings of European schools.

PLAYING THE RANKINGS' GAME?

We have seen how several rankings compete with each other as well as with other classification mechanisms for attention and authority as judges in management education, and how the European ranking is important for European business schools for several reasons. It is not clear from the above analysis, however, what the implications of this new European arena and of competing classification mechanisms are for the European field of management education. This relates back to the issue of templates discussed in Chapter 4, and begs a question: to what extent has the template (prescribed in the rankings) had an impact on the field? The main claim of this section is that the introduction of the European arena and the acknowledgement of assessments based on customer surveys have led to subsequent shifts in the attention of European business schools. Business schools place increasing resources and attention on satisfying customers and on securing support, not mainly from peers, but from entities outside the academic sphere, such as the public, alumni, and students. This is one of the effects of the fact that management education has entered the media and that arenas for boundary-work are in the public sphere.

The introduction of business school rankings as an arena for boundary-work has undoubtedly led to reactions in the business school world. Evinced in the many quotes from business school representatives above, rankings have become a fact of life for business school administrators and representatives. Interviews suggest that rankings have spurred an immediate reaction among business schools to change, not just in terms of offering new MBA programmes, but also in terms of other aspects of business school activities believed to influence the rankings. At the academic business school, for instance, efforts to change and adapt to the rankings are readily admitted:

> So, first of all engaging in them, and then of course looking at the criteria, thinking about how we might match up to those criteria and in some ways influencing our pattern of development so that we will not deliberately put ourselves in a situation where we are going to come low down in the rankings. (Director, 2001)

Measures taken by business schools to maintain high standings thus include adapting to the criteria and trying to change some of the features of the programme and the school to try to score well on the criteria used in the rankings. Some things are believed to be relatively easy to change, such as certain features that make up the diversity criteria, whereas others, such as research, require more time if they are to change and become more in line with the rankings criteria.

> [Rankings] do make you aware of areas in which to improve, because if you can see that you are being consistently lowly ranked in some particular area, obviously you have this in mind as an area in need of improvement. So in that sense they have a sort of useful effect on our thinking, and it is also in the back of the mind that if we improve in this area, we also improve in the next ranking. (PR officer, 2001)

Two more direct examples of immediate reactions to the rankings were provided in my interviews with European business schools. One school reports that after being ranked for the first time by the *Financial Times* in 2000, the school set up a senior task force to investigate what kind of criteria the rankings used, and find out how the school could make improvements in its activities in order to stay in or to climb the rankings. As news about this effort travelled, other business schools followed suit and put together reports and working groups to analyse the rankings criteria in order to figure out how the school could improve and what aspects of the programme they could influence to get a better result in the rankings.

One of the purposes of the task force at one of these schools was claimed to be to 'educate people here about what the rankings were, and how important they were' (external relations officer, 2002). It was believed that staff and faculty members of the organization did not understand the importance of rankings and the importance of reporting data and adapting to the demands of the rankings. The respondent suggested that a few individuals in the organization are pushing for the need and desire to participate in the rankings: 'One of the things I have been fascinated by is that nobody is really as interested in this as I am, because I think this is a huge opportunity!' (External relations officer, 2002). Similarly, the narratives in Chapter 3 suggested that there were mixed feelings about rankings among business school members, which created internal debates and discussions about changes and reactions to the rankings. Another director raised a similar idea: 'If you talk to most of the faculty here I think they will have a very sceptical view of it; they are not converted to the real significance of rankings, and not fully aware of what is at stake' (business school dean, 2001).

The pressures to change and adapt to the rankings thus originate both from inside the business schools and from outside. Once the system is in place, members inside business schools also appear to become proponents of the system, strengthening internal pressures to participate and to conform. But the exact character of the responses to business school rankings and the extent of changes undertaken by business schools have been difficult to capture in interviews. Business school members are very reluctant to admit that the rankings do influence the activities and identities of schools, and that rankings guide the development of management education organizations. Such changes will be investigated using survey data below.

Influencing MBA Recruitment and Building Brands

Before investigating the extent of changes undertaken in business schools, however, it is reasonable to make a short detour and ask why business school rankings are considered important enough to change activities and to adapt to the rankings and the outcome of the rankings. Although rankings have been shown to influence templates and positions, it is not so evident what business schools think that rankings contribute, or, in the words of the dean quoted above, what is 'at stake'.

At one business school, the rankings are seen as important because they are believed to influence strategically important questions and potential problems. For instance, a good ranking is assumed to positively influence the number of applicants to the MBA programmes and the ability of the school to attract good faculty.

> I think it is an important issue. Any area where there is introduced a ranking system by a creditable organization, particularly one that is in the media, always becomes important. So, yes, because it influences several things. It influences the key things that I've said are the most important to us: where are the best students going and where are the best faculty going. And rankings have an influence on that, so we have to be centrally involved with it. (business school director, 2001)

Another very important driving force identified in interviews at the academic business school, was a pressure to attract MBA recruiters and employers to the business school. For the MBA programme, having connections with good and well respected companies is believed to be important not only to secure external funding and get interesting guest lecturers, but also to have well-respected companies recruiting your MBA students when they graduate. Having the 'right' companies recruit at your school is perceived to be an important feature of a good MBA programme, and hence a good business school. MBA students are interested in good job opportunities and want employers that offer good and valuable career options, as well as good salaries.

At the academic business school, part of the job of the career advisors and the corporate relations officers is to recruit 'recruiters', that is, get companies to visit the school at recruitment events for graduating MBA students, and to get companies in general to consider hiring the school's MBA graduates. These experienced pressures from recruiters and MBA students have led the career advisors and corporate relations team to work actively to convince other members of the school that the rankings have to be managed and that the school has to participate in them. They claim other members of the business school need to understand that 'it is a business school issue, and not just a career service or a marketing issue' (Career advisor, 2001). Because of the influence the rankings are believed to have on the MBA recruitment process, they are considered a tool in the job of getting recruiters and students to the school.

Investigating these assumptions a bit further, the survey results suggest that they partly hold true for the larger population as well.[6] Table 6.4 confirms that rankings are considered important for the recruitment of MBA students and of MBA recruiters, while being less important for recruiting undergraduates, executive clients, and faculty to the business schools. A very important group of variables includes the three relating to the business school as a whole: building a brand, building alliances, and building corporate connections. These three variables are important not for a specific programme, but for the entire business school. The respondents nevertheless rate them high. Thus, the picture is not entirely consistent with the interviews, and these school features are considered more important than recruiting faculty, undergraduate students, and clients to the business schools.

These findings are important for the understanding of the changes undertaken in business schools as reactions to the rankings. I will hence resume with the argument above and move to investigate the changes undertaken by business schools in reaction to the rankings.

Table 6.4   The importance of rankings for business schools

	n	Mean	Median
Recruiting MBA students	29	4.4	4
Build a business school brand	30	4.2	4
Build business school alliances	30	3.7	4
Attracting MBA recruiters	29	3.6	4
Build corporate connections	30	3.4	4
Recruiting executive ed. clients	29	3.3	3
Recruiting faculty	30	3.2	3
Attracting financial resources	30	3.1	3
Recruiting undergraduates	20	2.8	3

Introducing Changes

Despite reluctance to specify changes, some of my respondents talked about a 'rankings game' and the necessity to 'play the game', indicating that changes are and have been made in business schools to better fit the demands of the rankings. One survey respondent expressed a concern about this 'game-playing' and the changes inferred from that: 'To achieve "success" in the rankings require too much "game playing" to meet the various criteria. This often distorts commitment to our real role as educators' (Survey comment, business school dean). The survey specifically investigated the perceptions of the character and extent of changes undertaken in European business schools in response to rankings. For the ranked business schools, the respondents were asked to state to what extent they have initiated changes in their schools in order to respond to the rankings; and for the non-ranked schools, the respondents were asked about the extent to which they have initiated changes in order to get into the rankings.[7] Note that the question was phrased to reflect changes that have been made in direct relation and response to the rankings.

The results presented in Table 6.5 show that European business schools have introduced significant changes to their organizations in response to rankings. Respondents indicated that most of the changes have been initiated in five areas: alumni relations, PR/media, career services, advertising/marketing, and recruitment of students. The variables for career services, alumni relations, and student recruitment relate directly to several of the ranking criteria, and to the belief, identified above, that business school rankings influence the recruitment of students and employers as well as the business school 'brand'. The handling of career services and alumni groups relates to several of the employability criteria used in the rankings, such as placement success and the number of firms recruiting on campus. Having well organized and resourced alumni relations and career-service offering may also indirectly relate to criteria for employment opportunities for graduates, international mobility of alumni, and of course graduate and alumni satisfaction in general. The variables advertising/marketing and PR/media are more difficult to relate to specific ranking criteria, but are related to the existence of rankings in general and to the belief in building business school brands (see below).

Lower ratings have been provided for the other variables in Table 6.5: advisory board, facilities, faculty recruiting, course content and offerings, and teaching materials. These provisions correspond to some extent with the conclusions drawn in Chapter 4, where it was stated that rankings are not primarily measures of course content and curricula design. We can therefore expect less influence on these criteria in response to rankings. However, the *Financial Times* rankings do measure advisory board composition and the satisfaction with facilities provided, and do also incorporate measures of

Table 6.5 Initiated changes in response to rankings

	Ranked schools			Non-ranked schools			Total		
	n	Mean	Median	n	Mean	Median	n	Mean	Median
Alumni relations	30	3.3	4	20	2.6	2	50	3.0	3
PR/media	30	3.2	3	18	2.6	2.5	48	3.0	3
Career services	30	3.0	3	20	2.2	2	50	2.7	3
Advertising/marketing	29	2.9	3	20	2.1	2	49	2.6	3
Recruitment of students	30	2.8	3	20	2.4	2.5	50	2.6	3
Advisory board	30	2.6	3	20	1.8	1	50	2.3	2
Facilities	30	2.2	2	20	2.3	2	50	2.2	2
Recruitment of faculty	30	2.2	2	19	2.2	2	49	2.2	2
Course offerings	29	2.1	2	21	2.3	2	50	2.2	2
Course content	30	1.8	2	21	2.2	2	51	2.0	2
Teaching materials	30	1.8	2	20	2.1	2	50	1.9	2

faculty characteristics, as for instance, publications, PhDs, and nationality. We would have therefore expected larger influences on these measures.

The data in this question are somewhat difficult to interpret, however. The relatively low mean values seem to indicate low levels of change, but this is slightly misleading. For all these variables, the responses are rather dispersed along the scale and are not normally distributed. This means that the perceptions of changes are rather diverse, particularly for the variables 'changes in advertising/marketing' and 'changes in career services'. Thus, there seem to be two kinds of responses to the question of rating the extent of changes: either the deans have rated changes 1 (i.e. acknowledging no changes in the business school), or have rated changes 4 or 5, thus moderately high or high. As an example of the first case, one dean stated that rankings have no influence on business schools: 'Rankings *reflect* developments, investment and changing strategy, rather than shape them' (Survey comment, business school dean). This pattern of responses has produced bimodal distributions that in turn make the interpretation of the central tendency measures more difficult, and contribute to low mean and median values overall.

These data have several problems that might have kept the mean and median scores down. The deans to whom the questionnaire was addressed may not be fully informed about all the changes made in the organization, as for instance, regarding changes in courses, teaching materials and marketing activities. This might mean that this question does not fully represent the extent of changes undertaken in business schools. One example is the criteria for course offerings that can include changes undertaken in order to get into the rankings, such as the starting of MBA programmes or executive MBA programmes. As was shown earlier, these changes have been undertaken in several schools, but might be related not only to the rankings but also to the existence and diffusion of a template for international business schools. Hence, changes such as these might not be attributed directly to the rankings, and therefore might not be reflected in this question.

Taking these concerns into account and also relating back to the results of the qualitative study in the previous section, I believe the extent of changes rated here can be regarded as quite high. Inasmuch as approximately half of the business schools have rated changes high, the responses suggest that the rankings do have an influence on business school activities and structures. Business school rankings are doubtlessly influencing the working of business schools, primarily initiating changes in the external relations functions of the business school. These changes are clearly linked to the fact that business school rankings are considered important for recruiting MBA students and employers, and for building brands and expanding connections with both corporations and other business schools.

One very interesting finding in these data is that, perhaps contradictory to what one would anticipate, changes seem to be more prominent in business schools that are already in the rankings than in schools that wish to be included. Pressures to change in order to adapt inside the system are thus stronger than those to adapt in order to enter the system. The results show that of the top five variables in Table 6.5, the ranked group of schools have rated changes higher or much higher than the non-ranked group. The difference in means and medians are largest for alumni relations, advertising/marketing, and career services. Quite a large difference can also be noted in relation to advisory board composition. Because of the large variances and bimodal distributions, further statistical analysis of these differences is difficult. It is reasonable to argue, however, that the differences in means and medians between the two groups are large enough to assert that the ranked schools have undertaken more changes in terms of external relations functions than have non-ranked business schools.

External Relations

The above section identified the largest changes in business schools in advertising/marketing and PR/media activities as well as in career services and alumni relations, as a response to business school rankings. These four categories reflect different aspects of what is often referred to in business schools as 'external relations'. Increasing focus on career services and alumni relations can be directly related to many of the rankings criteria, as noted above, while the increasing interest in PR/media and advertising/marketing activities is also connected to the general increase in media attention that, in part, preceded the development of rankings.

One effect of the rankings, expressed by business school representatives, is thus an increasing need being experienced to structure and provide information to the rankers and to other media sources. The media claim, however, that business schools don't quite know how to handle the increasing media attention and media coverage for business schools:

> there is loads of business education [in the media] that there wasn't five years ago
> ... and business schools really don't know what to do about it. They like the idea
> of rankings if they do well; they don't like them if they don't. They don't quite
> know the rules of media coverage. (Business education correspondent, *FT*, 2001)

However, the increasing media attention has not gone unnoticed among business schools, and they are learning. Schools have recognized an increased demand for information from the media, as the interest in business education has grown among national and international newspapers and magazines. Along with the pressure to submit information, a desire has grown within schools themselves to structure the information going out to the media more carefully, and to work actively to increase the press coverage of their school and programmes.

Several European business schools have identified a need to market their expanded management education activities more, and to become more active towards the press in general. Schools have started media and PR departments to work proactively to obtain press coverage, and both media and business school representatives recognize that there has been an 'influx of talent' into the media departments of business schools in the last few years (Director of public affairs, 2000; Business education correspondent, *FT*, 2001; PR manager, 2001). PR activities have thus increased dramatically at business schools in recent years. Business schools have, for instance, set up public affairs departments, hired PR and press managers, and generally increased efforts and resources on PR, press and media activities that fall outside traditional marketing efforts. Many schools have brought in journalists and PR professionals to these new departments; several of them had previous work experience from outside academia and management education organizations. The media and public relations issues thus seem increasingly to be handled more professionally by the business schools.

This increase in PR and media activities can be taken as evidence for what Gioia and Corley (2002, p. 107) call a 'Circean transformation from substance to image', implying that business schools only play to the concerns of looking good rather than actually being good when accommodating the rankings and striving for media attention. Although it may be true that to some extent media work has more to do with image than with what is taught and how it is taught in management education, there are more dimensions to rankings than simply enhancing the image, as was shown both in this chapter and in previous chapters. The media attention and the efforts by business schools to structure the information going out is rather an important feature that contributes to their identity-forming processes. Creating an image and working to convey that image to the international general public influences the identity of the organizations, and the perceptions that others as well as themselves hold. Business schools efforts in PR and media attention also suggest that they take an active part in constructing and diffusing a template of what proper and 'good' business schools should be like, and how they should present their work, and thus contribute to the template of a good international business school. The identity processes described above also illustrate, again, how 'superficial' changes such as an increase in media and PR activities pushes the institution to change in other dimensions as well, such as initiating quality discussions, structuring information, and influencing the role of media in these organizations.

The increasing interest in PR and media activities thus has a double role in the creation of a template for business schools. As more and more schools set up media departments and hire PR professionals, this function has become part of the 'business school' identity. As such, PR and media activities make up an important part of the identity formation of business schools and contribute to the continuous forming and re-forming of other aspects of the business school template. The starting of media and PR departments is thus a part of that template in itself, as well as contributing to diffuse and create a template for other business school activities.

European business schools have accepted the rankings as an arena and have been shown to adapt, at least partially, to the template, and to the criteria specified in the rankings. Efforts in PR and media among some business schools also show that schools have not only adapted to specific criteria, but have actively driven an increase in attention to media and PR aspects of education. By adapting to the rankings and to the template set by the rankings, business schools are not only accepting the system, but they are actively confirming the arena and the rules set by this arena. Business schools thus also confirm and promote the template and the positions of this rankings arena. Adapting to the rules and playing the rankings' game thus contribute to the forming and establishment of the rankings as authoritative judges of management education.

CONCLUSION

This chapter has shown how the rankings as a new arena for boundary-work have been accepted as an arena for field struggles, and how the development of a European-based ranking was driven by a demand for a new arena for field struggles. This demand is linked to a desire by European business schools to redraw the boundaries of the international field of management education organizations to include them, and to adapt the template to include aspects that are perceived to favour European schools. Competition between such arenas for boundary-work is both a driving force and a result of increasing scrutiny and regulation in the field. The development of rankings as arenas of field struggles has as one ramification a threatened autonomy of the European business school field. By incorporating customer-satisfaction criteria in the evaluation of education, business schools are evaluated by standards set from other interest groups, and by measures different from traditional peer-review assessments. By being evaluated by what are still perceived to be American criteria, despite efforts to incorporate European dimensions into the rankings, the perceived autonomy of European business schools in relation to American business schools is also threatened. This new arena has also led to more specific changes in business schools, most drastically in aspects concerning the external relations of business schools. More resources and more efforts are going into media/PR work, alumni relations, career services, and similar activities.

The introduction of this new arena in European management education has thus influenced the development of management education organizations, at least to some extent. By accepting rankings and adapting to the rules set by this arena, business schools have confirmed and legitimated the development of rankings as an arena for field struggles.

NOTES

1. The question asked was: 'How were you included in the rankings? We asked to be included; The *FT* approached us; Do not know'.
2. The question asked was: 'In your opinion, how well or poorly do the following rankings measure business school performance?' Rated on a 5-graded scale where 1 = Very poorly and 5 = Very well.
3. That schools answer 'no opinion' on this question can, in this context, mean two things: either the ranking/ranker is not well enough known for the respondents to have an opinion, or that they for various reasons do not want to give an opinion of the ranker in question. The responses here seem to indicate that most schools know about and have an opinion of the *Financial Times* rankings, while slightly fewer schools feel knowledgeable or motivated to rate the other rankers. This supports the finding that the *Financial Times* is considered the most authoritative ranker for European schools.
4. The question asked was: 'Which of the following ranking lists are the most important for your school? Please rank the three most important rankings, where 1 = most important.' Note: A few schools ranked more than three rankings lists, but I have only used the ones ranked 1 through 3. I have allowed tied ranks, but no more than four lists have been counted for each school (in other words, no more than one tie allowed for each school). Seven deans did not respond to this question.
5. This last note is in itself interesting. The fact that it is mainly non-ranked business schools that have rated the *Wall Street Journal* ranking high might reflect some characteristics of this ranking. In my interviews a strong displeasure with this ranking was voiced, mainly due to the fact that it was perceived to be very 'American-centred' in relation to business schools. Examples given were that efforts were mainly taken to secure the participation of American recruiters and that these were given special conditions for participation. Such, mainly practical, details about how the rankings were performed irritated European business schools. The methodology in the *Wall Street Journal* ranking has since then been altered to better reflect the position of international and European schools, partly by dividing the ranking into three groups, each attracting a similar group of recruiters. One ranking thus feature business schools that attract international recruiters, including international and US business schools, while two rankings feature only US business schools attracting American recruiters.
6. The question asked was: 'For your school, how important is a good ranking in order to: Attract MBA recruiters?; Attract financial resources?; Build a business school brand?; Build business school alliances?; Build corporate connections?; Recruit executive education clients?; Recruit faculty members?; Recruit MBA students?; Recruit undergraduate students?' Rated on a 5-graded scale where 1 = Not important and 5 = Very important.
7. The question asked was: 'As a result of the rankings, have you initiated changes in your school's: Advertising/marketing activities?; Advisory board composition?; Course offerings?; Curricula/course content?; Facilities?; Handling of career services?; Handling of alumni relations?; PR and media activities?; Recruitment of faculty?; Recruitment of students?; Teaching materials?'. For the non-ranked schools, the question asked was: 'In order to get into the rankings, have you made changes in your school's': (the same alternatives as above). Rating on a 5-graded scale, where 1 = Not at all and 5 = Very much.

7. Forming a field and making a market in international management education

This study has been driven by an empirical aim to understand the development of international rankings, particularly those featuring European schools, and to understand the attention they enjoy in the community of business schools. Furthermore, the book has attempted to provide an alternative view on what rankings are, and what the implications are of the proliferating rankings for European and international management education. In this chapter, I examine the driving forces behind the development of rankings in Europe in terms of boundary-work by recapturing some of the main empirical points from the previous chapters, and draw out the major implications of this development on the perceptions of boundaries in international management education.

The starting point for this work has been that, as in any field, in management education there is an ongoing process to define what 'good' and proper practice is and which organizations are considered to be inside and leading in a particular field. This has been described as a struggle to determine field boundaries. Classifications such as rankings take part in this struggle by attempting to evaluate practices and organizations. Rankings have been shown to be arenas for forming and reforming a business school template and setting criteria for how to evaluate business schools that conform to this template. Rankings are also important because they define and redefine specific positions in fields, which are used to create a stable sense of identity among business schools. The debates and discussions in relation to rankings, and the criteria and positions set by the rankings, contribute to shaping field boundaries in terms of who is inside and who is outside an elite group, and about which activities in management education are considered legitimate for business schools.

EXPLAINING THE EXPANSION OF RANKINGS

The introductory chapter opened with the observation that international business school rankings have proliferated rapidly in recent years, mainly from 1999 until 2004, when this study was concluded. Why have rankings proliferated? This study provides several answers to this question, focusing both on the context for such rankings and on the role that they play in international management education. Two answers were proposed in the introduction: one highlights the role of the media; the other relates to the development and expansion of management education internationally. The study has also suggested a third answer; that rankings are important classification mechanisms that help to structure and order the international field of management education, and are used by members of the field for such purposes. Let us take a closer look at these three explanations again.

Media attention to management and business education has increased significantly since the beginning of the 1990s, and with increasing competition rankings have become a way for newspapers and magazines to compete for readers and for the attention of the business community. Following this argument, this study shows that new international rankings have developed in response to other rankings – local, regional and global in focus – and the different rankings have thus been expanded and amended in response to other rankings and other efforts to compare and assess business schools and management education programmes. Also relating to an expansion of management education in Europe, particularly perhaps the MBA, the study shows how the *Financial Times* has agued for the need for increased information to students, the need for international comparisons between schools and between programmes, and the need for catering to a desire to hold universities and business schools accountable for performance. This way, rankings have become means for media organizations to increase their own influence and visibility among business and management professionals.

In a similar way, the expansion of management education has led business schools to compete for students and to conceptualize rankings as a way to attract attention and resources, mainly students, in an international and competitive market. Developed at a time when the European educational markets were opened, re-regulated and expanded, rankings and other forms of evaluations have provided ways to 'order' the field and guide business schools on how to compete in this field. The study has shown how the rankings have been driven by demands for increasing scrutiny and order in the field, and how the expansion of the MBA programmes has provided possibilities to compare management education organizations in diverse settings. The growing and increasingly competitive market for MBAs has also increased the interest in such comparisons and evaluations.

Not denying these contextual factors as important driving forces for the rankings, these general explanations of the development of rankings as results of an expanding market have been supplemented in this book with a more detailed analysis of the driving forces from within the management education field. While the interest by media organizations in management education issues and the expansion of management education in Europe paved the way for the expansion and proliferation of rankings, local and field specific processes have fuelled and exercised the rankings' development. The market for international management education has not been defined a priori; it has been constructed through the process of field creation. The argument is thus that perceptions of a market and 'market demand' has been formed partly through the rankings, and that rankings take part in forming perceptions of an international market for management education.

Attempting to explain the development of rankings from this perspective requires a different understanding of what rankings are. This study has conceptualized the rankings not as quality tools, reputation measures or performance indicators, but as arenas for field struggles and identity-formation processes. The driving forces from within the field have been described using the concept of boundary-work, which includes both explicit efforts to influence the forming of the ranking system and the less obvious forces of forming business school identities. This has created a view of rankings as arenas for the boundary-work of fields.

The development of rankings has thus been described here as driven by the identity formation of individual business schools and universities in that these organizations strive to develop a stable sense of self, an identity, and a secure position relative to other organizations in the field of management education. This identity work concerns aspects of belongingness as well as distinction and distinctiveness, driven by needs to belong to and define a group and to distinguish the organization from similar organizations outside as well as inside that group. The rankings have thus been driving, and been driven by, the forming of a business school template for management education organizations. Furthermore, rankings have been shown to provide positions within the field, which is believed to have distinguished ranked business schools from less well-known and less reputable members of the field.

The expansion and proliferation of rankings have been driven partly by their role as arenas for members of the field to set boundaries for the international management education field. Boundary-work as conceptualized here goes on in many arenas and is not restricted to rankings. For the field of management education, boundary-work is continuous through accreditation procedures, professional organizations, and other arenas for creating belongingness and distinction for members in the field. These forums constitute arenas for the boundary setting of fields, because within such arenas, the content and form of management education is debated and discussed. The media in general is also an important arena for boundary-work and field struggles (Gieryn, 1999, p. 24). This is not, however, to claim that everything is always boundary-work. The boundary-work discussed here is related to specific arenas, which have the ability to form and diffuse within the field ideas about the field, and which spreads to the important interest groups within the field. Arenas that claim to set standards, guidelines, provide evidence, evaluate, or in any other way form perceptions of what, in this case, management education is and who are included, have the ability to contribute to processes of boundary-work. They do so under the provision that they are used as arenas, and are acknowledged as arenas for boundary-work.

BOUNDARIES AND BOUNDARY-WORK FOR EUROPEAN BUSINESS SCHOOLS

I have argued above that the development of media rankings have been driven by the use of them as arenas to conduct boundary-work – to set boundaries for who are included in the field, which activities are legitimate, and which mechanisms and actors are allowed to judge the performance of members of the field. But the term boundary-work and the claim that a demand for a European arena for boundary-work has driven field developments seem to presuppose boundaries and existing, clear opinions about what the field currently is and is not. If this is true, we need to ask what these boundaries are and how they have been reformed. However, boundaries and boundary-work may also be a consequence, often unintended, of local identity-processes. Identity theory indicates that work to establish an identity often encompasses boundary-work of different kinds, to establish and 'patrol' the boundaries of the group that one belongs to, and to create comparison groups, and also to ally with individuals with whom one would like to be associated (Sevón, 1996, p. 57; Lamont, 1992, p. 11). Boundaries are thus, besides driving forces, consequences of boundary-work and of the identity-formation processes of actors in the field.

Even with this view, however, the question remains as to which boundaries the rankings are actually constructing and re-constructing in the field of European management education. There are at least three boundaries that have been drawn and redrawn in relation to the rankings in Europe: an academic–business boundary, a geographic boundary between the United States and Europe, and a boundary between a central, elite group of business schools and other management education organizations. These boundaries have both driven and been driven by the establishment of rankings.

An 'Academy–Business' Boundary

One of the prominent boundaries that has been discussed is the boundary for which kinds of activities and organizations are included in the field and, more specifically, for which activities are considered legitimate in the template for international business schools. This boundary has been described here as one between academic and business capital in management education. That there are tensions between these two forms of capital in management education is by no means a surprise; earlier studies have shown that this is an ongoing struggle and negotiation of value systems (cf. for instance Daniel, 1998; Engwall, 1992; Locke, 1989). The selection of business schools presented as narratives also seems to encourage such a finding, because these were chosen to represent the two proposed ends of the continuum. However, the focus here is not that this boundary exists, but on how the rankings work as arenas for business schools to influence the capital of the field and the boundaries drawn between academic and business values.

The business–academia boundary is important in relation to the formation of the business school template and the criteria set by the rankings to evaluate these organizations. The rankings have been shown to place demands on both academically-oriented organizations and business-oriented organizations. This study has shown that the relation between the business school template and the academic organization is not unproblematic, nor is the relation between the template and a business-oriented school. Both sides, however, use the rankings to argue conformity with the business school template, and both kinds of organizations are defined as prominent members of the field. There is still no clear definition of this template of business schools.

Taking the example of the debates concerning rankings criteria, the study showed that the boundary between academic and business values is clearly an issue for many members of the field. Academic research has been incorporated in the rankings largely because a number of business schools originally perceived the criteria to be business-oriented. The survey data confirm that the rankings have criteria that serve both academically-oriented schools, which are more inclined to like the academic criteria, and the business-oriented schools. However, a large share of the rankings criteria does not serve any one of the two perspectives exclusively, including criteria such as international features of school, experience of school and programmes, and diversity of students and faculty. Thus, the *Financial Times* rankings have also established criteria that schools from both ends of the continuum can agree on, or at least not object to. This clarifies the role of the template as laying somewhere in between the business and academic ends of the continuum drawn in the beginning of this book. The data showing that the MBA programme, which is central to the business school template, can be combined with both an academic orientation and with a business orientation of schools, and the fact that it is used to promote both a business and an academic view of management education, further support this finding.

The template thus supports various kinds of business schools, although the boundaries against other activities have been shown to be very important. The assumed continuum was perhaps even more important than I anticipated, and the desires even stronger to define the boundaries against the extremes of that continuum. The narratives illustrated that business schools cannot be overly academic nor overly business-oriented, as both schools showed strong needs to dissociate from the far ends of the continuum, or the outer boundaries of the field. For the academic business school, this meant a desire to dissociate the organization and draw boundaries against a university system that is too academically 'rigid' and 'departmental', and to associate with something closer to the middle: a business school with a large MBA programme and closer contacts with businesses. In the case of the business-oriented school, the desire was to dissociate from, and to draw boundaries against, consulting activities and corporate universities, and to associate with something not quite academic but still closer to the perception of academic organizations. This also included an MBA programme that was believed to foster an academic orientation, and a redefined use of academic research. The two narratives thus illustrate very clearly the importance of boundary-work and the way business schools unite around the business school template.

The business–academic boundary is important to a third kind of boundary-work as well, which relates to the autonomy of the field. Rankings introduce measures of customer satisfaction and attempt to measure the outcome of education, such as salaries and job opportunities, rather than assess the quality of teaching or educational programmes. The rankings are also clearly dissociated from the traditional peer-review processes that prevail in academia, and are therefore thought to introduce partly new means to compare and assess business school performance. The rankings are presented as being objective and public, and are aimed at increasing the flow of information to students and the public. The rankings, thus perceived to be business-oriented, are not considered to yield much academic reputation. Rather, they are said to contribute to general reputation and to the marketing of MBA programmes. Through these characteristics, rankings threaten the ability of the field to set its own standards for performance, and to define its own systems for assessments. Rather, the rankings make business schools more inclined to rely on public opinion and external measures of status.

The combination of business and academic values in the field as well as in the rankings illustrate the struggle over forms of capital of fields (cf. Bourdieu, 1988), and indicate that multiple logics or value bases can co-exist in fields (cf. Friedland and Alford, 1991). The construction of a ranking is in this sense a 'commensuration' process, which transforms different qualities into a common metric (Espeland and Stevens, 1998, p. 314). The template promoted through the rankings thus encompasses both academic and business values, without providing an immediate threat to either.

However, the incorporation of more and partly new means of assessing the organizations in the field contributes to the struggle between forms of capital, and creates a need to incorporate diverse standards and values. The academic business school provides an interesting example of how these systems influence the working of schools, and the need to conform to diverse demands and arenas. Being part of the academic environment of a large university was perceived to create a need and a pressure to do well in rankings, even though rankings are not by most business schools considered important for academic excellence. The academic standard of the university demanded a high ranking by all the available measuring mechanisms, regardless of which aspects they highlight. The rankings are thus consolidated with more traditional measures, such as assessment of research standards, which continue to be important for the business school. The introduction of rankings does not necessarily 'crowd out' other forms of assessments and standards, but does add to the number of arenas and judges in the field.

Boundaries between Europe and the United States

A second important boundary identified is the one drawn between European management education and its US counterpart. Although a geographical boundary, it is also a symbolic boundary for the international field of management education in terms of who counts and who is included in the international field of management education. The *Financial Times* ranking was driven by a desire among European schools to redraw the boundaries of the field of management education, largely in response to a perceived threat that American business schools were dominating and the American rankings were setting boundaries that excluded European schools. The rankings provided a means for European schools to place themselves in the group and to redraw the boundaries of the field to include them, thus to create and to re-create positions and prototypes in the field.

The debate about who are to be included in the field of management education illustrates both the boundary between Europe and the United States, and the business–academic boundary. While the so-called 'American model', with the business school inside or related to a university, such as Harvard and Stanford, is often referred to as inspiration for European management education, the European prototypes promoted through the rankings represent the independent business school as the model organizational form. The European schools most prominent in the rankings (with IESE and Rotterdam as exceptions) are independent business schools like INSEAD and IMD, and semi-independent schools like Cranfield and LBS. Some of these schools, such as INSEAD, IESE, and LBS, are often described as the most 'American' schools, but they have weaker links to traditional research universities than do many of the American prototypes. While promoting American ideals, the European prototypes are different. There are thus discrepancies in the organizational models promoted, and the organizations promoted as prototypes in the field.

Talking about a template is therefore more relevant than a specific model or than clear role models for the field. Some academically oriented business schools have noticed this discrepancy and refer directly to American business schools linked to research universities, for instance Stanford, Chicago, and MIT, than to the European prototypes.

The development of the *Financial Times* rankings illustrate more clearly the struggle to set boundaries between the United States and Europe. A need and desire for a particular European arena; an arena where European schools can influence, and an arena that takes account of European criteria in management education, have driven the development of rankings in Europe. This ranking as an arena, along with accreditation, was developed to strengthen the standing of European schools and to establish criteria that take care of the perceived European features of management education. In this context, we can understand the particular importance of a European ranking system, and the authority that the *Financial Times* enjoys among European schools for this purpose. The boundary between European and American management education is thus also visible in the boundary-work regarding the criteria used in the rankings. The discussions about these criteria showed that there is an ongoing debate about perceived European criteria, and criteria perceived to favour US business schools. The rankers continuously struggle to find criteria that balance European demands and American demands, as for instance, in the selection of journals for the research ranking and how international diversity is counted.

Despite the belief among European schools that the *Financial Times* takes care of European interests better than other rankings and rankers, there is still a perception that all rankings are based on an American model of management education. It is also a fact that it is still mainly schools from the United States at the very top of the international lists. Hence, quite paradoxically, the European-based rankings that were driven by demands to create an arena for European business schools and European criteria, confirm the dominant positions of American schools and the dominance of American criteria and models of management education. This is largely why European schools are unhappy about the rankings. The rankings confirm the dominant standing of US business schools largely because they have to confirm existing positions, and to partly conform to a pre-existing template of business schools, in order to be accepted and legitimate. Boundary-work by European schools, including encouraging the development of the *Financial Times* ranking and encouraging European criteria in the rankings, has been successful in the sense of getting the European schools onto the lists, but has failed in that they have not received the prominent positions they desired. Boundary-work is hence not always successful.

If participation in rankings is voluntary, which it is, and business schools hate it so much, which they often claim they do, why do they participate? European schools have encouraged the development of the rankings that feature European schools in order to become part of the international business school community and influence the boundaries of the field. But now that they feature in the rankings, they feel powerless and trapped in a system that is perceived to favour their counterparts. Rankings thus create a power relation between the European and the American business schools in the sense that very few actually have the possibility of breaking out and thereby threatening the authority of the rankings to represent the field. The rankers claim that the rankings would not be able to maintain their authority if the dominant American schools withdrew: 'You would need three business schools to pull out. You would need Harvard, Stanford, and Wharton to pull out and you would have it really. But will they?' (Selections interview 1, *Financial Times*, p. 3).[1] European schools, on the other hand, do not have that privileged postion, and therefore the rankings are not believed to be liable to collapse if those schools withdrew. If European schools do break out of the system, they are again left out of the field of management education, and they lose the ability to influence the boundary-work of the field.

European business schools thus find themselves to be both prisoners and 'prison guards' in the ranking system. They feel trapped because the rankings build on what is perceived to be an American model and to promote the US schools in the top, but they are also supporting the system in order to feature in the field themselves and to be able to promote their own positions. Once the arena is in use, European business schools experience little choice but to continue the boundary-work and use the arena to protect the interest of their group. This is also a threat to the autonomy of the field, although a slightly different autonomy than the one discussed above. The rankings threaten the ability of European management education organizations to set their own criteria and their own mechanisms to assess the performance of European management education. With the introduction of rankings, European business schools are assessed with criteria they perceive to be American and in a system that they believe favour American models and management education organizations. The ranking is nevertheless an arena for continued boundary-work, and a way for European business schools to debate and to influence, for instance, the criteria set and the symbolic boundaries that the rankings draw for the international field of management education.

Boundaries of an Elite Group

The rankings have been shown to contribute to a third kind of boundary as well, a boundary that is slightly different from the ones discussed above. The boundaries above relate to the entire field of management education; I have argued that the rankings contribute to setting boundaries against different kinds of management education organizations and different geographical regions of that field. This third boundary, however, distinguishes a group of business schools within this field and defines an elite group of business schools internationally. Rankings thus contribute to creating structures of dominance and of status hierarchies within fields (cf. D'Aveni, 1996), by creating and re-creating distinct positions for members in the field. These contributions to a third kind of boundary are thus about boundary-work for an elite group of schools.

Both the result of the ranking lists and the way they are constructed support the suggestion that rankings promote a small group of schools as leading schools and enhance the position of already prominent members of the field. The ranking lists confirm the position of some schools, but they are also modelled on business schools that are already perceived as leading. When constructing their rankings, the *Financial Times* consulted business schools in the United States and Europe that were considered to be leading, and let these schools influence the development of criteria for the rankings. Because the rankings also have to confirm the position of the leading schools, they are also implicitly modelled on the characteristics of a small group of schools internationally. Rankings thus confirm and enhance the standing of what is perceived to be a top group of international business schools.

Furthermore, the majority of the European business schools ascribe the importance of rankings to their ability to provide belonging to a top group of business schools internationally, and to create visibility and recognition for the school and its programmes. The desire to participate in the rankings is partly driven by their uncertainties of their identities in the field, and a desire to distinguish themselves from other business schools and from other forms of management education offerings. Rankings, which thus create distinct positions, are used to fight for the central positions in fields. Although other grouping mechanisms are also used, business schools ascribe particular importance to the rankings because of their specificity relative to, for instance, accreditation, and because rankings confirm conformity with the business school template. Business school rankings are thus linked to the template of an 'international business school', and consequently, business schools believe that rankings signal belongingness to the business school community.

It is in the relation to the rankings and the creation of an elite group of business schools that the comparisons between ranked schools and non-ranked schools are important. These comparisons aid the interpretation of how important the rankings are as a grouping mechanism and whether rankings are perceived differently by those participating, relative to those wishing to participate and belong to the 'top group'. The results indicate that variation is not large between ranked schools and non-ranked schools regarding beliefs about the rankings as a measuring technique, about what they measure, and about what they contribute collectively as a grouping and classification mechanism. The comparison indicates no large differences in the way the business schools regard the rankings criteria and in the way they rate the reasons they participate or would like to participate in the rankings.

Rather, the opinion about the importance of rankings differs between the ranked and the non-ranked groups of schools. The analysis has identified some differences in the perceived influence of schools, the importance of rankings relative other arenas, the use of positions and prototypes in the field, and differences in the rated changes in response to business school rankings. Non-ranked schools rate the importance of rankings slightly lower than the ranked schools, and the two groups of schools reference and use slightly different prototypes. Primarily, non-ranked schools rate the extent of changes in response to rankings considerably lower than the ranked schools for variables relating to external relations functions and changes in advisory board composition. This is perhaps not surprising, although one can argue that non-ranked schools would change more to be able to join than would ranked schools. The results indicate, however, that the rankings mainly influence those that are included, which comprise a relatively small group of business schools in the field. This finding also suggests that the importance of rankings as an arena for boundary-work, and the implications of this arena, is more evident for business schools that are participating. Business schools that have not yet participated are more likely to regard the rankings as an external mechanism that does not influence the work and values of management education organizations, than are those that participate.

This forming of an elite group of business schools means that there are a limited number of business schools that have access to the international business school rankings as an arena for this kind of boundary-work. Previous chapters showed that, partly because of selection procedures and minimum requirements for inclusion in the rankings, and partly because of the way the rankings are constructed, relatively few management education organizations have a chance to participate in the rankings. Even fewer have a chance of ranking high. Note, however, that the data also support the view that being ranked in the top is not the only important achievement: for many business schools, just being ranked is equally important. For lower ranked business schools, the rankings provide a means of being 'in', which confirms their conformity with the business school template. The elite group defined by the rankings can hence be defined differently depending on who does this boundary-work. This discussion thus notes boundary-work at a different level: boundary-work conducted inside the field, between an elite group versus the 'rest', as well as between those considered to be inside and those considered to be outside. The boundary-work processes are the same: business schools want criteria that serve their interests; they want a list that confirms the standing of the leading schools; and they strive for autonomy of this group relative others to influence the arenas used.

AN INTERNATIONAL MARKET FOR MANAGEMENT EDUCATION

Describing and explaining the proliferation and expansion of international rankings in these terms – as arenas for boundary-work, driven by and driving changed boundaries – means that new dynamics have been revealed. The expansion of rankings is coupled to the identity-formation of actors and their struggle for positions, and to political struggles and efforts of individual schools as well as concerted efforts to influence and change the perceptions of who is in the field and what is legitimate in management education. It is reasonable to ask in relation to this boundary-work, however, whether there is actually any change in the field in relation to the rankings and the discussions in this arena. Do the rankings contribute to changes in management education? This question is not, however, easy to answer.

I explained in the introduction, problems with dichotomizing the stability of boundaries and implicated changes in these boundaries due to rankings. I have instead, therefore, conceptualized boundaries as being continuously constructed and re-constructed in processes of field struggles and boundary-work. We can nonetheless describe and understand changes in local practices of business schools in relation to the rankings and the specifics of the bound-ary-work conducted – that is, in relation to the kinds of processes this bound-ary-work has started in European and international management education. Local and short-term processes of change and involvement in boundary-work may contribute to long-term changes in the field, but to assess such long-term implications for European management education is still too early. For now, I will limit the discussion to instances of boundary-work under way, and to the immediate implications of this boundary-work.

Change and No Change – Creating and Confirming Boundaries

My data suggest that business schools have changed in relation to the rank-ings, and that the rankings have influenced their identities and how they work as business schools and as management education organizations. Even though it is difficult to assess the extent of such changes, it is reasonable to argue that the rankings do in fact affect European management-education organizations. Business schools admit to making changes primarily in the external-relation functions of their schools, but also in student and faculty recruitment procedures, board compositions, and to some extent, in the courses offered. There is a noted clear increase in focus on PR and media relations in business schools, partly in response to rankings and demands from this public arena.

Researchers have claimed that such changes just imply an image game, or a 'Circean transformation' from caring about the educational aspects of management education to caring only about the image of the business school (Gioia and Corley, 2002). The narratives presented in this study clearly showed, however, that changes in PR and external relations functions also create pressures to change other aspects of education and values in the business school. The career advisor in the academic business school noted that rankings are 'a business school issue', rather than being simply a marketing issue for the business school, and that the external relations personnel have worked intentionally to influence other parts of the business school to take account of the issues raised by rankings. The incorporation of external relations functions in business schools has thus increased the pressure on business schools to also change educational aspects and to more clearly take into account the interest of the public in the decision-making process in business schools. The identified changes that business schools report in their perceived positions of schools corroborate the suggestion that rankings contribute to changes in business schools. Such changes in the perceived positions of schools lead to changes in identities that have implications for the working of business schools and the values in management education. The example of the Scandinavian school show that changes in positions sometimes spur needs to conform to the template and compare to prototypes of that template.

The study has also shown that a strong feature of the rankings is to reconstruct and re-create existing structures and perceptions. The rankings, in the manner of stabilizing agents, confirm existing positions, build on and diffuse existing templates and prototypes, and build on previous efforts to construct the field, and hence they tend to reproduce the field. It was shown, for instance, how the rankings build on the MBA and perceptions of established and well-known business schools in the field. This thus indicates stability rather than change in response to the rankings. Primarily, rankings appear to confirm positions of American business schools, while creating positions for other schools.

So the answer to the question of stability or change is that rankings contribute to both. The rankings form and re-form a template, and create and re-create positions, which all provide impetus for change in individual business schools. This way, rankings both confirm and contribute to shaping the field and the boundaries of the field of management education. This duality between continuity and stability on the one hand, and change and reformation on the other, is one of the driving forces for the rankings as an arena for boundary-work. The rankings must be sufficiently preserving to be accepted by those that are considered, by other means and arenas, to be leading in the field, and thus confirm the leading positions of these schools, in order to be trustworthy and authoritative. But rankings must also be innovative, and must introduce enough changes to attract interest and authority among those that aspire to become leading, or those that want to reform existing boundaries of the field. If rankings did not introduce any changes or reformed positions or templates in any significant way, they would most likely lose interest both among students and in the business school community. This way, rankings as an arena for boundary-work are a tool both to consolidate and secure positions and practices, and to change and reform positions and practices within fields. In this respect, the rankings serve as arenas for continuous adaptive change of business schools, individually and collectively, which will be discussed further in the next chapter.

More of the Same?

If we acknowledge some change in reaction to the rankings, it is also reasonable to ask if things are changing to become more alike or more different: in other words, are the rankings contributing to isomorphism in management education? There are indications of a movement towards the middle of an assumed continuum, that is, between business orientation at one end and academic orientation of management education organizations at the other end. Rankings contribute to the forming of a business school template that is perceived to be neither purely academic nor purely business, but rather a mixture of the two. The narratives illustrated that there are pressures from both ends of the continuum to conform to this template; to incorporate more business values in a university-based business school through MBA programmes and executive education, and to incorporate some academic practices in the business-oriented business schools through academic publishing and an MBA programme. There are thus indications that business schools will change to conform to the template. This way, it is not only leading members of the field that make others change, but 'peripheral' members of the field also influence the elite business schools to conform to a template that represents a larger share of business schools in the field. It is an interactive process where both top-ranked schools and other members of the field imitate and change to conform to the template and its prototypes.

The results of this study further suggest that business schools that are inside the rankings, and that to some extent already conform to the template, have changed their practices more than business schools that are not in the rankings and those wanting to get in. This indicates that the rankings do not push the entire field to become similar and conform to the template, but rather that the rankings influence a limited group of business schools to introduce change. Thus, there is no consistent evidence that the field as a whole is becoming more homogenous because of the rankings.

Just as the duality between stability and change has driven the rankings, a duality between similarities and differences in fields drives the development of rankings as an arena for boundary-work. Similarities between schools and between programmes are prerequisites for rankings to work and to be able to compare and set standards for management education programmes and organizations. Again, the two narratives are illustrative. One of the main effects of rankings is that it puts these two very different organizations in the same group and makes them part of the same field, thus making them compete for the same symbolic capital. Despite the differences in identities of the two schools, it is the recognition that both are business schools and that both have comparable MBA programmes that makes the rankings work. Similarities are thus part of what constitutes new boundary-work because they spur comparisons and desires to establish or protect the boundaries of the group.

At the same time, however, differences in the identities of business schools drives the rankings as an arena for boundary-work. Indeed, differences between business schools within the field give room for the rankings to develop as an arena and to contribute to boundary-work and changes in the capital of the field. Differences, moreover, make rankings an arena for debates, discussions, and negotiations about the character of the field and its boundaries, including discussions about which criteria are relevant, who should be included, and who should judge. Differences between business schools in terms of identities and opinion thus drive the rankings further as an arena for change and development. Differences, as such, also confirm and reinforce both similarities and differences of business schools in the field.

Making an International Market

The above account suggests that for European business schools, rankings imply changed positions in fields, changed perceptions of boundaries for who is included and who is not, and changed or reformed work practices and new activities in business schools. Local identity processes and the forming of both templates and positions are not just important for individual schools, but have been shown to be important aspects of the forming and structuring of a field of European management education. In the previous chapter, I argued that one important driving force for the development of an international ranking was that some business schools argued the need for an arena within which to conduct boundary-work. The *Financial Times* rankings has been shown to be used as an arena to position the community of European management education organizations in a more favourable comparison group, and to redraw boundaries for the field of management education. The international rankings were thus driven by boundary-work efforts, and a desire to establish order and to define a European field of management education.

While these changes have been described from the perspective of European business schools, the major implication of the introduction of rankings is perhaps more general than this, and includes the forming of the field that reaches beyond the European context. The main implication of the rankings thus relates to the forming of perceptions of an international field of management education; European business schools compare with other business schools around the globe, and they seem to find themselves competing increasingly with other international business schools. Thus, the perception of boundaries has changed, and European business schools perceive themselves to belong to, and identify with, an international field.

This has also meant that business schools believe they now act on and participate in an international market for management education. The changes described in the business schools as a response to rankings, mainly increasing external relations functions (including PR/media activities and efforts to create business school brands) suggest that the development of rankings in management education has contributed to forming perceptions of a market for business schools and management education programmes. The study has also shown that the development of rankings is intertwined with the forming of an international market for MBA-type programmes and executive education. In line with Fligstein (1996, p. 664), markets are social constructions that are formed through institutionalization processes. The market for international management education is thus not a given, but has developed in relation to the expansion of the MBA label and the international comparisons of such programmes that rankings, accreditation, and other systems have produced. The rankings rely largely on perceptions of a market (e.g., arguing the need for increasing information to students making choices about where to go to business school), and propagate a customer-approach to education and construct perceptions of who the customers are and what they want from business schools. This way, rankings contribute to perceptions of a market and of market demand, and hence to the construction of an international market for management education.

RANKINGS' PARADOXES

While the conceptualization of rankings as driven partly by efforts to construct the field and conduct boundary-work provides additional understanding of the development of rankings, it has also highlighted a few paradoxical situations for European business schools. This chapter will end with a recapitulation of some important empirical findings, illustrated by these paradoxes, which will be further explored in the subsequent chapter.

The first paradox is that while the rankings have been spurred by a need to participate and redraw the boundaries for the field, they have been shown to confirm the positions that were initially resisted. Boundary-work does not always lead to desired outcomes. As seen, the *Financial Times* ranking was driven by a demand for an arena for boundary-work, and a desire by some business schools to redraw the boundaries of the field of management education. There was a desire, experienced and expressed, to promote European interests and European business schools in comparison to American management education. Meanwhile, the rankings have been shown to confirm and consolidate the prominent position of American business schools, and to rely on what are perceived to be American evaluation criteria. Even though European business schools got the arena they asked for, the boundary-work was not fully successful. This deficiency spurs demand for more boundary-work. In a similar way, there is a contradiction between the experienced need and desire by business schools to participate in the rankings (to gain students, attention, and other resources), and the frustration of participating and being dependent on the rankings that is perceived to be high. Frustration is high over the positions assigned to European schools, but also about the variability and uncertainty of the rankings and problems of comparable criteria. This resulted from the creation of power relations and positions. European business schools cannot pull out even though the rankings are voluntary, as this would further confirm and establish the positions of American business schools. But while participating, European business schools further enhance the importance and influence of rankings. To participate or not to participate is thus an uneasy choice.

Another paradox is one between similarity and difference. The main complaint about rankings, at least in general terms, is that they compare apples and oranges, suggesting that they compare very different organizations. At the same time, they function as grouping mechanisms, used by business schools to create belonging to a group and to confirm conformity with the template. However, being driven by demands for distinctions, rankings are in essence classification systems that rely on measures that will show, with numbers, differences between organizations in the ranking. This study has shown that rankings do compare very different business schools in many aspects, illustrated mainly by the two narratives. While differences are important, the rankings also rely on similarities that make these organizations comparable, as for instance, MBA-type programmes. For business schools, rankings thus create the need to be both similar to other business schools perceived to be in the group, and different in order to distinguish themselves and their offers compared to other schools. It is, however, precisely the fact that rankings do compare very different organizations that make them arenas for boundary-work and that spur interest in them as well as their development. Rankings create distinctions and provide evidence of similarities as well as differences within the group.

NOTE

1. This statement was made in 2001, when all of the leading business schools participated in the rankings. Since then, Harvard and Wharton have several times threatened to pull out of the rankings, and have not provided rankers with access to alumni and student contact information. In 2005, the two schools refused to supply statistical data to the *Financial Times* ranking of executive education programmes. Thus, there are indications that the relations between the rankers and the prominent American business schools are changing, although it is too soon to tell what this implies for the authority of the rankings and for the business school field. It seems clear, however, that the rankings threaten the position of the top American business schools as the most prominent members of the international management education field.

8. Arenas for forming identities, fields and boundaries

I argue in this book that we need to step away from a view of rankings as an independent, external examination of business education organizations and programmes, and of rankings as an assessment of business school quality. The rankings are not just reflections of the field; they are also part of creating the field and the boundaries of the field. Hence, rankings are conceptualized as constitutive systems that help shape and form both mental and social structures. I have argued that the rankings are important in creating and re-creating the field of business education that we observe, that is, the order of things we experience. Considering classification systems, such as rankings, as constitutive systems means that we need to investigate the implications of them: not just for individual units or organizations, but also for the relations between organizations that make up the complex web of social interactions.

Two main theoretical concepts have guided my presentation of the development as well as the effects of rankings: arena and boundary-work. A careful reading of the previous chapters reveals a shift from considering rankings as techniques and mechanisms – as measuring techniques, audit activities, and classification mechanisms – to considering and conceptualizing them as arenas for debate, conflict, and identity-work. These latter aspects are part of what has been termed boundary-work. This implies a shift from looking at rankings as an outcome, full stop, to considering the outcome of rankings as an input in larger processes of field formation. The issue then is not whether the rankings are true or false, or whether the methodology is right or wrong, or whether they are, per se, good or bad, which seem to be the underlying questions in many of the previous articles and work on rankings (for instance Dichev, 1999; Gioia and Corley, 2002). Rather, the conceptualization of rankings as arenas for field struggles has focused our attention on questions of (1) why rankings look like they do and are constructed the way they are; (2) what the implications are of the chosen methodologies and the presented lists; and (3) what possible influence the rankings have on broader aspects of the field. The criteria as well as the outcome of the rankings are thus important because they contribute to the forming of fields and field boundaries.

The main thesis in this work is that rankings are arenas for structuring and setting boundaries for fields, and that they are important for the ongoing struggle to define capital and the distribution of capital in fields. Rankings as arenas contribute to constructing and forming a business school template and specific positions within the management education field. The previous chapter showed how the template and the positions assigned through rankings are part of the identity-work of business schools. As arenas for debates and identity-work, rankings contribute to setting boundaries for the field in terms of which activities are appropriate, who are included and central in the field, and how management education should be evaluated. The concept of boundary-work, which has been used to describe such processes of setting boundaries for fields, implies that field processes include active members and active work (Gieryn, 1999, p. 23). In this chapter I develop the theoretical argument about the role of classification systems as arenas for field struggles, and recapture some of the main points made throughout this book.

CLASSIFICATION SYSTEMS AS ARENAS FOR FIELD STRUGGLES

The concept of arena is borrowed from other studies of the structuration and institutionalization of fields. Greenwood et al. (2002) conceptualized professional associations as arenas for organizations to interact – arenas that host debates about the jurisdictional claims of a community of organizations. Conceptualizing rankings as arenas, and the debates connected to them as field struggles, extends this understanding of the role of arenas in field structuration processes and theorizes the role of ranking lists and the media in such processes. It extends the concept of arena to encompass mechanisms and actors that are not commonly theorized, and involves settings that are not as highly organized and structured as communities controlled by laws or by professional standards (cf. Greenwood et al., 2002, p. 74). Despite modest claims to provide information to prospective students and other interest groups and to simplify the choice of students applying to business schools, business school rankings, as arenas for field struggles, have implications for the structuring and forming of the field.

Professional organizations as arenas have been shown to contribute to delineating the domain of the profession and to specify conditions for membership and behaviour of members in that domain (Greenwood et al., 2002, p. 62). Just like professional associations as arenas help determine professional jurisdiction and membership in the community, classification mechanisms contribute by linking identities to specific groups and by separating these from other groups. Sahlin-Andersson and Sevón (2003, p. 256) state, 'Classifications are the bases for identification, and a match of identities, therefore, contains a judgement that something is similar to something else'. Part of the identity-forming process is thus concerned with placing oneself (the organization) in a group and comparing with others perceived to be similar. This is the essential work of classifications as well as the effects of classifications (cf. Bowker and Star, 1999; Foucault, [1970] 2002). More than identifying with things that are similar, classifications also separate groups from other groups, thus creating distinction and distinctiveness. Sameness and distinction are two sides of the same coin: at the same time as a category is shared with some, it is different and distinct from other categories and other individuals (Alvesson and Willmott, 2002; Rao et al., 2000). By putting somebody in one category, pointing to similarities between those in the group, that group has to be distinct and different from other categories and groups. The processes of boundary-work described in this book clarify the role of classifications in such processes of creating belongingness and distinction within and between groups.

Three Interrelated Processes of Boundary-work

One aspect of structuration is placing in a group, defining membership, and creating 'awareness of belonging together' (cf. DiMaggio and Powell, 1983; Greenwood et al., 2002). The conceptualization of boundary-work has specified the processes whereby this belongingness is reached, and the specific role of classification mechanisms in such processes. The two main contributions are the way classifications contribute to the forming of a template and of positions in fields. The creation of a template refers to the process whereby rankings create and make visible criteria for evaluating performances. They thus contribute to the forming of a template, as a general notion of what, in this case, business schools are and what they should do, and to the re-forming and diffusing of a template that already exists. In this sense, rankings are Aristotelian classifications that use predefined criteria and measurements as the bases for classification and grouping (cf. Bowker and Star, 1999). The role of classifications in forming positions refers to the process of defining insiders and prototypes within fields. Classifications such as rankings not only produce perceptions of who is inside and who is outside, but have also been shown to produce a hierarchy of schools within this field. The top schools have become prototypes for the field. This corresponds to the role of prototypical classifications (Bowker and Star, 1999, pp. 61–2).

Through such prototypical classifications, the distinction between templates and positions is not clear-cut, and the processes of creating templates and positions are often intertwined. The promotion of a specific template or of organizational characteristics may also include, and generate, the promotion of certain organizations as prototypes for that template.

Similarly, the promotion of certain organizations as central or leading organizations often implies the celebration of certain characteristics and qualities judged as suitable and desirable by other organizations. Although Bowker and Star (1999) show that the two principles of classification, Aristotelian and prototypical, are often used simultaneously, it is important to separate them analytically because they contribute slightly differently to the processes of boundary-work and to the creation of symbolic boundaries in fields.

The first way that rankings contribute to defining field boundaries is thus to define the capital required for participation in the field, or in other words, to define what is considered to be included in the field of management education. Capital, in Bourdieu's (1988) terms, defines the characteristics recognized as useful in field struggles. This definition sets the boundaries for which activities are considered proper and good, and thus sets the limits for legitimate activities in the field. This involves boundary-work in terms of expansion in Gieryn's (1999) work, where authorities contest the definitions and the characteristics of, for instance, science. This is the main function of the template; it specifies which characteristics and activities are appropriate for field members. Rankings contribute to setting boundaries for legitimate activities by providing a set of criteria and measurements for how business schools are to be evaluated and for determining which characteristics are to be valued.

Closely related to this, and thus the second way that rankings contribute to the boundary-work of fields, is the definition of membership of fields. For both Bourdieu and Gieryn, boundaries also seem to define a group of organizations/actors that 'count' as authoritative members of a certain field. This perspective sets boundaries for who are included in the field. The boundaries drawn between these units and others are constantly created and redefined, making boundary-work a process of expulsion, in Gieryn's terms (cf. Gieryn, 1999, pp. 15–16). This process of expulsion has been shown to be more complex than just drawing boundaries towards 'outsiders', and to be involved in contributing to creating prototypes within the field and in defining a status hierarchy (cf. Benjamin and Podolny, 1999; D'Aveni, 1996). Thus, the obvious way the rankings create boundaries is to produce a list of a number of schools/programmes, which are ranked in terms of a perceived status order. Rankings also promote prototypes of the template that further enhance the boundaries of an elite group of business schools.

The third way that a ranking contributes to the construction and reconstruction of boundaries and fields is related to its ability to attract interest and authority as a classification system in the field; thus, a ranking obtains its authority as an arena for defining templates and positions. As such, rankings also compete with other arenas for the authority to judge management education organizations. Both Bourdieu and Gieryn are concerned with the question of who has the authority to judge members of the field, and to set criteria and capital for the field. According to Bourdieu (1988), the struggle over hierarchies of classifications within fields implies a struggle over who has the authority to judge: an increase in the number of judges may threaten the autonomy of the field. This corresponds to boundary-work conducted by members of the field to protect the autonomy of epistemic authority, in Gieryn's (1999) terms. The media rankings are arenas that claim the authority to judge business education, although these have not traditionally been considered important judges of the performance of management education organizations. The more such judges there are in fields, and the less linked they are to established measures of performance, the more difficult it is for members of the field to have an influence on the criteria and the standards used to evaluate performances in the field. More and new judges thus threaten the autonomy of the field, and the ability of field members to set criteria for their own performance. These attempts to claim authority to judge are perhaps particularly important in the field of business and management education, because of the apparent lack of state regulations and ratings of schools and education organizations in the field.

Note here a slight paradox. While threatening the autonomy of the field as a whole, the proliferation of rankings may increase the autonomy of individual actors in the field. The proliferation of rankings leads, to some extent, to an increase in autonomy for individual actors, who can choose to relate to different forms of evaluations and to the different rankings in different ways. Elsbach and Kramer (1996) argue that business schools form their identities around the comparisons that highlight their core features, and that put them in a favourable comparison group. The increasing number of rankings can thus allow business schools to choose rankings that are favourable to them, and use these for image and identity-work. This study has shown, however, that many forms of assessments and rankings are used and that business schools feel the need to incorporate several rankings and evaluations, and to relate to many of them simultaneously. Despite allowing for the possibility to choose, the autonomy of individual actors is thus not necessarily strengthened. For the field as a whole, however, the increasing number of judges threatens the autonomy to control the way performance is evaluated and assessed.

Classifications as Credibility Contests

The conceptualization of arenas and the distinction between the three different forms of boundary-work clarifies the role of classification systems in field processes. It is often unclear in neo-institutional studies of fields whether regulations, regulatory agencies, and classification mechanisms should be considered as part of the field, or as separate entities that work from 'outside' the field to influence organizations in the field. They have, however, been conceptualized as being outside, particularly in studies of the state as a regulatory agent (for example Fligstein, 1996). In opposition to this view, I have argued that classification mechanisms, as arenas, are part of the field, and take part in the struggles of the field to determine the form and distribution of capital within fields (cf. Bourdieu, 1988).

Classification systems such as rankings are part of the struggle about who, and about which mechanisms, have the authority to judge members of the field; thus they are an arena for field struggles, and as such, take part in the struggle for authority. I have argued that they are part of the second-order boundary-work that determines the autonomy of the field. By constituting arenas, they are also important for forming and diffusing templates and positions in fields, and thus they are important for the struggle between management education organizations that want to be part of the field. Without being a member of the management education community, they are thus influential in forming such a community, and defining its boundaries.

This conceptualization thus widens the conceptualization of fields and provides a distinction between the forming of fields and the forming of communities of organizations (Hoffman, 1999, p. 352; Greenwood et al., 2002, p. 58). Classifications, as parts of the field, contribute to the shaping of ideas and symbolic boundaries, and to the shaping and diffusing of templates and positions, and to struggles about the autonomy of the field. As arenas, classifications take part in all three forms of boundary-work of fields. As such, they contribute to the structuration of fields in terms of defining membership and of creating an awareness of belonging together, as well as defining a status hierarchy and structures of domination within fields (cf. DiMaggio and Powell, 1983).

Highlighting the role of rankings as arenas for field struggles, and as arenas for boundary-work, supplements earlier conceptions of them, as parts of reputation building and image control of organizations (Elsbach and Kramer, 1996; Gioia and Corley, 2002; Miller, 1996; Schulz et al., 2001). The role of rankings in identity-formation processes has also been specified, which made clear that rankings do not just threaten individual positions and identities – they also have implications for the working of business schools. More importantly, by influencing the identities of business schools, rankings also influence the field of management education and the capital of the field. In this way, rankings are not simply beauty contests for members of fields; more importantly, they are the credibility contests that make up the field.

IDENTITIES, FIELDS AND BOUNDARY-WORK

The conceptualization of rankings as arenas for field struggles and the boundary-work of fields has allowed me to specify the role of classification systems in fields, and to elaborate on processes involved in the forming of fields and field boundaries. Conceptualizing classifications and rankings as arenas has brought together local identity-formation processes of organizations, with field-formation processes and the boundary-setting of fields. This increases our understanding of the micro-processes of fields, and, as highlighted in the previous chapter, issues of power and interests among field members. Furthermore, the three-part analysis frame presented here aids the understanding of what field boundaries are, how they are created, and how they are sustained and transformed. This contributes to our understanding of incremental changes in fields and field boundaries, and of the continuous forming and structuring of organizational fields. I now review and specify the main contributions of this framework and the boundary-work identified in the European field of management education to studies of fields and field formation.

Incremental Field Change

Focusing on the role of classifications in forming fields and field boundaries highlights some important features and characteristics of boundary-work processes such as those described above. A first feature is that different classification mechanisms, and different processes of boundary-work, are intertwined and interconnected. Competing systems of classification comprise an important feature of fields (cf. Bourdieu, 1988, p. 113). Primarily, rankings intertwine with each other and with other types of arenas. Competition between newspapers has increased the interest in rankings, generally, and has contributed to giving the media overall a strengthened position to evaluate and judge management education institutions, by increasing the attention and legitimacy of rankings overall. As the American rankings gained increased attention and authority, some European schools demanded an international ranking that would draw new boundaries for the field. Processes of boundary-work thus create the need to do more boundary-work and to set new boundaries for fields. The interconnectedness of rankings with other arenas for boundary-work also drives the definition of new boundaries, and yet more boundary-work. The rankings use accreditation in their own classification system, and contribute to redrawing and refining the boundaries already established. Thus several actors contest and redraw existing boundaries, and spur the development of yet more boundary-work.

Related to this interconnectedness of different arenas is that boundary-work needs to be recognized by others. No one does boundary-work alone. Classifications need to be accepted and used by individual organizations in their identity-forming processes as well as shared and recognized by members of the field in order to contribute to institutional and field development (cf.

Sahlin-Andersson, 1996). Such needs make arenas dependent on previous efforts to construct the field, on existing templates and positions, and on competing attempts at boundary-work. The fact that the rankings must be accepted as fair implies that they must conform to implicit or tacit classifications and standards that already exist among business schools and their constituents. The rankings are thus largely based on taken-for-granted assumptions about management education organizations and their programmes, created in previous processes of boundary-work.

The fact that rankings are based on previous boundary-work efforts has two important implications. First, the rankings are an act of classification that objectifies standards and assumptions that already exist and that make these assumptions public and accessible outside the field of management education. This implies that the need to do boundary-work is enhanced. Second, formalized classifications such as rankings may replace otherwise random classifications that are used by various members of the field, and which reflect a variety of viewpoints and criteria (cf. Bourdieu, 1988, p. 268). The rankings hence create and strengthen the template of business schools and centre the attention on certain criteria and ways of classification. Both these processes mean that some aspects and criteria of management education are highlighted, while others are rendered invisible (cf. Bowker and Star, 1999). This means that classifications both produce and reproduce structures and existing orders within the field.

Theoretically, this suggests a different conceptualization of stability and change in institutional theory. We often assume either stability or change to be the 'normal' case, and seek to explain why things nevertheless change or remain unchanged. Concepts such as institutions (Meyer and Rowan, 1977), habitus (Bourdieu, 1988), and taken-for-granted and institutionalized practices (Scott, 2001), tend to emphasize the stability and the reproductive capacity of fields. Concepts of identity and boundary-work on the other hand, stress the continuous and fluid aspects of fields and of field boundaries, thus arguing for continual and constant change (Gieryn, 1999; Lamont, 1992; Oakes et al., 1998). The bringing together of these two conceptualizations of fields, as well as the combining of institutional theory and identity theory, thus provide a more balanced view of change and stability in organizational fields. Both stability and change are inherent properties of fields, through the productive and reproductive capacities of classification mechanisms in fields.

Change in fields is often described as a result of changes in the external variables (Oliver, 1992), or 'jolts' that destabilize established practices in fields (Greenwood et al., 2002, p. 59). Such external disruptions include, for instance, regulatory change, social and technological change, or political pressures. Another conceptualization of change is the role assigned to institutional entrepreneurs (DiMaggio, 1988), or prominent members of fields, that by

innovation, drive processes of field change. Rao (1998), for instance, highlights the role of institutional entrepreneurs in a study of the construction of
consumer watchdog organizations. He shows how institutional entrepreneurs
legitimate new organizational forms by infusing them with cultural value and,
in political processes, mobilize support for institutional and field change.

The role of institutional entrepreneurs as well as a focus on logics of fields
stress revolutionary and distinct changes in fields, rather than evolutionary and
step-by-step processes of field formation and change. This study has shown,
however, that field change is brought about not necessarily by external shock
or by institutional entrepreneurs, but is the result of much more incremental
processes and less intentional attempts to break with norms and values. The
boundary-work and identity-work conducted by field members in response to
classifications and mechanisms for assessment have been shown to influence
a continuous struggle for capital that makes up the field. A focus on capital
rather than logics thus allows a more detailed understanding of change: the
distribution of capital and the struggle between different forms of capital is
continuous and incremental, while shifts in logics are large scale and seemingly more revolutionary. However, incremental changes in the forms and
distribution of capital may well contribute to more large-scale changes in
fields over time.

Classification systems, as arenas for change, thus capture micro-processes
involved in both the construction of such systems, and the construction and reconstruction of fields and boundaries for fields. It also leads us to conclude
that issues of boundaries and the work to set boundaries for fields are not
peripheral activities engaging only organizations balancing on or near the
boundaries. Rather, boundary-work as described here is a central activity to
field formation and to field change and is the concern of most organizations in
a field, although not necessarily at the same time.

The Mediating Role of Templates

The concept of arena and boundary-work has implied a focus on local identity
processes, and the reactions and responses to field processes and the development of classification systems. A focus on identities and the identity formation
of actors in the field has pointed to different drivers for the development of
new classification mechanisms, as pointed out in the previous chapter. One of
these was the duality between stability and change, highlighted above, which
drives continuous and incremental changes of fields. Anther such driver is the
duality between the construction of similarities and differences, both of which
are an essential part of the identity-formation processes of actors. While often
stressing conformity, isomorphism and the need and desire to be similar to
others, identity theory also tells us that organizations strive toward distinction

and to differentiate their specific character from other members of the field (Alvesson and Willmott, 2002; Bourdieu, 1988; Czarniawska, 2004). This is also an essential part of boundary-work (Lamont, 1992).

The rankings have been shown to create a rather fuzzy template, while creating very specific positions, thus supporting both aspects of belongingness and distinction, and similarity and difference, among members of the field. The template contains several broad characteristics of business schools including a focus on MBA and/or executive education programmes, some aspects of research, criteria for the employability of students, and the output of education, and a focus on customer-satisfaction aspects of management education. Little attention is thus paid to the content and form of educational programmes. This means that the template is a generalized notion of what a business schools is, instead of being a specific model of organization. It contributes to identity-forming processes, and to the creation of belongingness in the field. Contrary to this, however, rankings create very clear positions for members of the field through the hierarchical ordering of schools on the list. This precision in the assigned positions is different from most other arenas, and creates uncertainty and particular conditions for boundary-work. The specificity of the rankings has been shown to be a reason for some business schools to prefer this arena before others because it provides distinction from competitors and gives greater rewards for those that do well. Thus, the 'mathesis' of rankings is a distinct feature that separates it from grouping mechanisms that build on taxonomic models (cf. Foucault, 1977, p. 181). The mathesis of the rankings provides both the attribute of belonging to the group, and thus conformity to the template, and the distinction of being good schools within that group. Some business schools demand this specificity, while others fear its consequences.

The study has shown that there are strong pressures to adhere to the template, and to conform to the values and characteristics prescribed through this template. Isomorphism can thus be assumed to follow from the forming of this template, both as a result of changes in the field (i.e., business schools changing and imitating each other to become more alike) and from aspects of stability, including the fact that rankings confirm the positions of top schools and make these even more prominent as prototypes for imitation. The rankings also confirm the template that defines an elite group that encourages more schools to conform to prescribed characteristics.

But pressures to conform to the template do not necessarily imply that business schools become similar, partly because of processes of decoupling, which imply that images and ideals may change while the core of the organization (teaching, research, etc.) remains unchanged (cf. Meyer and Rowan, 1977). Conforming to the template can just mean to appear to be more like a general model by incorporating certain aspects of the template while not changing the entire organization. Note again that it is not primarily aspects of, for instance, course content or teaching matters that are described in the rankings; these can hence vary in individual schools irrespective of the template and the rankings. However, as suggested above, the rankings are not simply image-games; they lead to further changes in identities and in the identity-forming processes of business schools. Thus, decoupling is not the full answer to variations in the field.

The template (and the prototypes promoted through the template) also has a mediating role that filters demand for change in response to rankings and that makes up an important part of the identity-forming process in business schools. Even with the template and pressures to conform to that template, there is room for large differences and great variation within the field. Variations can be the result of ambiguity that leaves room for translation and interpretation of models and concepts (cf. Sahlin-Andersson and Engwall, 2002; Sahlin-Andersson, 1996). The narratives showed that despite the fact that both business schools conform to the template, they are very different in almost all respects. The rankings confirm both the business perspective and the academic perspective by placing both these organizations in the top group of business schools. The interpretation of the role of the MBA and the practice of research varies between these two organizations; both believe they can conform to the template without threatening their perceived core identity. This way, the template itself does not necessarily lead to isomorphism.

Theoretically, this reasoning leads us to question the assumption of isomorphism. It is not so straightforward that regulations and classification mechanisms, such as rankings, automatically contribute to isomorphism and increasing homogeneity within fields. The reason presented here is that classification systems such as rankings often rely on, and contribute with, templates rather than specific models. A template, as opposed to a model, does not oblige an organization to implement specific practices and charac-teristics, but rather, a template provides an abstract notion of whether some-body belongs to a category or not and what that category then represents. This template influences organizations through identity-forming processes of members in the field, where the template is used as a comparison of a gener-alized other. This is a slightly different process from the three conceptualiz-ations of coercive, normative, and mimetic isomorphic processes in institutional theory (cf. DiMaggio and Powell, 1983). The concept of template, and the notion that it is a template rather than a model that is diffused through the rankings, thus provide room for differences and diver-gence in fields and in our conceptualization of field formation. This has also illustrated that the process of field change is incremental, and takes place in processes of identity-formation in individual schools and in relation to vari-ous arenas for boundary-work.

Arenas for Power and Agency

One of the features of the rankings as an arena for boundary-work is that they are public, and have moved the boundary-work of management education, and the credibility contests of business schools, into the public domain. Rankings, at least those prominent so far, are driven by the media and are adapted to the aims and demands of the media field. This includes demands for 'easy-to-read' presentation of results, a certain dynamic (i.e., schools moving slightly up and down in the list) that secures interest over time, and the use of certain criteria that are relevant for readers of business newspapers as well as students and other perceived customers. These activities, which incorporate new audiences for management education evaluations, are distinctly different from traditional peer-review assessments in academic organizations. The rankings thus make standards and evaluations accessible outside the immediate field of management education organizations. Because of these characteristics, arguing for a threatened, or at least questioned, autonomy of the management education field is relevant.

These characteristics of the rankings contribute to yet a third dynamic that has driven the rankings as an arena for boundary-work. This is the uncertainty of identities of business schools, and the desires to establish stable identities and clear positions of members within the field. Uncertainty of identities is partly a result of the diversity of the field discussed above, as for example, different forms of capital, unclear boundaries of the field, and unclear models for organizing business schools, and classifications such as rankings are thus used for creating certainty and stability. However, the specificity of the rankings, that is, the way they assign specific positions to business schools within the field, and the fact that they are volatile and change over time, contribute to still more uncertainty among business schools, and create the need to do more boundary-work through the rankings and other arenas.

This inherent duality of certainty and uncertainty, which thus links boundary-work to processes of identity-formation, also relates to aspects of the voluntary character of the rankings. Participation in the rankings is voluntary for business schools, but it was shown above that this voluntarism instead creates power and power relations. Few business schools have the power to withdraw without losing their influence within the arena. Classification systems are thus also arenas where power is played out, and where power relations are made visible (cf. Foucault, [1970] 2002; Townley, 1993). For the majority of business schools, participating in the rankings can thus be assumed to create less uncertainty than not participating because the implications of being outside are unknown. Participating, and hence using the rankings as an arena for debate and negotiation of, for instance, criteria, values, and positions, is a way to reduce uncertainty and to influence the forming of the field.

This leads us to yet another paradox linked to the rankings. The study has noted a clear focus on the MBA programme in the rankings as well as in the general template for business schools. At the same time, however, I have identified an increasing interest and desire by business schools to define and promote the business school as a whole – through marketing, PR, branding exercises, and the like – and to clearly define the 'business school' unit. Thus despite the focus on specific programmes, the rankings seems to promote the need to be a business school. This is linked to the development of rankings as arenas for boundary-work, which creates power relations and instances where power becomes apparent.

With the enactment of power and construction of power relations, it follows that the creation of power also creates needs and desires to define a unit that can exercise this power. An important result of power relations is the experienced need to create an object of power, or a unit that can use the system to strengthen power positions. In other words, the rankings as an arena for power, and where power relations have been formed, have driven a desire to define the business school as a unit that can formulate interests, can influence positions, and can use the rankings as an arena for both power and boundary-work. This implies the formation of an actor and the construction of an agency for that actor (Meyer and Jepperson, 2000). The process of constructing organizations as actors is linked to the development of evaluations and audits, in that such technologies define the units to be evaluated (Power, 1997; Townley, 1993). Brunsson and Sahlin-Andersson (2000, p. 740) show that incentives to construct public entities as 'organizations' and as actors are linked to the introduction of market mechanisms, or market-like conditions, and the belief in customers in the public sector. The belief in markets and market conditions seems to require autonomous and self-interested actors that are intentional and rational (Brunsson and Sahlin-Andersson, 2000). The rankings have thus contributed to forming perceptions of an international market for management education, and have at the same time also defined the entities or the actors of this market; that is, constructing the business school unit.

PLAYING THE RANKING GAME

I end this concluding chapter with an observation about the character and role of rankings in processes of field creation and boundary setting. As noted in the empirical chapters, several business school representatives, in both interviews and survey comments, have referred to the rankings as a 'game' and the need for game-playing in relation to rankings. Rather than implying cheating, these references express the experienced need to participate and 'play' according to the rules set by the rankings, and the powerlessness that business schools feel when faced with rankings. It is, however, not always clear what it entails for participants to play this ranking game.

The study has shown that European business schools have clearly chosen to play the game of rankings; business schools have submitted to the rules set up by the rankings, and have adapted and changed in relation to them. Incorporating external relations functions, media/PR managers, and changes in advisory board compositions, are some examples of adaptations undertaken in relation to rankings. Besides contributing to legitimizing the rankings as an arena, these adaptive responses to the rankings also make pulling out of them more difficult. Not participating in the rankings would leave European business schools partly outside of the field, and without influence on how the game is being played. Individualistic responses to identity-threats and playing the game weaken the power of actors to collectively change or transform the structures of the power-relations that created the insecurity (cf. Knights and Willmott, 1985, pp. 22, 39). To play the rankings game thus contributes to legitimizing the game, and to acceptance of the influence that the game brings. By playing the game, business schools also make themselves more vulnerable to changes in the rankings. If criteria change, business schools have to change correspondingly – and adaptively – in order to defend the position and their identity within the field. European business schools are thus trapped between the need to participate and adapt to the rankings – to be able to influence and be a part of the field – and the desire for the rankings to 'go away', or at least not have an influence on the organization.

For Mead (1934), playing games is a way for children to learn about the self and to create a generalized other, a process through which the child can learn about the game and about all the roles and relative positions in the game. Through the generalized other, the child learns to take and to understand the roles of all other people in the game. This seems to be similar to the role of classifications in field processes. Through the rankings, business schools create a generalized other that contributes to creating a sense of self, and an identity, and that contributes to learning about the roles and positions of all other business schools in the field. It is a way to define positions relative to others, and to become like a generalized notion of player of the game. Unlike children's games, however, rankings are also a means for business schools to influence the game and the rules of the game, through discussions and debates and the ongoing boundary-work of the field. Business schools are thus not primarily victims of this game, but important players that participate in forming the field and in defining the rules of the game. This is an important driving force for this game to continue.

Trying to capture the drivers for the development of international rankings, I have thus focused on those business schools that are playing the game; on the business schools and universities that participate in rankings and those that would like to participate. This study has investigated the development of international rankings from the perspective of European business schools and management education organizations, focusing on the European initiatives, debates, and reaction to rankings, and the drivers for boundary-work in a European context. However, the processes uncovered in this analysis have implications that reach beyond the specific European context. We are witnessing an expansion of rankings in many other parts of the world, and international rankings are increasingly taking account of management education around the world. Although this development is salient in management education, other areas of education are increasingly handling international rankings and international comparisons of schools, programmes and research, thus making this analysis relevant in a number of contexts and settings.

Conceptualizing and understanding game-playing is not only important in relation to rankings, the present study has also described and analysed dynamics and processes that are important for understanding social order and interactions in other settings and contexts. The case of rankings has highlighted the role of classifications in forming and reforming social order and some of the dynamics of fields and field formation processes. Particularly, the role of classifications in forming symbolic boundaries of the field; in setting rules for the game, defining participants of the game, as well as forming winners and losers of game-playing. Thus games are part of credibility contests that make up a field and the struggle to determine the boundaries of it.

Appendix A

The survey was sent to a total of 74 deans/directors of European business schools and management education organizations. The sampled population for this survey was the European schools that have received accreditation from at least one of three international accreditation organizations: EQUIS (the efmd), AACSB International, or AMBA (the Association of MBAs). The reason I used accreditation for defining and delimiting the population was to arrive at a group of schools that are reasonably comparable across countries and regions, and that have the possibility of being included in international rankings. The *Financial Times* and other rankings use accreditation from these three international organizations as a screening mechanism for their rankings, thus letting only accredited business schools participate in the survey for the rankings. Accredited schools can thus be assumed to know what the rankings are and to have taken a decision, conscious or otherwise, whether to participate or not. Only schools offering more than one programme or course in management education were included in the survey, because several of the questions were aimed at the school rather than at specific programmes. Technical universities and schools offering only an MBA programme were thus not included in the survey (two schools in total).

This survey can hence be divided into two separate groups, or populations. One group is that of accredited schools that are ranked (or that have been ranked) by international ranking magazines, and the other group is that of schools that are eligible to participate in the rankings (i.e., accredited) but have not yet appeared in the league tables. For both groups, the entire population of European schools was surveyed.

One survey was thus sent to all the deans of European business schools that are or have been ranked in international ranking lists in 2000, 2001, or in the spring of 2002. Hence, this population includes all European schools that are ranked by at least one of the three international rankers, the *Financial Times*, the *Wall Street Journal*, and *Business Week*. Another prominent ranking, *The Economist*, was first published in the fall of 2002 and was thus not available at the time of the survey. The total population for this group is 40 schools, of which 30 have returned the questionnaire (75 per cent response rate).

A similar survey was sent to all the deans of European business schools that are accredited but have not yet appeared in the published league tables and rankings. This group consists of 34 schools, of which 23 have answered and returned my questionnaire (68 per cent response rate). The slightly lower response rate for this group was expected, based on the belief that more schools in this population can be assumed to be less affected and concerned about the rankings, and hence less motivated to answer questions about it. This has implication for some of the responses, as will be indicated in the empirical section, although the difference in response rate is very small.

For the entire population of 74 schools, the response rate is thus 72 per cent. The schools are located in 14 different countries, with an overrepresentation of schools from the UK and France (34 and 15 schools, respectively). The survey further includes schools from Belgium, Denmark, Finland, Germany, Ireland, Italy, the Netherlands, Norway, Poland, Spain, Sweden, and Switzerland. Several factors can explain the large share of schools from the UK. Although global today, the Association of MBAs (the MBA accreditation used here to define the population) was originally British, and a large number of British MBA programmes are accredited by the association. This is also, however, a reflection of the fact that the UK market for MBAs is proportionately larger than any other European market, and second in the world after the United States. A total of 271 management education organizations in the UK offer MBA programmes, to be compared to France in second place with 75 organizations. This can be compared to, for instance, 39 in the Netherlands, seven in Sweden, and six in Denmark (Moon, 2002, p. 81). The distribution in my sample thus corresponds well with the size of the respective MBA markets. Twenty-one schools have chosen not to participate in the survey. Of the 21 schools that are not included, 11 are from the UK and five from France. The non-responses are fairly proportionate to the total number of schools from each country.

A limitation to this survey approach is that it is addressed only to one respondent in each organization, the dean or director of the business school. It does not therefore reflect other views or opinions in the business schools, and one could argue that people in other positions may have different views. However, this survey covers the opinions and views of deans from a large share of European business schools and provides a good supplement to the interview study, where the views of representatives from different positions within the business schools are expressed. The main argument for this choice of representative is that the dean is the person who is most likely to have an overall view of the business school, its focus, and its activities, and the person who would be able to provide 'opinions' for the entire business school. Because many of the questions ask about opinions and viewpoints, it was important to find respondents who could be assumed to have opinions based on an overall perspective.

Through the survey, the interviews, and the printed material used for this book, there is thus a triangulation of data in the sense that information is collected from many different sources and from different viewpoints. The interview study and the survey are complementary, both in number of cases and in diversity of respondents. A combination of quantitative and qualitative data is useful for avoiding or minimizing the risk of selective interpretation of data. The use of simple counting techniques and quantitative data analysis can support the qualitative data reporting by adding instances of observation about a particular phenomenon. The use of numbers, and survey data, in this book is thus not aimed at proving things, but at providing additional views and representations of the whole dataset, yielding a broader picture of the data at hand.

While opposing a positivistic reliance on numbers and the operationalization of concepts, Silverman (2001) proposes that quantitative data and simple counting techniques can supplement and strengthen qualitative analyses. The aim is to measure what it is possible to measure, preferably in terms of the categories used by respondents themselves, rather than to create constructs and categories. Counting such natural categories with simple counting techniques and tabulations is a way to achieve a more rich and trustworthy representation of the social reality (Silverman, 2001, pp. 35–7, 246). The questionnaire used in this study was designed for this purpose, with empirically generated questions largely based on initial findings and impressions from the interviews. Rather than theoretically deduced concepts, and hence operationalized constructs, the questions and the specified alternatives relate to concepts and issues that respondents used in interviews and in texts.

This, of course, creates specific problems for the quantitative data analysis. Because of the desire to keep the variables and concepts 'close', and true, to the empirical reality and to my respondents, the use of some of the results for statistical analysis is limited. The survey data cannot be used to illustrate or prove the validity of any theoretical constructs or concepts, but they can illustrate empirical findings. This does not exclude, however, the use of simple summary and correlation statistics to discuss patterns in the data, and to identify the similarities and the divergence between groups. The statistics employed are thus simply used as an accepted method to identify and illustrate patterns in quantitative datasets.

Given these aims and the limited scope of this survey, the statistics used throughout this work are non-parametric tests for ordinal data, chosen largely because they make fewer demands on normal distributions, equal variances, and size of samples than do equivalent parametric tests (Bryman and Cramer, 1997, pp. 117–18). Statistical methods have been used to compare differences between groups, for unrelated and related samples. Correlation measures have been used to identify relationships between ordinal variables. Factor analysis is commonly used to identify groups of variables that are related and that measure a particular aspect of a phenomenon (Bryman and Cramer, 1997, pp. 276–7).

Exploratory factor analysis has been used here to simplify the presentation of results by limiting the number of variables to analyse. This way, we can benefit from the complexity of answers while simplifying the presentation. Factor analysis is not used, however, to confirm theoretical propositions or to combine variables into theoretical constructs.

Appendix B

The factor matrix shows the loadings of each criterion on each of the identified factors (or groups of criteria). Tables B.1 and B.2 show the rotated factor matrix and the communalities table for the factor analysis. The factor analysis for the ranking criteria shows that all variables except one load significantly on one factor each; thus the factor result is rather clear. I have used 0.600 as the level of factor loadings to be considered significant. Sometimes a higher level is recommended for a sample of 50, usually 0.750, but factor loadings as low as 0.3 are often accepted (Hair et al., 1998, Chapter 3). I have allowed 0.600 to be the minimum level because the practical validity and relevance of the factor solution presented here is high, and each variable loads high on only one factor. Furthermore, because the number of variables analysed is relatively large, allowing a lower value for the factor loadings to be considered significant is reasonable (Hair et al., 1998, Chapter 3). 'Career progress', the one variable that does not load significantly on a single factor, was omitted from the subsequent analysis. The overall factor solution was not affected by leaving out this variable. With one exception all variables had commonalities above 0.6, which is considered good. The exception here is also the variable 'career progress', with communality of 0.582, thus slightly lower than the other variables.

The factor analysis thus produces seven groups of variables used for ranking, here called factors. The first factor contains five variables: required languages, international experience during programme, number of programmes run in other countries, number of joint programmes with companies, and number of joint programmes with other business schools. I have labelled this factor 'experience', because it measures the experience during the time spent at the business school in terms of programme features, languages, international experience, and business school features (such as the scope of programmes available at the school). The second factor contains three variables that measure the female diversity of the school and of the programme: number of female students, faculty and advisory board members. This factor is labelled 'gender diversity'. The third factor contains four variables that measure the international diversity and international profile of the school: international mobility of alumni, number of international students, number of international faculty, and number of international advisory board members.

Table B.1   Rotated factor matrix for factor analysis of ranking criteria

	1	2	3	4	5	6	7
Salary and salary increase	0.317	5.165E-02	-4.252E-02	0.173	-9.048E-02	-0.124	0.706
Value for money	-8.908E-02	-5.295E-02	0.107	2.187E-02	0.269	0.199	0.710
Employment opp.	6.364E-02	0.211	6.631E-02	0.704	5.358E-02	5.877E-02	0.405
Placement success	0.144	-0.130	7.727E-02	0.832	1.725E-02	-1.520E-02	0.171
Career progress	-6.369E-02	0.303	0.147	0.157	0.178	0.532	0.353
Firms recruiting	0.175	4.299E-02	0.321	0.725	0.151	0.119	-0.196
Usefulness of skills	0.118	0.168	-4.631E-02	0.310	0.710	0.110	-0.142
Languages	0.742	0.312	-1.682E-02	0.287	0.127	-8.009E-02	3.449E-02
International experience	0.742	0.165	5.655E-02	0.145	0.362	4.234E-02	-0.121
International mobility	0.208	0.325	0.652	0.284	-0.171	5.529E-02	0.267
Programmes in other countries	0.773	2.906E-02	0.218	-5.728E-02	0.170	7.708E-02	0.151
Joint programmes schools	0.809	-3.448E-03	0.275	1.769E-02	-3.384E-02	6.580E-02	0.130
Joint programmes companies	0.605	-0.167	0.362	0.326	0.135	0.194	-2.703E-02
Food and accommodation	0.282	3.298E-02	5.164E-02	-1.317E-02	0.806	4.604E-03	0.250
Facilities	0.110	0.133	0.202	-2.856E-02	0.816	3.329E-02	9.922E-02
International students	0.225	0.113	0.840	-2.208E-02	0.224	-3.566E-02	6.043E-02
International faculty	0.146	0.169	0.861	9.692E-02	-1.311E-02	-8.015E-03	-4.365E-02
International board	0.184	0.197	0.608	0.408	0.297	0.145	-1.074E-02
Female students	4.349E-02	0.899	0.120	-0.128	0.147	0.126	-4.153E-02
Female faculty	7.705E-02	0.914	0.217	1.771E-02	9.251E-02	0.145	3.690E-02
Female board	0.189	0.710	0.295	0.176	8.303E-02	0.276	8.874E-02
PhD programme	0.193	0.103	3.065E-02	-0.353	0.190	0.715	8.684E-02
Doctorates	-7.072E-03	0.474	-0.194	0.336	0.217	0.632	-7.059E-02
Research output	5.138E-02	0.125	3.657E-02	0.152	-0.150	0.822	-4.254E-02

Notes: Extraction method: Principal component analysis; rotation method: Varimax with Kaiser normalization.

Table B.2 Communalities table for factor analysis of ranking criteria

	Initial	Extraction
Salary and salary increase	1.000	0.657
Value for money	1.000	0.639
Employment opportunities	1.000	0.719
Placement success	1.000	0.766
Career progress	1.000	0.582
Firms recruiting	1.000	0.737
Usefulness of skills	1.000	0.677
Languages required	1.000	0.754
International experience	1.000	0.749
International mobility	1.000	0.758
Programmes run in other countries	1.000	0.707
Joint programmes with schools	1.000	0.752
Joint programmes with companies	1.000	0.688
Food and accommodation	1.000	0.795
Facilities	1.000	0.748
International students	1.000	0.824
International faculty	1.000	0.803
International board	1.000	0.718
Female students	1.000	0.880
Female faculty	1.000	0.919
Female board	1.000	0.749
PhD programme	1.000	0.728
Doctorates	1.000	0.826
Research output	1.000	0.742

Note: Extraction method: principal component analysis.

This factor is labelled 'international diversity'. The fourth factor measures 'employability', with three variables: employment opportunities for graduates, placement success, and number of firms recruiting on campus. The fifth factor is labelled 'other' because it contains three variables that seem a bit odd in the context: food and accommodation offered to executive clients, facilities, and the usefulness of skills taught in the programme. This factor thus contains both clearly business school features and a specific programme feature. The sixth factor contains three variables that measure academic performance: size of PhD programme, number of faculty with doctorates, and the research output for the school. This factor is thus labelled 'academic orientation'. The seventh and last factor is related to the two variables that measure the value or the 'financial gain' of programmes: salary and salary increases, and value for money.

Appendix C

The same reasoning about significance levels as described in Appendix B was used for this factor analysis. The rotated component matrix and the communalities table are shown in Tables C.1 and C.2. Here also one variable, in this case 'executive MBA programme', which had a low communality, did not load significantly on a single factor. This variable was thus omitted from the analysis. Leaving out this variable did not influence the results of the analysis.

Table C.1   Rotated component matrix for school features

	1	2	3
Academic research	0.421	0.678	0.231
Applied research	0.776	0.165	0.194
Custom-made executive education	0.854	–0.103	0.104
Open executive education	0.789	3.593E-02	1.154E-02
Executive MBA programme	0.558	0.174	–0.307
MBA programme	4.651E-02	2.226E-02	0.894
PhD programme	7.008E-02	0.857	4.406E-02
Undergraduate programme	–0.191	0.760	0.436

Note: *Extraction method: principal component analysis; rotation method: Varimax with Kaiser normalization.*

Table C.2   Communalities table for factor analysis

	Initial	Extraction
Academic research	1.000	0.691
Applied research	1.000	0.667
Custom-made executive education	1.000	0.751
Open executive education	1.000	0.623
Executive MBA programme	1.000	0.436
MBA programme	1.000	0.802
PhD programme	1.000	0.741
Undergraduate programme	1.000	0.804

Appendix D

Table D.1 *Correlation 'academic focus' of business school and groups of ranking criteria*

	Correlation coefficient	Significance (two-tailed)
Salary	0.082	0.570
Employability	−0.003	0.985
Other	−0.005	0.975
Features	−0.051	0.723
International	−0.129	0.361
Female	0.205	0.154
Academic	0.437	0.001

Note: Non-parametric correlation statistics: Spearman's rho.

Table D.2 *Correlation 'business focus' of business school and groups of ranking criteria*

	Correlation coefficient	Significance (two-tailed)
Salary	0.312	0.027
Employability	0.307	0.030
Other	0.285	0.052
Features	0.101	0.480
International	0.107	0.450
Female	0.067	0.641
Academic	0.031	0.831

Note: Non-parametric correlation statistics: Spearman's rho.

Table D.3   Correlation 'MBA programme' and groups of ranking criteria

	Correlation coefficient	Significance (two-tailed)
Salary	0.191	0.179
Employability	0.023	0.870
Other	0.186	0.205
Features	−0.224	0.111
International	0.166	0.234
Female	−0.039	0.783
Academic	0.143	0.311

Note: Non-parametric correlation statistics: Spearman's rho.

Appendix E

Table E.1 Comparing reasons for participation in rankings and accreditation

	Z	Significance (two-tailed)
Marketing reason	−0.373	0.709
Academic reputation	−2.655	0.008
International recognition	−0.210	0.834
External visibility	−0.887	0.375
Quality development	−4.489	0.000
Quality control	−4.923	0.000
Distinction	−0.074	0.941
Demanded students	−1.525	0.127
Demanded corporate clients	−0.744	0.457
Competition	−2.315	0.021

Note: Non-parametric statistic: Wilcoxon Signed Ranks Test.

References

LITERATURE

Abbott, Andrew (1988), *The System of Professions. An Essay on the Division of Expert Labor*, Chicago: University of Chicago Press.

Abbott, Andrew (1995), 'Things of boundaries', *Social Research,* **62** (4), 857–82.

Albert, Stuart and David Whetten (1985), 'Organizational identity', in L.L. Cummings and Barry M. Staw (eds), *Research in Organizational Behavior*, vol. 7, Greenwich, CT: JAI Press, pp. 263–95.

Alvesson, Mats and Hugh Willmott (2002), 'Identity regulation as organizational control: producing the appropriate individual', *Journal of Management Studies*, **39** (5), 619–45.

Ashforth, Blake and Fred Mael (1989), 'Social identity theory and the organization', *Academy of Management Review*, **14** (1), 20–39.

Baldwin, John D. (1986), *George Herbert Mead: A Unifying Theory for Sociology*, Baldwin, CA: Sage.

Benjamin, Beth A. and Joel M. Podolny (1999), 'Status, quality, and social order in the California wine industry', *Administrative Science Quarterly*, **44** (3), 563–89.

Borgatti, Steve P., Martin G. Everett and L.C. Freeman (2002), *UCINET for Windows: Software for Social Network Analysis*, Natick, MA: Analytic Technologies.

Borum, Finn and Ann Westenholz (1995), 'The incorporation of multiple institutional models: organizational field multiplicity and the role of actors', in Richard Scott and Søren Christensen (eds), *The Institutional Construction of Organizations: International and Longitudinal Studies*, Thousand Oaks, CA: Sage, pp. 113–31.

Bourdieu, Pierre (1984), *Distinction. A Social Critique of the Judgement of Taste*, Cambridge, MA: Harvard University Press.

Bourdieu, Pierre (1988), *Homo Academicus*, Stanford, CA: Stanford University Press.

Bourdieu, Pierre (1993), *Kultursociologiska Texter*, Stockholm: Brutus Östlings Bokförlag.

Bourdieu, Pierre (1996), *The State Nobility: Elite Schools in the Field of Power*, Stanford, CA: Stanford University Press.

Bowker, Geoffrey C. and Susan Leigh Star (1999), *Sorting Things Out: Classification and its Consequences*, Cambridge, MA: MIT Press.

Brunsson, Nils and Kerstin Sahlin-Andersson (2000), 'Constructing organizations: the example of public sector reform', *Organization Studies*, **21** (4), 721–46.

Bryman, Alan and Duncan Cramer (1997), *Quantitative Data Analysis with SPSS for Windows*, London: Routledge.

Burke, Peter J. and Donald C. Reitzes (1991), 'An identity theory approach to commitment', *Social Psychology Quarterly*, **54** (3), 239–51.

Clark, Burton R. (1998), *Creating Entrepreneurial Universities: Organizational Pathways of Transformation*, Oxford: IAU Press and Pergamon.

Clegg, Stuart (1989), *Frameworks of Power*, London: Sage.

Crainer, Stuart and Des Dearlove (1999), *Gravy Training: Inside the Business of Business Schools*, San Francisco: Jossey-Bass.

Czarniawska, Barbara and Bernward Joerges (1996), 'Travel of ideas', in Barbara Czarniawska and Guje Sevón (eds), *Translating Organizational Change*, Berlin: Walter de Gruyter, pp. 13–48.

Czarniawska, Barbara and Guje Sevón (eds) (1996), 'Introduction' in *Translating Organizational Change*, Berlin: Walter de Gruyter, pp. 1–12.

Czarniawska, Barbara (1997), *Narrating the Organization: Dramas of Institutional Identity*, Chicago: University of Chicago Press.

Czarniawska, Barbara (2004), 'Gabriel Tarde and big city management', *Distinktion*, **9**, 81–95.

Dacin, Tina, Jerry Goodstein and Richard Scott (2002), 'Institutional theory and institutional change: introduction to the special research forum', *Academy of Management Journal*, **45** (1), 45–57.

Daniel, Carter (1998), *MBA: The First Century*, London: Associated University Press.

D'Aunno, Thomas, Robert I. Sutton and Richard H. Price (1991), 'Isomorphism and external support in conflicting institutional environments: a study of drug abuse treatment units', *Academy of Management Journal*, **34** (3), 636–61.

D'Aveni, Richard A. (1996), 'A multiple-constituency, status-based approach to interorganizational mobility of faculty and input–output competition among top business schools', *Organization Science*, **7** (2), 166–89.

Davis, Gerald and Walter W. Powell (1992), 'Organization–environment relations', in Marvin Dunnette (ed.), *Handbook of Industrial and Organizational Psychology*, vol. 3, Palo Alto, CA: Consulting Psychologists Press, pp. 315–76.

Davis, Joseph E. (2000), 'Introduction: social change and the problem of identity', in Joseph E. Davis (ed.), *Identity and Social Change*, New Brunswick, NJ: Transaction Publishers, pp. 1–10.

Davis, Joseph E. (ed.) (2000), *Identity and Social Change*, New Brunswick, NJ: Transaction Publishers.

Dichev, Ilia D. (1999), 'How good are business school rankings?', *Journal of Business*, **72** (2), 201–13.

DiMaggio, Paul J. (1987), 'Classification in art', *American Sociological Review*, **52** (4), 440–55.

Di Maggio, Paul J. (1988), 'Interest and agency in institutional theory', in Lynne G. Zucker (ed.), *Institutional Patterns and Organizations: Culture and Environment*, Cambridge, MA: Ballinger, pp. 3–21.

DiMaggio, Paul J. (1991), 'Constructing an organizational field as a professional project: U.S. art museums, 1920–1940', in Walter W. Powell and Paul J. DiMaggio (eds), *The New Institutionalism in Organizational Analysis*, Chicago: University of Chicago Press, pp. 267–92.

DiMaggio, Paul J. (1997), 'Culture and cognition', *Annual Review of Sociology*, **23** (1), 263–87.

DiMaggio, Paul J. and Walter W. Powell (1983), 'The iron cage revisited: institutional isomorphism and collective rationality', reprinted in Walter W. Powell and Paul J. DiMaggio (eds) (1991), *The New Institutionalism in Organizational Analysis*, Chicago: University of Chicago Press, pp. 63–82.

Durand, Rodolphe and Jean McGuire (2005), 'Legitimating agencies in the face of selection: the case of the AACSB', *Organization Studies*, **26** (2), 165–96.

Dutton, Jane E. and Janet M. Dukerich (1991), 'Keeping an eye in the mirror: image and identity in organizational adaptation', *Academy of Management Journal*, **34** (3), 517–54.

Elsbach, Kimberly D. and Roderick M. Kramer (1996), 'Members' responses to organizational identity threats: encountering and countering the Business Week rankings', *Administrative Science Quarterly*, **41** (3), 442–76.

Emirbayer, Mustafa and Ann Mische (1998), 'What is agency?', *American Journal of Sociology*, **103** (4), 962–1023.

Engwall, Lars (1992), *Mercury Meets Minerva. Business Studies and Higher Education, the Swedish Case*, Oxford: Pergamon Press.

Engwall, Lars (1995), 'Management research: a fragmented adhocracy?', *Scandinavian Journal of Management*, **11** (3), 225–35.

Engwall, Lars and Vera Zamagni (eds) (1998), *Management Education in Historical Perspective*, Manchester: Manchester University Press.

Espeland, Wendy N. and Mitchell L. Stevens (1998), 'Commensuration as a social process', *Annual Review of Sociology*, **24** (1), 313–43.

Fligstein, Neil (1985), 'The spread of the multi-divisional form', *American Sociological Review*, **50** (3), 377–91.

Fligstein, Neil (1996), 'Markets as politics: a political-cultural approach to market institutions', *American Sociological Review*, **61** (4), 656–73.

Foucault, Michel [1970] (2002), *The Order of Things*, London and New York: Routledge.

Foucault, Michel (1977), *Discipline and Punish. The Birth of the Prison*, London: Penguin.

Foucault, Michel (1991) 'Governmental rationality: an introduction', in Graham Burchell, Colin Gordon and Peter Miller (eds), *The Foucault Effect: Studies in Governmentality*, London: University of Chicago Press, pp. 1–51.

Friedland, Roger and Robert R. Alford (1991), 'Bringing society back in: symbols, practices, and institutional contradiction', in Walter W. Powell and Paul J. DiMaggio (eds), *The New Institutionalism in Organizational Analysis*, Chicago: Chicago University Press, pp. 232–66.

Galaskiewicz, Joseph (1991), 'Making corporate actors accountable: institution-building in Minneapolis-St. Paul', in Walter W. Powell and Paul J. DiMaggio (eds), *The New Institutionalism in Organizational Analysis*, Chicago: University of Chicago Press, pp. 293–310.

Gemelli, Guiliana (1998), 'The enclosure effect: innovation without standardization in Italian postwar management education', in Lars Engwall and Vera Zamagni (eds), *Management Education in Historical Perspective*, Manchester: Manchester University Press, pp. 127–44.

Giddens, Anthony (1984), *The Constitution of Society*, Cambridge: Polity Press.

Gieryn, Thomas F. (1999), *Cultural Boundaries of Science. Credibility on the Line*, Chicago: University of Chicago Press.

Gioia, Dennis A. and Kevin G. Corley (2002), 'Being good versus looking good: business school rankings and the Circean transformation from substance to image', *Academy of Management Learning and Education*, **1** (1), 107–20.

Gioia, Dennis A. and James B. Thomas (1996), 'Identity, image, and issue interpretation: sensemaking during strategic change in academia', *Administrative Science Quarterly*, **41** (3), 370–404.

Gioia, Dennis A., Majken Schulz and Kevin G. Corley (2000), 'Organizational identity, image, and adaptive instability', *Academy of Management Review*, **25** (1), 63–81.

Goffman, Erving (1963), *Stigma. Notes on the Management of Spoiled Identity*, New York: Simon & Schuster.

Greenwood, Royston, Roy Suddaby and C.R. Hinings (2002), 'Theorizing change: the role of professional associations in the transformation of institutionalized fields', *Academy of Management Journal*, **45** (1), 58–80.

Hair, Joseph F., Rolph E. Anderson, Ronald L. Tatham and William C. Black (1998), *Multivariate Data Analysis*, London: Prentice Hall International.

Haveman, Heather A. and Hayagreeva Rao (1997), 'Structuring a theory of moral sentiments: institutional and organizational coevolution in the early thrift industry', *American Journal of Sociology*, **102** (6), 1606–51.

Hedmo, Tina (2002), 'The Europeanization of management education', in Rolv Petter Amdam, Ragnhild Kvålshaugen and Eirinn Larsen (2002), *Inside the Business School: The Content of European Business Education*, Lund, Sweden: Liber-Abstrakt, pp. 247–66.

Hedmo, Tina (2004), 'Rule-making in the transnational space: the development of European accreditation of management education', doctoral thesis no 109, Department of Business Studies, Uppsala University.

Hedmo, Tina, Kerstin Sahlin-Andersson and Linda Wedlin (forthcoming), 'The emergence of a European regulatory field of management education', in Marie-Laure Djelic and Kerstin Sahlin-Andersson (eds), *Transnational Governance: Institutional Dynamics of Regulation*, Cambridge: Cambridge University Press.

Hoffman, Andrew J. (1999), 'Institutional evolution and change: environmentalism and the U.S. chemical industry', *Academy of Management Journal*, **42** (4), 351–71.

Kipping, Matthias (1998), 'The hidden business schools: management training in Germany since 1945', in Lars Engwall and Vera Zamagni (eds), *Management Education in Historical Perspective*, Manchester: Manchester University Press, pp. 95–110.

Knights, David and Hugh Willmott (1985), 'Power and identity in theory and practice', *Sociological Review*, **33** (1), 22–47.

Lamont, Michèle (1992), *Money, Morals, and Manners. The Culture of the French and the American Upper-middle Class*, Chicago: University of Chicago Press.

Lamont, Michèle and Virág Molnár (2002), 'The study of boundaries in the social sciences', *Annual Review of Sociology*, **28** (1), 167–95.

Locke, Robert (1989), *Management and Higher Education since 1940. The Influence of America and Japan on West Germany, Great Britain, and France*, Cambridge: Cambridge University Press.

Lounsbury, Michael (2002), 'Institutional transformation and status mobility: the professionalization of the field of finance', *Academy of Management Journal*, **45** (1), 255–66.

Lounsbury, Michael, Marc Ventresca and Paul M. Hirsch (2003), 'Social movements, field frames and industry emergence: a cultural–political perspective on U.S. recycling', *Socio-Economic Review*, **1** (1), 71–104.

Martin, John Levi (2003), 'What is field theory?', *American Journal of Sociology*, **109** (1), 1–49.

Mazza, Carmelo, Kerstin Sahlin-Andersson and Jesper Strandgaard Pedersen (forthcoming), 'European constructions of an American model: developments of four MBA programs', *Management Learning*.

Mead, George Herbert (1934), *Mind, Self, and Society from a Standpoint of a Social Behaviorist*, Chicago: University of Chicago Press.

Meyer, Heinz-Dieter (1998), 'The German "Handelshochschulen" 1898–1933: a new departure in management education and why it failed', in Lars Engwall and Vera Zamagni (eds), *Management Education in Historical Perspective*, Manchester: Manchester University Press, pp. 19–33.

Meyer, John W. (1994), 'Rationalized environments' in W. Richard Scott and John W. Meyer (eds), *Institutional Environments and Organizations: Structural Complexity and Individualism*, Thousand Oaks, CA: Sage, pp. 28–54.

Meyer, John W. and Ronald L. Jepperson (2000), 'The "actors" of modern society: the cultural construction of social agency', *Sociological Theory*, **18** (1), 100–120.

Meyer, John W. and Brian Rowan (1977), 'Institutionalized organizations: formal structure as myth and ceremony', *American Journal of Sociology*, **83** (2), 340–63.

Meyer, John W., John Boli, George M. Thomas and Francisco O. Ramirez (1997), 'World society and the nation-state', *American Journal of Sociology*, **103** (1), 144–81.

Miller, Peter (1994), 'Introduction' in Anthony Hopwood and Peter Miller (eds), *Accounting as Social and Institutional Practice*, Cambridge: Cambridge University Press, pp. 1–39.

Miller, Peter (1996), 'Dilemmas of accountability: the limits of accounting', in Paul Hirst and Sunil Kihlnani (eds), *Reinventing Democracy*, Oxford: Blackwell, pp. 57–69.

Miller, Peter (2001), 'Governing by numbers: why calculative practices matter', *Social Research*, **68** (2), 379–96.

Moon, Hyeyoung (2002), 'The globalization of professional management education, 1881–2000: its rise, expansion and implications', unpublished doctoral dissertation, Stanford University.

Nader, Laura (ed.) (1996), *Naked Science. Anthropological Inquiry into Boundaries, Power, and Knowledge*. New York: Routledge.

Oakes, Leslie S., Barbara Townley and David J. Cooper (1998), 'Business planning as pedagogy: language and control in a changing institutional field', *Administrative Science Quarterly*, **43** (2), 257–92.

Oliver, Christine (1991), 'Strategic responses to institutional processes', *Academy of Management Review*, **16** (1), 145–79.

Oliver, Christine (1992), 'The antecedents of deinstitutionalization', *Organization Studies*, **13** (4), 563–88.

Perrow, Charles (1986), *Complex Organizations. A Critical Essay*, New York: McGraw-Hill.

Powell, Walter W. (1991), 'Expanding the scope of institutional analysis', in

Walter W. Powell and Paul J. DiMaggio (eds), *The New Institutionalism in Organizational Analysis*, Chicago: University of Chicago Press, pp. 183–203.

Powell, Walter W. and Paul J. DiMaggio (eds) (1991), *The New Institutionalism in Organizational Analysis*, Chicago: University of Chicago Press.

Power, Mike (1997), *The Audit Society: Rituals of Verification*, Oxford: Oxford University Press.

Prichard, Craig and Hugh Willmott (1997), 'Just how managed is the McUniversity?', *Organization Studies*, **18** (2), 287–317.

Ragin, Charles (1994), *Constructing Social Research*, Thousand Oaks, CA: Pine Forge Press.

Rao, Hayagreeva (1994), 'The social construction of reputation: certification contests, legitimation, and the survival of organizations in the American automobile industry: 1895–1912', *Strategic Management Journal*, **15** (8), 29–44.

Rao, Hayagreeva (1998), 'Caveat emptor: the construction of consumer watchdog organizations', *American Journal of Sociology*, **103** (4), 912–61.

Rao, Hayagreeva, Gerald F. Davis and Andrew Ward (2000), 'Embeddedness, social identity and mobility: why firms leave the NASDAQ and join the New York Stock Exchange', *Administrative Science Quarterly*, **45** (2), 268–92.

Rose, Nikolas and Peter Miller (1992), 'Political power beyond the state: problematics of government', *British Journal of Sociology*, **43** (2), 173–205.

Røvik, Kjell-Arne (1996), 'Deinstitutionalization and the logic of fashion', in Barbara Czarniawska and Guje Sevón (eds), *Translating Organizational Change*, Berlin: Walter de Gruyter, pp. 139–72.

Røvik, Kjell-Arne (1998), *Moderne Organisasjoner. Trender i Organisasjonstenkninger ved Tusenårsskiftet*, Oslo, Norway: Fagbokforlaget.

Røvik, Kjell-Arne (2002), 'The secrets of the winners: management ideas that flow', in Kerstin Sahlin-Andersson and Lars Engwall (eds), *The Expansion of Management Knowledge*, Stanford, CA: Stanford University Press.

Sahlin-Andersson, Kerstin (1996), 'Imitating by editing success: the construction of organizational fields', in Barbara Czarniawska and Guje Sevón (eds), *Translating Organizational Change*, Berlin: Walter de Gruyter, pp. 69–92.

Sahlin-Andersson, Kerstin and Lars Engwall (eds) (2002), *The Expansion of Management Knowledge*, Stanford, CA: Stanford University Press.

Sahlin-Andersson, Kerstin and Guje Sevón (2003), 'Imitation and identification as performatives', in Barbara Czarniawska and Guje Sevón (eds), *The Northern Lights: Organization Theory in Scandinavia*, Malmö: Liber, pp. 249–65.

Schultz, Majken, Jan Mouritsen and Gorm Gabrielsen (2001), 'Sticky reputation: analyzing a ranking system', *Corporate Reputation Review*, **4** (1), 24–41.

Scott, Richard W. [1981] (1998), *Organizations: Rational, Natural and Open Systems*, 4th edn, Englewood Cliffs, NJ: Prentice-Hall.

Scott, Richard W. (1994) 'Institutions and organizations: toward theoretical synthesis', in Richard W. Scott and John W. Meyer (eds), *Institutional Environments and Organizations: Structural Complexity and Individualism*, Thousand Oaks, CA: Sage, pp. 55–80.

Scott, Richard W. (1995), *Institutions and Organizations*, Thousand Oaks, CA: Sage.

Scott, Richard W. (2001), *Institutions and Organizations*, 2nd edn, Thousand Oaks, CA: Sage.

Scott, Richard W. and John W. Meyer (1983), 'The organization of societal sectors', in J.W. Meyer and W.R. Scott (eds), *Organizational Environments: Ritual and Rationality*, Beverly Hills, CA: Sage, pp. 129–53.

Segev, Eli, Adi Raveh and Moshe Farjoun (1999), 'Conceptual maps of the leading MBA programs in the United States: core courses, concentration areas, and the ranking of the school', *Strategic Management Journal*, **20** (6), 549–65.

Sevón, Guje (1996), 'Organizational imitation in identity transformation', in Barbara Czarniawska and Guje Sevón (eds), *Translating Organizational Change*, Berlin: Walter de Gruyter, pp. 49–67.

Shore, Cris and Susan Wright (2000), 'Coercive accountability: the rise of audit culture in higher education', in Marilyn Strathern (ed.), *Audit Cultures. Anthropological Studies in Accountability, Ethics and the Academy*, London: Routledge, pp. 57–89.

Silverman, David (2001), *Interpreting Qualitative Data. Methods for Analysing Talk, Text and Interaction*, 2nd edn, London: Sage.

Strang, David and John W. Meyer (1993), 'Institutional conditions for diffusion', *Theory and Society*, **22** (4), 487–511.

Strathern, Marilyn (ed.) (2000a), *Audit Cultures. Anthropological Studies in Accountability, Ethics and the Academy*, London: Routledge.

Strathern, Marilyn (2000b), 'The tyranny of transparency', *British Educational Research Journal*, **26** (3), 309–21.

Suddaby, Roy and Royston Greenwood (2001), 'Colonizing knowledge: commodification as a dynamic of jurisdictional expansion in professional service firms', *Human Relations*, **54** (7), 933–53.

Thornton, Patricia H. and William Ocasio (1999), 'Institutional logics and the historical contingency of power in organizations: executive succession in the higher education publishing industry, 1958–1990', *American Journal of Sociology*, **105** (3), 801–43.

Tiratsoo, Nick (1998), 'Management education in postwar Britain', in Lars Engwall and Vera Zamagni (eds), *Management Education in Historical Perspective*, Manchester: Manchester University Press, pp. 111–26.

Townley, Barbara (1993), 'Foucault, power/knowledge, and its relevance for human resource management', *Academy of Management Review*, **18** (3), 518–45.

Trieschmann, James S., Alan R. Dennis, Gregory B. Northcraft and Albert W. Niemi, Jr (2000), 'Serving multiple constituencies in business schools: MBA program versus research performance', *Academy of Management Journal*, **43** (6), 1130–41.

Trow, Martin (1998), 'On the accountability of higher education in the United States', in William G. Bowen and Harold T. Shapiro (eds), *Universities and their Leadership*. Princeton, NJ: Princeton University Press, pp. 15–61.

Tsoukas, Haridimos (1997), 'The tyranny of light: the temptations and the paradoxes of the information society', *Futures*, **29** (9), 827–43.

Walgenbach, Peter and Nikolaus Beck (2002), 'The institutionalization of the quality management approach in Germany', in Kerstin Sahlin-Andersson and Lars Engwall (eds), *The Expansion of Management Knowledge*, Stanford, CA: Stanford University Press.

Wedlin, Linda (2004), 'Competing for employability – the media ranking of graduate business education', in Christina Garsten and Kerstin Jacobsson (eds), *Learning to be Employable. New Agendas on Work, Responsibility and Learning in a Globalising World*, Basingstoke: Palgrave, pp. 252–73.

Whitley, Richard (1984), 'The fragmented state of management studies: reasons and consequences', *Journal of Management Studies*, **21** (3), 331–48.

Zilber, Tammar B. (2002), 'Institutionalization as an interplay between actions, meanings, and actors: The case of a rape crisis center in Israel', *Academy of Management Journal*, **45** (1), 234–54.

NEWSPAPERS AND INTERNET SOURCES

Academy of Management News, October 2000.

Business Week, 19 October 1998, special report, 'The best b-schools', pp. 80–98.

Business Week, 2 October 2000, special report ,'The best b-schools', pp. 64–80.

Business Week, 21 October 2002, special report 'The best b-schools', pp. 47–72.

Efmd Bulletin, February 2002.

Financial Times, 19 January 1998, 'Opting for a broadened outlook. Survey: Business Education'.

Financial Times, 25 January 1999, 'Rankings can both help and rankle', *FT* Survey.

Financial Times, 24 January 2000, 'A high degree of diversity at top schools', *FT* Survey.

Financial Times, 4 June 2001, 'Some painful lessons for the e-learning sector', *FT* Survey.

Financial Times, 21 January 2002, 'Class of 2002 faces jobs uncertainty', *FT* Survey.

Financial Times, 20 January 2003, 'Schools look at ways to put their house in order', *FT* Survey.

Financial Times, 19 March 2003, 'Making courses measure up', *FT* Survey.

Financial Times, 20 October 2003, 'Top brands shape market for MBA's', *FT* Survey.

http://mba.eiu.com, Economist Intelligence Unit, 12 September 2002, 22 September 2003.

MBA Info, 2003, www.mbainfo.com, 13 October 2003.

Selection interview 1, *Financial Times*, Della Bradshaw. http://www.gmac.com/selections, 18 December 2001.

Selections interview 2, *Financial Times*, Parminder Bahra. http://www.gmac.com/selections, 18 December 2001.

Selections interview 3, *Business Week*, John Byrne. http://www.gmac.com/selections, 18 December 2001.

Wall Street Journal, 30 April 2001, 'Top business schools: a special report'.

Wall Street Journal, 9 September 2002, 'A global journal report: examining M.B.A.s'.

www.businessweek.com, *Business Week*, 12 November 2000, 29 February 2004.

www.forbes.com, *Forbes* magazine, 4 September 2003.

www.ft.com, *Financial Times*, 23 June 2002, 9 November 2003.

www.gmac.com, GMAC, 27 November 2003.

www.wsj.com, *Wall Street Journal*, 21 November 2002, 22 September 2003.

Index